British Politics in the Suez Crisis

UNIVERSITY OF ILLINOIS PRESS, URBANA, 1964

British Politics

by Leon D. Epstein

in the Suez Crisis

For S.G.E.

Preface

Work on this book stretched over several years, and I am grateful to several sources for enabling me first to begin the study and then finally to complete it. Thanks to help from the Rockefeller Foundation and the Graduate Research Committee of the University of Wisconsin, I spent the academic year of 1958-59 in Great Britain and, at that time, gathered most of the material for the study. Subsequently I had support from the National Security Studies Group (financed at the University of Wisconsin by the Carnegie Corporation) to conduct additional research concerning a special aspect of my study. Since the writing of most of the book unfortunately coincided with my tenure as department chairman, I owe a special debt of gratitude to our department secretary, Mrs. Jeanne Burull, whose unusual ability and willingness to assume responsibilities allowed me enough time for writing the last portions of the study.

I cannot name all of the Englishmen who helped me secure information. Most of them would, in any case, have to remain anonymous as interviewees. Without their help, and especially the help of selected M.P.s, I would have made little progress, particularly with reference to Chapter Six. I should also thank the staff of the Library of the British Museum, at the newspaper collection in Colindale, for so fully responding to my need for local newspaper files, which proved a rich source of political information. The help of the British Institute of Public Opinion I have explicitly acknowledged in Chapter Seven.

For research assistance at crucial points I am grateful to Paul Beckett and John Kingdon, graduate students at the University of Wisconsin. And for most efficient typing from a very rough draft, I want to thank Mrs. Norma Lynch and Mrs. Sandra Nash. My wife helped me in more ways than I can describe.

Critical comments of the most useful kind have been made by Professor Harold Sprout of Princeton University and by three of my Wisconsin colleagues, Professors John Harrison and George Mosse in history and Professor Austin Ranney in political science.

I want also to thank the editors of the *American Political Science Review* and of *World Politics* for permission to use material previously appearing in article form in those journals.

Madison, Wisconsin, March 1963   LEON D. EPSTEIN

Contents

Tables and Figures

CHAPTER ONE

Introduction

This is primarily a study of the British political system. The Suez issue provides the subject matter, but the issue as such is not of central concern. Attention is focused on the place of the issue in British politics and, even more emphatically, on the way in which the political system worked during the critical period of late 1956. What happened at Suez, including British policy itself, is described only as an essential preliminary to the analysis of British politics.

Choosing the Suez issue for a political case study requires an explanation. It might be said that the issue was too unusual and that the accompanying internal political events too untypical of British behavior. Certainly the whole affair was the most dramatic British experience since World War II. It would be no exaggeration to label the experience "Seven [or possibly "Ten"] Days That Shook Britain." This was the crisis proper: from the Anglo-French ultimatum of 30 October through 6 November, when the cease-fire was accepted, or perhaps through 8 November, when the last critical parliamentary division took place. Those were the days of political trauma. Suez was of overwhelming concern. But the issue also tended to dominate British politics during much of the longer period from late July, when Egypt nationalized the canal company, until the spring of 1957. In this respect, as in the intensity of the shorter crisis, the British situation was special. Elsewhere in the West, including the United States, the Suez issue was seldom so dramatic or even so important relative to other contemporary events as to be labeled a domestic

1

political crisis. Englishmen, however, responded to Eden's interventionist decision by dividing against each other with unusual passion.

Why so much passion existed in Britain is one of the things that ought to be explained in the course of the study. But the fact that it existed does not destroy the usefulness of the experience as a case study. The unusual features of the Suez affair do not necessarily mean that the British political system responded untypically or even abnormally. It is equally possible that the response was simply a more intense and, therefore, at most a somewhat exaggerated version of ordinary behavior. There is no a priori basis for expecting the system to display basically different characteristics under stress than it displays in quieter circumstances. On the contrary, it is more reasonable to believe that unusual stress may simply bring into sharper focus certain regular aspects of the system. For example, party solidarity, ordinarily strong in Britain, was manifest during the crisis in especially striking and vital ways. A crisis, although by definition involving an abnormal event, may not produce political responses that are aberrant in essential respects. Even if it did, however, there would be an obvious importance to learning how a political system works in the exceptional situation.

In other words, the Suez issue presents no greater methodological difficulties than most case studies.[1] The case-study method itself has limitations as a means of understanding any larger generality of political experience. A single case, no matter how usual it might seem, provides a risky basis for generalizing. Of course, one does not even attempt to generalize solely from a case on its own, but instead against a background of already existing generalizations which can be tested by the particular case study. Even this procedure, however, does not produce the scientific certainty that we should like to have, but seldom possess, with respect to the larger questions of political inquiry. Not only can we establish no more than probabilities, but these too are likely to be conditioned by the given issue and the

---

[1]The problem of typicality always confronts the maker of a political case study. It is discussed with sophistication by James B. Christoph in the introduction to his *Capital Punishment and British Politics* (London: Allen & Unwin, 1962), pp. 7-8. He explains that capital punishment, admittedly untypical in its legislative history, may nevertheless illustrate the typical in the British political process by indicating the limits of independent parliamentary law-making as opposed to cabinet leadership. Thus his case, in its very different way, seems to support a view of British politics similar to that derived, as will be observed, from the Suez experience.

given period of time. Thus the way in which the British political system worked during the Suez crisis may be partly the product of the Suez issue itself, or perhaps more broadly of an important foreign or imperial issue. It may also be partly the result of a particular set of British political circumstances having to do with parties and their leaders in the mid-1950's.

The difficulties in the way of suggesting generalizations from a case study seem so great that one might be tempted to forego the effort altogether and simply tell the story of what happened in Britain during the Suez crisis. Unhappily, perhaps, this would not be enough to satisfy a political scientist. By whatever methods, narrowly or only loosely scientific, he is ambitious to understand how a political system works in more than a given situation. Moreover, he wants this understanding in order to throw light on the operation of other political systems. His purpose must always be comparative. Accordingly the objective is not just to learn, from the Suez crisis, something about *Britain's* Parliament and parties, but hopefully also something about types of parliamentary and party systems.

Another and very different kind of question could be asked about the choice of Suez as case-study material. It may seem either too late or too soon to review Britain's experience in the crisis of 1956. Too late surely to be topical, and too soon for definitive diplomatic history. Why then discuss again an incident embarrassing to Anglo-American relations, humiliating to British pride, and untypical of Britain's conduct in the postwar world?[2] The answer to this apparently forbidding question must rest in part on the usefulness of a study that is neither strictly topical nor definitive diplomatic history. The latter is not an objective of the present work. Nor is topicality in the reportorial sense. But we are still close enough to 1956 so that what happened then is topical at least in the sense of being relevant to an existing political system. The politics of the 1960's, and very likely those of subsequent decades as well, cannot be entirely different from the 1950's. Moreover, what is now sacrificed by way of immediacy of interest is compensated by the advantage of several years' perspective

[2]Englishmen have often expressed a wish to forget about the Suez affair even while reviving controversy by stating or restating their own views. For instance, Lord Tedder began his important speech not long after the immediate crisis by saying: "I have no desire whatever to stir up unnecessary mud in this unhappy affair. The sooner the subject can be neatly filed away as one for students the better, but we must get the records right first." 200 *H. L. Deb.* 1083 (12 December 1956).

on the events of 1956. Such emotional involvements as even an American observer might have had in 1956 or 1957 are diminished. His views of Britain's Suez action are now much less likely to be influenced by his own partisan response, pro or con, to the Eisenhower administration's opposition to that action. It is a curious but understandable feature of the Suez crisis that many American liberals tended to criticize Eisenhower and Dulles, thus sympathizing with Eden, while almost all British liberals (in and out of the Labour party) principally blamed Eden. At the time, it might have been almost as difficult for an American to escape his partisan outlook in writing about Suez as it was for an Englishman. By no means, however, is the diminution of partisanship the only advantage derived from the lapse of time since 1956. Several years are always useful to the scholar in need of many facts and much time to think about them.

It is easy thus to claim an advantage for the perspective of one writing several years after an event. It is harder, as well as immodest, to claim a similar advantage for the perspective of an American. On this score, one must begin by saying that there is a decided disadvantage in a foreigner's study of British politics. Despite some years, in and out of Britain, with this and related subjects, an outside observer may still miss nuances that an English scholar would be sure to comprehend. What can be said on the other side is that an American has some special equipment when, as in the present case, he seeks to explain the British system primarily to an American audience. He should understand what his fellow Americans need to have made explicit and how best to do so in American terms. Also, perhaps it may not be too grossly immodest to add that an American, because he is an outsider, is not necessarily in a bad position to discuss the British imperial experience—so plainly important to an understanding of the Suez crisis. In light of the decline of British imperialism, even the hard legacy of American anticolonialism should not prevent one from viewing Britain's imperial tradition with sympathy as well as objectivity.

There can be no doubt that the importance, in the British community, of this tradition must be presented as an essential aspect of the background of the politics of the Suez crisis. What is needed here is a Western counterpart of the many efforts, often by Westerners, to explain the politics of Asian and African nations in terms of anticolonialist or anti-imperialist biases. Just as many of the people of those nations are said to respond as formerly subject peoples, so some Englishmen can be said to have responded, at least in the 1950's, as a formerly master people. This is not solely a matter of Englishmen still thinking of themselves as masters. There may have been some of that, but there was also a reaction against a very recent loss of the master role. The British seem, in this respect, to have had to undergo a trying period of adjustment to a new status in the world. Mostly this adjustment, in relation to the rest of the world, has been smooth and gracious since World War II. No nation has ever given up so much so fast and, with exceptions, so peacefully. Suez was an exception. Truly Britain did then, in relation to most of its postwar policies, act out of character. But at Suez it may have been acting as desired by a still significant portion of the national population. The otherwise unbroken record of imperial retreat may simply have overridden or ignored the preferences and traditions of many Englishmen. Something significant in the British community seems to have required a last effort in the old style.

This is not to say that the Anglo-French intervention at Suez should be viewed as itself old-style imperialism. The policy objectives were well short of nineteenth-century conquest even though residual imperial sentiment supported the intervention. Rupert Emerson has aptly called the intervention "one of the early reactions to the post-imperial period" rather than a "recrudescence of imperialism."[3] For Britain, or for France, 1956 was not 1882, when Alexandria was bombarded and Egypt subsequently occupied. Nor was it 1899, when Britain began its campaign to defeat the Boers in South Africa. Now Britain did not have the imperial opportunity, the imperial power, or the imperial will.

The whole matter of Britain's imperial background is discussed at some length in the next chapter. The chapter is designed chiefly for Americans unfamiliar with this vital aspect of British experience. Englishmen may find it unnecessary. There follows in Chapter Three, also as background, a summary of the events leading to the crisis and a brief commentary on crisis actions, which are detailed in an accompanying log. Chapter Four describes the relation to these

[3]*From Empire to Nation* (Cambridge: Harvard University Press, 1960), p. 401. Emerson went on to say: "It seems clear that neither Britain nor France wanted any extension of power or domain and hoped at best not to lose too much of what they had formerly had. What was essentially at stake was that each felt that the time had come to call a halt to the attack upon what it considered its legitimate interests."

actions of the most forthrightly imperial group, and its place in British politics of the period. The next four chapters, constituting the bulk of the book, show how the British political system operated in Parliament, in constituency associations, and in selected nongovernmental and nonparty ways. Finally, in Chapter Nine, an effort is made to bring together what has been learned about the functioning of the political system in response to the Suez issue.

CHAPTER TWO

Imperial Legacy

Britain's imperial greatness is still recent. Certainly it was so in 1956. No visitor to London could fail to be impressed by its monumental landmarks. But he could miss the significance of the imperial past in the national consciousness. So completely has British supremacy now disappeared that outsiders, particularly Americans, may fail to appreciate that most British adults of the mid-twentieth century had been born and raised in the era when their nation ruled huge portions of the world. Many had even experienced the last great expansion of the British Empire at the turn of the century. They knew the pre-1914 glory as well as the great withdrawal after 1945.

For the observer in the late 1950's, the continuing importance of the imperial experience was neatly illustrated in the National Portrait Gallery's room for twentieth-century statesmen. On one wall were portraits of eight major empire-builders: Evelyn Baring (Earl Cromer), the financial expert who established British influence in Egypt; Major F. D. Lugard, exponent of indirect rule in West Africa; Sir Henry Durand, the Indian civil servant who negotiated the Afghan frontier settlement of 1893; Viscount Milner, whose South African service in establishing British supremacy over the Boers was the most notable of several contributions; Joseph Chamberlain, the expansionist Colonial Secretary who sought to popularize and consolidate imperial interests; Earl Kitchener, the general whose reputation was first established by the conquest of the Sudan and later by his Indian command; Dr. Jameson, the Cecil Rhodes associate who was the Cape Colony's Prime Minister and the leader of the famous raid preliminary to the

South African war; and Taubman Goldie, the founder of Nigeria. These names and deeds, as objects of contemporary British pride, symbolize an imperial tradition central to an understanding of the Suez affair. Much of the affair, after all, turned on the manner in which that tradition should be discharged.

1. IDEOLOGY

Imperialism in modern history, despite earlier, more limited connotations, has meant chiefly the overseas expansion of the European nations.[1] The expansion was both by settlement of fairly open spaces—colonialism proper—and by conquest and rule of large native populations. Accompanying this expansion, but occasionally on its own, was an extension of economic interests. That these interests, particularly capitalist profit-seeking interests, explain the imperialist movement is a familiar theory, but it is not settled that the theory provides a sufficient explanation for the vigor and popularity of imperialism.[2] It has been argued, cogently and forcefully, that imperialistic motivations were precapitalist and atavistic.[3] No matter how this issue is settled with respect to primary motivations, there is no question that imperial ideology, like the nationalism of which it was an extended expression, came to have noneconomic elements. To believe in empire was to believe in the greatness of one's nation.

Englishmen did not always, even in fairly modern times, think in these terms. Early in Britain's overseas expansion, and even in the last half of the eighteenth century, when India was won and much of North America first won and then largely lost, the building of empire may have seemed merely the wayward task of a few adventurers outside the mainstream of British life. Yet the "will to empire" has been dated from Clive's Indian campaign of 1756. It was then that Britain's role began to change from mere trading in Asia

[1] A detailed etymological account of "imperialism" is provided by Richard Koebner, "From Imperium to Empire," in *Studies in Medieval and Modern Thought and Literature* (Jerusalem: Magnes Press, 1955), pp. 119-75.

[2] E. M. Winslow, *The Pattern of Imperialism* (New York: Columbia University Press, 1948), presents and criticizes the several economic theories of imperialism.

[3] Schumpeter's argument along this line has been well known since 1919, when it was first published in German. See Joseph A. Schumpeter, *Imperialism and Social Classes* (Oxford: Blackwell, 1951). The essay on imperialism is indeed a classic work, and it is rightly accorded a prominent place in contemporary discussion of the subject, as by Klaus Knorr, "Theories of Imperialism," *World Politics*, Vol. 4, pp. 402-31 (April 1952).

and Africa, and from farm settlement in North America, to imperial government of large native populations.[4] The change, however, came slowly, and for more than half of the nineteenth century the British outlook was dominated by a free-trade philosophy in which colonies were often regarded as burdensome. The already discovered sense of "Britain's supreme mission to civilize the world" was not yet predominantly in an imperial mold.[5] But the belief in Britain's greatness and power was very much alive. This was characteristically expressed by Palmerston in his famous mid-century speech defending the high-handed British naval intervention in behalf of a British subject's claims against Greece. Just as the Roman, asserted Palmerston, had held himself free from indignity when he could say *Civis Romanus sum*, "so also a British subject, in whatever land he may be, shall feel confident that the watchful eye and the strong arm of England will protect him against injustice and wrong."[6] The Roman parallel was to become even more appropriate later in the century when and where British authority was directly imperial and not merely episodic as in the Greek incident. It was in this later period, starting with the response to the Indian mutiny of 1857, that Britain, as Churchill has aptly declared, "gradually and consciously became a world-wide Imperial Power."[7] The nation, as we would now say, accepted the responsibility flowing from its power.

This power, as of 1870, was that of the most highly developed industrial nation in the world. Never after 1870 was Britain's own relative position so strong. Thus the imperial expansion of the last decades of the nineteenth century, when the Empire's territory increased by one-third, was achieved after the island kingdom itself had begun to lose its industrial leadership to Germany and the United States. This loss of status has been used to explain Britain's last imperial surge as essentially a defensive reaction in which empire-building was substituted for the vanishing supremacy derived from the sale of manufactures in a free-trade world.[8] Perhaps this view is valid only retrospectively. The self-confidence exhibited by the late

[4]John Strachey, *The End of Empire* (New York: Random House, 1960), pp. 23-24.

[5]Klaus Knorr, *British Colonial Theories* (Toronto: University of Toronto Press, 1944), pp. 246-47.

[6]*Hansard's Parliamentary Debates*, Third Series, Vol. 112, col. 444 (25 June 1850).

[7]Winston S. Churchill, *The Great Democracies*, Vol. 4 of *A History of the English-Speaking Peoples* (New York: Dodd, Mead & Co., 1958), p. 80.

[8]Elie Halevy, *Imperialism and the Rise of Labour*, Vol. 5 of *A History of the English People in the Nineteenth Century*, tr. by E. I. Watkins (London: Ernest Benn, 1951), pp. 10-12.

nineteenth-century imperialists was not that of men deeply aware of their nation's decline. They had the buoyant optimism of a nation accustomed to success. Yet it was the imperial achievement that made it possible for Englishmen, especially after 1900, to regard their country as a great power and even as *the* great power in the world at a time when such a claim for Britain alone would have been an exaggeration. National consciousness of greatness, there can be no doubt, now depended heavily on the Empire.

Probably Disraeli sensed this as early as 1872 when, in his famous Crystal Palace speech, he officially proclaimed Britain's imperial position.[9] For him the Empire was already a matter of prestige. So it seemed to be presented to the British people in the 1880's and 1890's, particularly in the great Jubilee celebrations in London. Enthusiasm at this stage was largely unchecked by the problem of costs. "Painting the map red" was still inexpensive. Kitchener's conquest of the Sudan, for example, cost British taxpayers less than £1,000,000 and caused no increase in the standard income tax rate.[10] Only at the turn of the century, with the South African war, did the price in men and resources begin to seem high. Then, after an almost frenzied imperialism, the expansionist spirit declined and consolidation became the order of the day.

The content of the ideology accompanying British imperialism, both during its expansion just before 1900 and during its consolidation just afterward, reveals a state of mind that, except superficially, is very different from our own current view of the West's relation to what we call underdeveloped nations or, latterly and even more politely, developing nations. The terminology itself is significant. British imperialists, circa 1900, had no doubt that they were dealing with backward peoples. At their best, imperialists accepted a mission to civilize on Western terms. There was an idealism, even a romanticism, about this mission. At least this was characteristic of the governing classes, and it was expressed, for example, in the unconsciously arrogant phrase, "serving India," used by British imperial officials.[11] The con-

[9]The importance of Disraeli's speech as a mark of the new imperialism of the late Victorian period is made clear in William L. Langer's full account of "The Triumph of Imperialism," chap. 3 in Vol. 1 of his *The Diplomacy of Imperialism* (New York: Knopf, 1935).

[10]Philip Magnus, *Kitchener* (London: Murray, 1958), p. 136.

[11]Justification in this way of the imperial mission is objectively described by A. P. Thornton, *The Imperial Idea and Its Enemies* (London: Macmillan, 1959), especially at pp. 38, 72, 211-13, 227.

sciousness of responsibility for the welfare of subject peoples was no doubt genuine. Serving British interests alone was not enough to justify the task. Rather, the Empire became a trust for Englishmen to manage on behalf of the civilized world. Crudely put, this was the "white man's burden." For Kitchener, for instance, shouldering this burden was a missionary duty imposed on the British race.[12] The more sophisticated and enlightened imperialists used a different language. Still, a national self-confidence in the overseas mission was a common element. Thus Major Lugard wrote of "moral obligations to the subject races," and said that African countries were held "because it is the genius of our race to colonise, to trade, and to govern."[13]

Winston Churchill, whose own early years involved experiences in the Middle East, India, and South Africa, provides the most significant example of the imperialist ideology. The significance lies not so much in his writing at the turn of the century, when Britain's civilizing mission was so widely accepted, but in his retention of imperial idealism later in his career. Churchill's long-running battle against Indian independence is striking. He persisted in his view that to hand over power to Indian political leaders, presumed to be an unrepresentative faction, was for Britain to fail to discharge "a supreme moral duty."[14] That the leadership of the Conservative party in the early 1930's was willing to accept a large measure of Indian self-government was the well-known cause of Churchill's break with Stanley Baldwin and the bulk of his party. "Its mission in India" was what Churchill wanted the British nation to maintain.[15] He was pained that so many of his fellow countrymen now seemed to lack the will power to do so.

It is usual among admirers of Churchill to regard his Indian views as an unfortunate aberration from an otherwise largely brilliant farsightedness. And it is more flattering to his career to remember his opposition in the late 1930's to the Conservative party's unsuccessful German policy and armaments program than it is to remember the original cause of his defection earlier in the decade. But it is wrong to separate the two cases. The basis and spirit of Churchill's views on

[12]Magnus, *op. cit.*, p. 24.

[13]F. D. Lugard, *The Dual Mandate in Tropical Africa* (London: Blackwood, 1929), pp. 58, 618-19.

[14]Winston S. Churchill, *India* (London: Butterworth, 1931), p. 78.

[15]*Ibid.*, p. 47.

India and on appeasement were essentially similar. It was because he believed in Britain's greatness in the world that he wanted to retain India as well as to stand firmly against Germany. For that matter, the same imperial self-confidence that caused Churchill to believe Britain could continue to govern India caused him to believe in Britain's destiny even in the dark days of 1940. Perhaps only a leader whose optimism was fixed by the halcyon British days of 1900 could have sustained his nation's faith in ultimate victory against staggering odds.

Underlying the imperial ideology, especially during the expansionist phase, was a tone of racial superiority. Often this was tacit and polite but not thereby less offensive. In some sense, feelings of racial superiority must have been required for the imperial task. Probably it was less essential for a faith in an ability to conquer a native population than it was for the belief in the rightness of imposing an alien rule for what was, at first, thought to be an almost interminable period. Preparation for self-government was not characteristic of imperialism in its expansionist phase. Natives, although the proclaimed beneficiaries of civilized rule, were often ignored as even potentially active participants in the governing system. For example, Viscount Milner, surely intelligent and intellectual, wrote of South Africa in 1909 that there was "no question, at least not in my opinion, of the black population ever becoming a danger to the political supremacy, to the government of the whites."[16] The assumption here as to the durability of white supremacy may now appear fantastic (except, to be sure, to white South Africans), but at least before World War I it was so widely accepted that only seldom did anyone have to be as explicit as Milner.

Bolstering the assumption were the then popular social Darwinian theories about the survival of the fittest.[17] In 1900 it was indeed intellectually respectable to believe in racial superiority. For the British, the concept was often more specific than "race" in the present anthropological sense. Not only was there an Anglo-Saxon race, but even a British or an English race. No matter how inexact these terms seem to our ears, attuned to the usage of mid-twentieth century social science, they added a level of significance to the extended nationalism

[16]Viscount Milner, *Imperial Unity* (London: Hodder & Stoughton, 1909), pp. 56-57.

[17]Langer, *op. cit.*, p. 85; Crane Brinton, *English Political Thought in the Nineteenth Century* (London: Ernest Benn, 1933), pp. 282-92.

of the earlier period. Englishmen, in particular, thought themselves fit to rule many supposedly inferior whites as well as Negroes. Certainly the British did not distinguish sharply between peoples whose skins were slightly darker and those much darker than Englishmen's. Even when a nation was hardly darker at all, like the Irish, Englishmen could be convinced of an evidently inherent inferiority that justified British rule.[18]

Yet the import of racial superiority doctrines was chiefly to support imperial rule over nonwhite populations. These doctrines may well have been essential to the confidence that sustained the sense of national mission. The relativism of contemporary cultural anthropology would hardly have provided useful ideological support for imposing British rule and British customs. Racism seems an almost inevitable component of imperialism.[19] In its crude form, as that the only good Indian is a dead Indian, it accompanied cruel and bloody conquests, and in its less ferocious form it went along with benevolent paternalism.

No doubt the imperial ideology was less directly important for the bulk of the British population than it was for those who actually constructed and ruled the Empire. It was the British ruling classes who, as Nehru said, viewed the Empire as their "earthly Kingdom of Heaven."[20] Certainly it provided great and challenging tasks which could be endowed with a religious fervor. An unsympathetic critic may view this spirit as the romantic fancy of men who refused to reject their boyhood idealism.[21] In this perspective, empire-building is seen as the means of escape from a domestic society in which one would have to grow up. But, mature or immature, romantic or realistic, imperialism was an article of faith in the ruling classes.

Popularizing this faith in larger sections of the community posed another problem. Here the experience of empire would have to be enjoyed vicariously. Only a privileged minority could have the pleasure of conquest and rule. But the pride of national accomplishment could be shared. Imperialism, for this purpose, was an extension of national patriotism. Thus it was presented to the newly politicized

[18]Magnus, *op. cit.*, p. 4, writes of Kitchener having been raised in Ireland as a member of an English "master race."

[19]E. Franklyn Frazier, *Race and Culture Contacts in the Modern World* (New York: Knopf, 1957), p. 98.

[20]Jawaharlal Nehru, *Toward Freedom* (New York: John Day, 1941), p. 271.

[21]Hannah Arendt, "The Imperialist Character," *Review of Politics*, Vol. 12, p. 307 (July 1950).

mass of the British population late in the nineteenth century. Even
if imperialism, as Schumpeter has written, was only a slogan or a
catch phrase, without any genuine value to the working class, it
assuredly gained a popular standing.[22] The Conservative party, in
particular, found it useful to identify itself with imperial success. The
new mass journalism, notably the immediately successful *Daily Mail*,
made the same identification. The 1890's were plainly jingo years,
and even school textbooks took pride in what Britain held through
"right of conquest."[23] More striking still in expressing and fixing the
imperial mood was popular literature. Kipling's role, of course, is
well known. At least as important as a communicator, although not
so significant a literary figure, was G. A. Henty. Primarily a writer
of immensely popular stories for boys in the 1880's and 1890's, Henty
blended exciting adventure with idealistic imperial accomplishment.
His stories are the British imperial counterpart of the American
winning-of-the-West tales. *With Roberts to Pretoria* and *With Kitchener
in the Soudan* are typical titles. And a typical viewpoint is expressed
in a prefatory remark, in the latter volume, that the Sudan was
"wrested from barbarism and restored to civilization. . . ."[24] The
Henty stories retained their vogue at least until World War I, or long
enough to influence the thinking of a generation still very much alive
in the middle of the twentieth century. Although the story of imperial
adventure, unlike the American Western, was no longer being produced, the impact lingered from the days when pride in empire had
been gloriously established.

That pride, it must be emphasized again, had been established
fairly recently. Old but still active men in the 1950's had been school-
boys when the 1897 Jubilee, at the high tide of imperialism, brought
troops from all parts of the Empire to impress London with Britain's
ascendancy. Thus Earl Attlee, to take a nonimperialist example,
could recall "the memorable day" on which he watched the great
imperial procession. "Most of us boys at that time were imperialists
with an immense pride in the achievements of our race."[25]

[22]Schumpeter, *op. cit.*, chap. 2.

[23]A good example is George Gill's *The Geography and History of the British Colonies*
(London: George Gill and Sons, 1891), which described for secondary students the
vast territories held by British power.

[24]G. A. Henty, *With Kitchener in the Soudan* (London: Blackie & Son, 1903), p. vi.

[25]Earl Attlee, *From Empire into Commonwealth* (New York: Oxford University
Press, 1961), p. 3.

2. GREATER BRITAIN

A special imperialist element, having little to do with the late nineteenth-century African expansion and in fact originally preceding it, was the concept of Greater Britain. It rested not on British rule over large African or Asian populations, but rather on a projected union, under British leadership, of the areas actually colonized by European and chiefly British settlers. Greater Britain was to be white and English-speaking, thus literally an extension of Britain overseas. Other peoples, like the Indians, who happened already to be governed by Britain, might remain so, or perhaps be governed by the new Greater Britain. But their place in the scheme was never clear or certain. They were not of prime concern. Canada, Australia, New Zealand, and perhaps South Africa were to be the components, with Britain itself, of the new unified community. The rise and decline of this concept, like that of the broad imperialist ideology, are important for understanding subsequent British perceptions of the nation's role in the world.

In the beginning, just after the middle of the nineteenth century, the Greater Britain idea represented a rejection of the earlier belief that colonies, especially English-speaking ones, were rightly destined to become independent of the mother country. In reversing this disinterest in empire, the advocacy of Greater Britain loosely resembled the spirit of imperial expansion. Or at least the reaction against "little England" was the same, although the direction of the reaction differed markedly. In both cases Britain's destiny in the modern world was to be found in a larger entity than that provided by the island nation itself. Britain alone was simply too small to be great in what was already coming to be an age of continental powers. Uniting with the English-speaking colonies was one route to strength and status.

The Greater Britain concept was usually loosely expressed, although schemes for imperial federation did develop later. The first famous work on the subject, Charles Dilke's *Greater Britain* (1869), was largely a record of travel in English-speaking countries. What distinguished it from other such records, besides Dilke's perceptiveness, was his vision of a single though geographically dispersed community. He wrote about the idea, which had guided his travels, "of the grandeur of our race, already girdling the earth, which it is destined, perhaps, eventually to overspread."[26] So general was his concept that the

[26]Charles W. Dilke, *Greater Britain* (London: Macmillan, 1869), Vol. 1, p. vii.

United States was included among the nations of his English race. In fact, Dilke thought of the United States as a most important member of a subsequent "confederation of the English race."[27] The vague hopefulness of this idea was eventually modified, even by Dilke himself, so that Greater Britain rested exclusively on the components of the existing Empire.[28] The scheme was thus less grandiose and, seemingly at least, more practical.

The most widely influential presentation of the Greater Britain case, that by Sir John Seeley in 1883, was specific enough. He would simply have united Englishmen beyond the sea with those at home, making a population total he estimated as large enough to rank with Russia and the United States.[29] Science was rapidly making possible, as Seeley correctly said, the governing of large geographically separate areas. Since the future seemed to belong to larger nations, why not a large British nation as well? After all, Britain, Australia, New Zealand, and Canada did have largely common institutions and a common language.

This kind of reasoning was at the basis of the movements for imperial federation in the late nineteenth and early twentieth centuries. Advocates sought to convince Englishmen as well as colonial or dominion citizens that they belonged to a larger nation. The Empire, in other words, represented a greater nationalism. Its institutional expression was to be a federation of what were already largely self-governing units. An imperial parliament would be created, at least for foreign affairs and defense problems. The Imperial Federation League, started in the 1880's, devoted itself to this cause directly,[30] and the Royal Empire Society, started even earlier, also encouraged imperial unity but less directly.[31] Often mingled with the political arguments for federation were economic reasons, and the movement eventually concentrated heavily on the more limited objectives of a customs union or mutual tariff concessions among the units of the Empire. Originally, however, the primary purposes were political and these purposes did not entirely die out even during the early twentieth

[27]*Ibid.*, Vol. 2, p. 157.

[28]Charles W. Dilke, *Problems of Greater Britain* (London: Macmillan, 1890).

[29]Sir John Seeley, *The Expansion of England* (London: Macmillan, 1883). India he treated as a case to one side, and Africa was not yet an area of major British responsibility.

[30]J. E. Tyler, *The Struggle for Imperial Unity* (London: Longmans, Green & Co., 1938).

[31]Alvaline Foster, *The Royal Empire Society* (London: Allen & Unwin, 1933).

century, when the chances for political federation had dimmed. These chances diminished as the separate national consciousness of the dominions increased. Mainly they had never been anxious for imperial federation anyway. Although at certain stages the dominions pressed for tariff preferences, the history of the federation movement is largely one of dominion resistance to occasional British advocacy, at successive imperial conferences, of various unification schemes.[32] Instead of being willing to move closer together, the dominions sought, with eventual success, to achieve their own status as foreign policy–makers— the very thing that the federationists wanted most to avoid.[33] In retrospect this seems inevitable, as it did to Ernest Barker when he observed that the "ingrained idea of each self-governing State of the empire" was that "its own parliament is its own last word and final expression."[34] An imperial parliament, Barker thought, would have been a step away from the road to liberty that the dominions were taking.

Yet the advocacy of imperial unity by Englishmen was zealous and persistent. And it was carried on by important statesmen. Joseph Chamberlain's work for the cause is well known, particularly during his tenure as Colonial Secretary. So is Lord Milner's early twentieth-century campaign, and it is a significant one to examine because of a relatively full doctrinal development untempered by much adjustment to strictly vote-getting considerations. It is true that Milner was realistic enough not to expect an imperial parliament as a first step; he hoped it would come later with the growth of imperial patriotism in various cooperative endeavors.[35] But imperial unity in some almost immediately realizable and useful form was unquestionably his objective. His reasons were plain. "These islands by themselves," he said, "cannot always remain a Power of the very first rank. But Greater Britain may remain such a Power. . . ."[36] His definition of Greater Britain was usually the familiar one of the white dominions, but occasionally he held out the even grander prospect that imperial patriotism might develop among races not of British

[32]Eric A. Walker, *The British Empire* (Cambridge: Bowes & Bowes, 1953), pp. 133-50.

[33]Lionel Curtis, *The Problem of the Commonwealth* (London: Macmillan, 1915), pp. 130-32.

[34]Ernest Barker, *The Ideas and Ideals of the British Empire* (London: Cambridge University Press, 1941), p. 81.

[35]Milner, *op. cit.*, p. 30.

[36]Milner, *The Nation and the Empire* (London: Constable & Co., 1913), p. 140.

origin.[37] The latter, however, was evidently not crucial to Milner's desire to preserve "the unity of a great race"[38] so that it could fulfill its mission in the world. This was the vision that he urged his countrymen as well as his overseas brethren to adopt.

Milner and others like him became voices in the wilderness, especially after World War I. Despite hopes engendered by the Imperial War Conferences during that conflict, the subsequent results were greater dominion autonomy and a much looser imperial arrangement. Virtually no substantive imperial institutions survived. Plans for a constitution for the Empire were specifically put aside.[39] It was appropriate, therefore, for a later biographer of Milner to entitle his work *The Forsaken Idea*.[40] It is worth remembering, while Milner's ideal was forsaken, that it was an ideal of considerable appeal within the British community itself. It was one way that Englishmen sought to give their nation a destiny as a great power in the twentieth-century world. The new enlarged British nation could be a substitute for status to be lost through the surrender of imperial possessions, or it could be a means of strengthening the British capacity to hold such possessions. Certainly the belief in a Greater Britain was entirely compatible with the imperial ideology, and it is not surprising that men like Chamberlain and Milner were imperialists, in the sense of justifying British domination over native populations, and also advocates of the imperial unity of the English-speaking parts of the Empire. The intellectual origins of the two points of view were different, but by the turn of the century they went together as the means by which Englishmen hoped to maintain their nation's greatness.

Much the same regret, therefore, is to be found in British reactions to the dissipation of the Greater Britain concept as in the reactions to loss of imperial possessions. The new Commonwealth was not an adequate replacement for either loss. Obviously it was not so for

[37]"Certainly I am the last person," Milner wrote, "to question the importance of the racial bond. Without it there would be no British Empire. But I do not admit that Imperial patriotism of a kind may not be developed among the races that are not of British origin." *Ibid.*, p. 492.

[38]*Ibid.*, p. xxxii.

[39]The history may be traced in the proceedings of the *Imperial War Conference of 1917* (Cmd. 8566), the *Imperial War Conference of 1918* (Cmd. 9177), the *Conference of Prime Ministers and Representatives of the United Kingdom, the Dominions, and India in 1921* (Cmd. 1474), and the *Imperial Conference of 1926* (Cmd. 2768).

[40]Edward Crankshaw, *The Forsaken Idea* (London: Longmans, Green & Co., 1952).

those who cherished British domination of an empire. And for those who wanted a unified English-speaking imperial state the Commonwealth was both too loose and too diverse. The looseness seems inevitably to go with the diversity. Whatever slight chance there was for unity with the old white and largely English-speaking dominions surely disappeared with the inclusion after World War II of the newly self-governing units of Asia and Africa. Not only did their Commonwealth membership mean that nonwhites were now overwhelmingly preponderant, but these new nations were plainly more unwilling to merge any substantial part of their identity or authority in a larger imperial whole. The Commonwealth could exist only so long as it was really disunited. To be fair, however, this was already its interwar condition in all practical respects. The additions after World War II only made the truth obvious. For example, the word "British" was dropped from the term "British Commonwealth," just as earlier that term had replaced "British Empire." Now it was neither imperial nor British.

The Commonwealth, however, remained of great significance to Englishmen. The preservation of any bond at all between the old imperial units was at least a reminder of past glories and of a special British influence in the world.[41] The Commonwealth idea has been highly cherished for emotional, cultural, and historical associations. Only when judged in the harsh light of power, and in comparison with the older imperial vision, has the Commonwealth bond appeared pale and insipid. Significantly, this is the way the Commonwealth, in its late form, has appeared to the few who continue, wishfully, to cherish genuinely Greater Britain notions.

3. RESIDUAL BELIEFS

Along with the development of the new Commonwealth, there persisted, for those who found its looseness and vagueness insufficient substitutes for the old faith, other residual elements of the imperial order. London was still the center for the numerous organizations that had been started to promote various activities on an empire or a commonwealth basis. In 1953–54, for example, a list of such boards, committees, and societies in the United Kingdom totaled 57, many of which were comparatively recent creations while others had their

[41]As the *Sunday Times* (London) reminded its readers in an editorial marking the change from Empire Day to Commonwealth Day. 24 May 1959, p. 10.

origin in an earlier, more optimistic era.[42] Among these were several devoted to the establishment of trade and tariff preferences among Commonwealth nations. Perhaps they represent the most significant residual imperialist cause, since their ideological base is descended from the earlier imperial federation efforts. Much of the attempted justification for imperial preference in trade and tariffs has not been limited to economic arguments but has also involved the belief in the usefulness of contributing to Commonwealth solidarity. Economic preferences were both an expression of an old bond and a means, it was hoped, of building a new one that would also have political implications.

As such, it is not surprising that the imperial preference movement has been closely linked to the Conservative party. Generally the Conservatives have sought to maintain the traditions of empire. It was their leader, Disraeli, who first proclaimed Britain's modern imperial destiny. And it was their party that defended the cause against its critics, beginning especially with the South African war. At one point, imperialism seemed to be offered to the working class as a counter to socialism. More generally, in relation both to the liberals and to the Labour party, Conservatives presented themselves as conservers of Britain's greatness. The cause was emotive for rank-and-file party activists, and evidently useful in appealing to voters at large. Regularly, into the 1950's, Conservative party conferences passed resolutions urging closer ties to Commonwealth and Empire.[43] Significantly the phrase "imperial policy" continued to be used in party statements. A program of trade preferences was simply the most tangible of the party's general imperialist convictions.

Tangibility derived from the fact that some preferential arrangements had actually been made among the self-governing portions of the old Empire. The dominions were willing, even anxious, for such arrangements, and originally, at the turn of the century, they took the initiative in extending tariff preference to British manufactured goods. Britain itself, largely a free-trade nation until after World War I, reciprocated later with respect particularly to primary products. Since meaningful British preferences to the dominions required a general British tariff from which concessions could be granted, advocates of

[42]Ronald S. Russell, *The Empire and Commonwealth Yearbook* (London: Rolls House Publishing Co., 1953), pp. 22-40.

[43]For examples, see the *74th Annual Report of the Conservative Conference* (1954), pp. 51, 58, and the *75th Annual Report of the Conservative Conference* (1955), pp. 27, 33.

such preferences were necessarily also advocates, in the first place, of a new British tariff policy. The greatest triumph for the cause came with the Ottawa agreements of 1932. Preferences not only among the self-governing nations of the Commonwealth, but also for the colonial empire, were established. An imperial economic union to replace the old Empire now seemed a distinct possibility. But Ottawa, and its immediately following arrangements, turned out to be the high point of the imperial preference cause. As early as the late 1930's, the British government retreated slightly from protectionism and accompanying preferences in return for concessions obtained in the American market under reciprocal trade negotiations.[44] After World War II, further concessions were made to the United States under terms of the Anglo-American Loan and the General Agreement on Tariffs and Trade (GATT). Existing preferences were scaled down and a no-new-preference rule went into effect. Without these concessions, representing the price paid for American aid and American markets, Britain might still have been unable in the new postwar environment to arrange a much larger preference program than that achieved at Ottawa. Nevertheless the result looked like an American victory over imperial preference advocates.

Before the retreat, enough had already been achieved to encourage the advocates of imperial preference to believe that theirs was an entirely feasible economic scheme with decidedly political overtones. And the achievement, at Ottawa, was so recent as to be fresh in the recollections of the postwar years. Advocates of imperial preference persisted in the belief that at least one major step had been taken on the route to imperial unity. Preference agreements had by no means accomplished Chamberlain's imperial *Zollverein*,[45] but the hope had been rekindled. Economic arguments minimizing the actual accrued advantages of the Ottawa agreements had little effect on this hope.[46] Statistics could also be interpreted so as to associate Britain's economic recovery of the 1930's with the new preferential arrangements. And this was surely the way statistics were interpreted by the true imperial believers. They were sustained, in any case, by

[44]The interwar history of imperial preference is fully and clearly presented by W. K. Hancock, *Survey of British Commonwealth Affairs*, Vol. 2, Part 1 (London: Oxford University Press, 1940).

[45]*Ibid.*, p. 85.

[46]There is a careful statistical accounting by Sir Donald MacDougall and Rosemary Hutt, "Imperial Preference: A Quantitative Analysis," *The Economic Journal*, Vol. 114, pp. 233-57 (June 1954).

a faith that transcended purely economic considerations. As L. S. Amery, a Conservative leader of the imperial preference school, said: "The issue between Free Trade, on the one side, and Protection and Preference, on the other, was not a mere detail of trade policy. It was essentially a conflict between two wholly different philosophies of national life."[47] For his preferential philosophy, Amery and his supporters had as much ideological zeal as the Manchester school had had for free trade. Only the British public needed to be convinced of the virtues of preference. The remainder of the Empire was assumed, rather optimistically, to be ready and waiting for preferential arrangements. The United States, it is true, was classed as an inveterate enemy of imperial preference, but Amery and his friends believed that Britain should stand up to American objections. The last of Britain's imperial opportunities was at stake. Unless economic preference united the already self-governing nations of the Commonwealth, nothing of the old dream of a Greater Britain would remain.

Almost nothing of this old dream was left by the mid-1950's. Frustration, rather than hope, now characterized the advocates of imperial preference. Chances to extend preferential arrangements seemed nonexistent. Thus, although established preferences did not yet have to be surrendered, as they would later if Britain were to enter the European Common Market, the battle had already become an almost entirely defensive one.

4. MIDDLE EASTERN ADVENTURES

British imperial experiences in the Middle East obviously deserve special attention here because of their direct relevance to the Suez crisis. Also there is another reason for separate consideration. The Middle East, despite Britain's great interest in the area, remained largely outside of the formal limits of the Empire. In most Middle Eastern nations, British influence and even control were real enough, but they did not take the form of outright imperial acquisition. Egypt, for instance, was not technically a dependency of the British Empire. On the other hand, British imperial experience in the Middle East did develop in the same period (the late nineteenth century) as the great expansion in Africa. Pride in recent accomplishment is therefore similar. In fact, the Middle Eastern accomplishment bulked

[47]L. S. Amery, *My Political Life*, Vol. 3 of *The Unforgiving Years 1929-1940* (London: Hutchinson, 1955), p. 95.

so large in British consciousness as to make national pride seem especially strong.

The Middle Eastern achievement began in 1875 with Disraeli's purchase from the debt-ridden Egyptian ruler of almost half the shares of the Suez Canal Company. Until then the recently completed canal, originally opposed by Britain, had been largely a French affair.[48] French private interests remained, but the British government now became the dominant element on the company's board. Britain's interest in Egypt and the Middle East was thus substantial. That Egypt should have a stable and friendly government was now of prime concern, but the canal was not the sole reason. The Egyptian government was in debt to British and other European bondholders, and it was a matter of moment that such debts should be honored. In the late 1870's, Earl Cromer was already in Egypt as "British Commissioner of the Public Debt." His task was to straighten out Egyptian finances. Ensuing difficulties, particularly a premature Egyptian nationalist revolt against the ruler who was cooperating with Britain, led to a British military landing and occupation in 1882. The occupation included the Suez Canal zone. Cromer became British Agent and Consul General, from which post he exercised effective rule until 1907. His successors operated similarly, and British occupation was continuous until 1956. Only from 1914 to 1922, however, was Egypt's status formally that of a British protectorate. Before 1914, Egypt was technically under a loose Turkish sovereignty. After 1922, Egypt, now nominally independent, began the long process of negotiations which eventually produced a British agreement for withdrawal. No such agreement was concluded before World War II, when Britain again used Egypt as a military base. By this time, Britain had, as a consequence of victories in World War I, become dominant in much of the rest of the Middle East as well as in Egypt.

Much has been written about the significance for Egyptians, and Middle Easterners generally, of this long British domination. Something must also be said for its significance in the British community. Englishmen had fought in one world war to win the Middle East and in the other to hold it. They were surely convinced of its importance. The Suez Canal emerged as the imperial lifeline, the basis of Britain's world trade, and the route to India. Then there was also

[48]Hugh J. Schonfield, *The Suez Canal in World Affairs* (New York: Philosophical Library, 1953).

the growing national stake in Middle Eastern oil. But Britain not only had interests in the Middle East, it also had a sense of belonging there. It was part of the civilizing mission. Englishmen thought they had done something *for* Egypt and Egyptians, not just to them.

A good example of this attitude was provided by a defender of the imperial tradition when, in 1954, the British government agreed to evacuate its Suez Canal base. Referring to the whole period of British experience in Egypt, he spoke of "72 years in which Cromer, Milner, Allenby, Kitchener, Lloyd and Killearn built modern Egypt as we now know it; 72 years in which we built the foundations of what became a British Empire in the Middle East after the First World War and has remained so until the other day. It is an area to which the forces of the Commonwealth came twice in a generation to defend freedom and civilisation."[49] All this may seem a surprisingly late statement of what Milner took for granted as the value of "the guiding hand of Great Britain,"[50] but out of date as it may be in the modern world of rising Asian and African nationalism, there is no reason to think that its meaning had been lost for the British.

With this continued sense of mission went an assurance of the basic gratitude of the subject peoples if not of their political leaders. Egyptians were not exceptions. As one Conservative M.P. said in 1956: "The Egyptians are a kindly, friendly, simple, though emotional people. . . ."[51] This was the basis for distinguishing between an anti-British ruler and his people. It was also the basis for justifying British action against an unfriendly government. The assumption was that the British really acted for the good of the native population. Nowhere was this conception more persistent than in relation to Arabs, often highly romanticized anyway. British soldiers were thought to serve the Arabs as well as Britain.[52] As one of the most famous of these soldiers, Glubb, wrote even after he was removed by nationalist forces from his command of Jordan's army: "I have already referred to the instinctive mutual sympathy which often seems to draw British and Arabs together, even when political relations are bad."[53] Glubb was not the only British imperialist to like Arabs. The manner may

[49]Julian Amery, 531 *H. C. Deb*. 772 (29 July 1954).

[50]Viscount Milner, *England in Egypt* (London: Edward Arnold, 1904), p. 360.

[51]Sir Thomas Moore, 558 *H. C. Deb*. 1674 (1 November 1956).

[52]Thus C. M. Woodhouse wrote of Glubb Pasha in reviewing his book. *Sunday Times* (London), 12 April 1959, p. 14.

[53]John B. Glubb, *Britain and the Arabs* (London: Hodder & Stoughton, 1959), p.394.

have been patronizing, but it seemed so friendly that Englishmen expected friendship in return. And many could never quite believe that it was not there.

As a symbol of the maintenance of British status in the Middle East, the Suez Canal assumed a strikingly great significance in British minds. To control the canal, or at least to prevent anyone else from controlling it, came to be regarded as a matter of life and death. Whether it was so in point of economic fact may be doubted. But certainly the British thought it was. This alone was sufficient cause for keeping troops in Egypt as long as possible.[54] And it was cause for reinforcing British forces there even in 1940, when the island kingdom itself was threatened. As Churchill wrote of this decision: ". . . the War Cabinet were determined to defend Egypt against all comers with whatever resources could be spared from the decisive struggle at home."[55] The fact that the canal was successfully defended, as it had been on a smaller scale in World War I as well, contributed to the subsequent emotion that could be aroused by a threat of some kind of enemy control. As one old canal defender said about Nasser's threat: "Having fought in two wars to stop the Canal from falling into unfriendly hands, I am not going to stand by and see just that happen today."[56]

The nature of Britain's wartime experience in the Middle East was such as to leave, even in the 1940's and 1950's, an especially strong sense of identification. More than elsewhere, the Middle East, even in World War II, had been an area where British arms seemed to have been dominant and decisive.[57] Here the command and the bulk of the forces were not American. The wartime accomplishments were British, and they were considerable. Egypt and the canal were successfully defended; most of the rest of the Middle East was retained by British arms. From Egypt, at El Alamein, the one great *British* overseas victory of World War II was launched. Indeed, at the end of the war Britain seemed as strong as ever in the Middle East. The

[54]Churchill made the point during the discussion in 1946 about Britain's negotiations with Egypt. 422 *H. C. Deb.* 894 (7 May 1946). He had made the same point in 1929. 233 *H. C. Deb.* 1998 (23 December 1929).

[55]Winston S. Churchill, *The Second World War* (Boston: Houghton Mifflin Co., 1949), Vol. 2, p. 418.

[56]Sir J. Hutchison, 558 *H. C. Deb.* 82-83 (12 September 1956).

[57]As Thornton has said, the Middle East was the last place in which the British felt "imperial." *Op. cit.*, pp. 330-31.

appearance was misleading. Britain's dominant postwar position was, as has aptly been said, "by default and on borrowed strength."[58] It rested on American reluctance to intervene and on the temporary nonintervention of Russia. But the British cannot have been expected to have foreseen the rapid end of their recently re-established dominance. And certainly they cannot have been expected to abandon to anyone else the one area which their own forces had just rewon. The imperial tradition here was still very much alive. It was really the area of a last great emotional commitment.

5. ANTI-IMPERIALISM

There is a sense in which it has been accurate to consider the imperialist tradition as widely shared by the British community. Yet a sturdy anti-imperialism has endured as well. Its traditions may be found in the mid-nineteenth century, before the rise of modern British imperialism. The free-trade school argued against empire both as a financial burden and as an impediment to British commerce with the rest of the world. These arguments were bolstered by the broader liberal belief that the spoils and aristocratic ways accompanying imperial rule would have an adverse effect on constitutional government at home.[59] Resembling this was the later Gladstonian attitude that colonies should achieve their independence or at least their free self-government.[60]

Even in the imperialist heyday of the 1890's, when increasing British domination seemed the order of the day, an important minority remained critical. Notably was this true during the South African war. Supported though this war was, at least during its early stages, by an overwhelming majority, a section of the then opposition Liberal party was openly critical—sufficiently so as to be labeled pro-Boer.[61] Afterward their views became more respectable when the British Empire ceased to expand. Sharp and unpopular criticism belonged to the last expansionist period; Hobson's famous critique is a case in point.[62]

[58]A. H. Hourani, "The Middle East and the Crisis of 1956," in St. Antony's Papers No. 4, *Middle Eastern Affairs No. 1* (London: Chatto & Windus, 1958), p. 22.
[59]Knorr, *British Colonial Theories*, chap. 11.
[60]Paul Knaplund, *Gladstone and Britain's Imperial Policy* (London: Allen & Unwin, 1927).
[61]Halevy, *op. cit.*, pp. 93-110.
[62]J. A. Hobson, *Imperialism* (London: Allen & Unwin, 1902).

With the decline of the aggressive imperialist spirit after the South African war, there was temporarily less cause for criticism. Surrender of large imperial parcels, already held, was not yet widely advocated. It was one thing to oppose the further extension of British rule to unwilling subjects, and quite another to suggest withdrawal from responsibilities already assumed. Also, an anti-imperialist could still believe in a Greater Britain based primarily on an association of English-speaking nations.[63] The difference from the imperialist was in a willingness to accept a relatively loose association.

This idea of a loose association, eventually identified with the emerging Commonwealth, was often at odds with particulars of the imperialist belief after World War I. This was certainly true of imperial preference. Liberals of a free-trade persuasion preserved their bias against preference. They mustered strong arguments and lost only temporarily, as it turned out, in the early 1930's, when the Ottawa agreements came into force. For liberals, the attempt of Britain to secure a preferred position in the markets of imperial dependencies was a violation of the trust by which Britain was supposed to govern backward peoples; preferential arrangements seemed to substitute imperial self-interest, especially on Britain's own behalf, for the general interest of the dependencies presumably served by international free trade.[64] Even preference among self-governing Commonwealth nations was objected to on the ground of its essentially nationalistic character. "Imperial self-sufficiency" was criticized as an idea projected from the state-of-siege mentality characteristic of World War I and its aftermath. Furthermore, its opponents were sure that the growth of strictly Empire trade would be at the expense of foreign markets that Britain and most of the other Commonwealth nations could not afford to lose. For this reason, doubt was expressed as to the economic feasibility of any substantial move toward imperial preference. Commonwealth nations were expected to view such a move as impractical. Such steps as were taken, particularly under the Ottawa agreements, did not appear so momentous as advocates of preference claimed. Opponents even denied that any increase in Empire trade resulted from Ottawa; they argued that there was a greater percentage of increase in such trade before 1932 than after,

[63]As did G. P. Gooch, "Imperialism," in *The Heart of the Empire* (London: T. Fisher Unwin, 1901), pp. 308-97.
[64]Hancock, *op. cit.*, p. 308.

and that following Ottawa non-Empire trade increased faster than Empire trade.[65] The facts plainly were in dispute. The important thing to note here is that imperial preference remained debatable even when its establishment seemed to have begun in earnest, and that this debate was largely a reflection of the larger dispute over the imperial tradition.

Imperialism was a target not only for liberals. It also became an important enemy for the newly enlarged socialist movement. Drawing variously on Hobson as well as Lenin, British socialists opposed the imperial tradition on a broad front. Often they became identified with the cause of colonial independence. Their anti-imperialism tended to be strengthened in reaction to the Conservative champions of empire. On this subject as on so many others, socialists, through the Labour party, represented the interwar opposition. However, there was more than this by way of intellectual support for socialist anti-imperialism. The British experience over the past century was seen in a different perspective from that held by imperialists. Thus a socialist could say in 1956, in sharp contrast to the Conservative pride in imperial accomplishment, that "no country has committed so many crimes against Egypt as this country has . . . " and "let it be remembered that for many years we imposed the Government of Egypt upon the people of Egypt."[66]

A significant aspect of this well-known anti-imperialist attitude was that its exponents also believed in the continued greatness of the British role in the world. Forcible domination of other countries was rejected, to be sure, but for this traditional basis for British influence the anti-imperialists almost always sought to substitute a new moral force that would be just as British as that which had gone before. As Earl Attlee said, ". . . in these days Great Britain's influence in the world depends far more on moral leadership than on force."[67] Socialists argued that they were best equipped to supply this leadership, presumably because of their break from the nation's imperial past. The act of freeing colonial dependencies supplied a basis for "giving a lead" to the rest of the world in standards of international morality. The paradox is that this very policy of moral leadership depended on Britain having an empire to surrender. Anti-imperialism

[65]*Ibid.*, pp. 230 ff.
[66]Wedgwood Benn, 558 *H. C. Deb.* 1699-1700 (1 November 1956).
[67]199 *H. L. Deb.* 733 (13 September 1956).

required an imperialist past and present. Britain's claim to lead the world morally derived from the fact that it had recently led by other means. British leadership in any form, through the new Commonwealth concept for example, was simply the last and the least substantial of the old imperialist ideas of Britain's destiny in the world. The imperial experience thus left its mark on the attitudes of its critics as well as of its champions. Both, in the mid-twentieth century, hankered for a national greatness that had only recently seemed certain to be Britain's destiny.

CHAPTER THREE

Policy Record

Useful, along with the general imperial experience, for following the internal politics of the Suez crisis, is the policy record that was the subject of controversy. Unfortunately, this record is not entirely clear with respect to all negotiations and motivations,[1] but this matters less here than it would in a study of international relations. Certain crucial external events are not in dispute, and these are listed, beside the relevant British political events, in the detailed log at the end of this chapter. All that remains to be done is to describe Britain's Suez policy just before 1956, to note Prime Minister Eden's position, and to comment briefly on the most significant of Britain's actions in 1956-57. On other events, such as the simultaneously important Hungarian crisis, the log supplies the crucial chronology.

Until the time that President Nasser nationalized the Suez Canal Company in 1956, the British government had continued, however reluctantly, its postwar policy of gradual retreat from Egypt as from other imperial outposts. The most signal mark of this retreat was the 1954 agreement of Britain to evacuate its large military base in the Suez Canal zone. This had been the base which the British regarded

---

[1]A perceptive observer has said of the lack of knowledge of Suez policy-making: "Perhaps we shall never know; the essential discussions may never have been recorded, and it may be that those who took the decisions have obscured even to themselves the real reasons for which they took them, by the excuses which they later invented to prove that they were right." A. H. Hourani, "The Middle East and the Crisis of 1956," in St. Antony's Papers No. 4, *Middle Eastern Affairs No. 1* (London: Chatto & Windus, 1958), p. 10.

as the means for the defense of their interests in the canal, in Egypt, and in the Middle East generally. Withdrawing troops from Suez seemed significant militarily as well as symbolically. Under the agreement, the last British troops were to be withdrawn (and they actually were) early in 1956. The long history of the British military presence in Egypt was evidently ended. The base itself, with technical installations, was to be maintained, but it was subject to British reactivation only in the event of armed attack by an outside power (not Israel) on Egypt, other Arab nations, or Turkey. Even on this matter, any British return was plainly contingent on Egyptian cooperation. But cooperation, in general, Britain now hoped to obtain from Egypt. It was on this prospect that Eden had staked some of his reputation when, as Foreign Secretary, he defended the 1954 agreement against Conservative critics of withdrawal.[2]

Even before the nationalization of the canal, there were signs that Egyptian cooperation was limited. Verbal attacks on British and Western imperialism continued, particularly in conjunction with Nasser's hostility to Israel as the supposed Middle Eastern outpost of the imperialist powers. President Nasser arranged for arms from the Soviet bloc. Nevertheless, into mid-1956, Britain, along with the United States, pursued a generally conciliatory policy. Britain fulfilled her agreement to evacuate the last of her troops from the canal, and joined the United States in the commitment of funds to help finance Nasser's projected Aswan Dam. This effort ended on 19 July 1956 when the American Secretary of State, John Foster Dulles, told the Egyptians ("abruptly,"[3] Eden later said) that the Aswan Dam deal was off. So it was for Britain too. This was the immediate backdrop for the nationalization of the canal company. Nasser's speech to this effect was on 26 July, and he coupled the nationalization announcement with the statement that funds obtained from operating the canal would be used to finance the Aswan Dam. He promised to compensate the share-

[2]531 *H. C. Deb*. 818-19 (29 July 1954). The agreement had been called "a piece of paper" and a "give-away" by Captain Waterhouse, 531 *H. C. Deb*. 738, 739 (29 July 1954). His views are treated in the next chapter.

[3]Sir Anthony Eden, *Full Circle* (London: Cassell & Co., 1960), p. 422. This was the first volume of his *Memoirs* to be published although it covers his last years of office, 1951-57. Eden might have preferred to have handled the matter so as to avoid wounding Nasser's pride, but Eden seems to have agreed with Dulles in withdrawing the offer. It has even been suggested that Eden had known of the prospective American withdrawal and had approved of it. Erskine B. Childers, *The Road to Suez* (London: MacGibbon & Kee, 1962), pp. 161-62, 191.

holders. What was nationalized, of course, was the Universal Suez Maritime Canal Company. Technically this was a legitimate exercise of Egyptian sovereignty. The company had operated under Egyptian law according to a 100-year concession due to expire in 1968. Nasser, it is true, had ended this concession 12 years early, but it was not this narrow issue that chiefly aroused Britain. It was the anti-imperialist hostility implied in the act and circumstances of nationalization. Much was made of the unilateral and arbitrary features of Nasser's move. These, the British thought, threatened the free use of the canal as guaranteed by the 1888 Convention. That convention, recognizing the international character of the canal, had made the great European powers of the day jointly concerned with Turkey (then acting for Egypt) for the maintenance of free use of the canal. Nasser had not denounced this convention, but his good faith in observing it was doubted. This was now the case although he would not have had to nationalize the company in order to interfere with free use of the canal. Egypt had for some years barred the canal to Israel. And the canal did not have to be owned by Egypt for this to be done to the ships of other countries as well. Yet it was evidently nationalization that convinced the British that Nasser was capable of interfering with their shipping too. Even without such interference, however, the hostility involved in nationalization of so important a British-dominated concern was a major psychological blow.

The difference between Britain and Egypt was sharply drawn over the issue of control subsequent to nationalization. Britain took the position that Egypt, regardless of its new ownership, should allow an international authority to control the operation of the canal.[4] This was the very principle that Nasser would not accept. It would destroy the entire effect of nationalization if he were now to be left only with ownership but not control. The nationalist base for the seizure would be abandoned if he were to yield the just-asserted Egyptian sovereignty to an international authority. The Egyptian idea was for Egyptians to manage the canal themselves. The most they would concede was a promise to manage the canal in the general interest as provided by

[4]In measured words, repeated twice in the Commons within a week of nationalization, Prime Minister Eden proclaimed: "No arrangements for the future of this great international waterway could be acceptable to Her Majesty's Government which would leave it in the unfettered control of a single Power which could, as recent events have shown, exploit it purely for purposes of national policy." 557 *H. C. Deb.* 919, 1603 (30 July, 2 August 1956).

the 1888 Convention. Nasser refused to accept any international supervision over Egypt's management, and he refused to share this management with any non-Egyptian authority.

Between July and the end of October 1956 Britain pursued various policies designed to get Nasser to yield on the issue of international control. These policies were of two different but related types. Negotiation was pressed, and at the same time Anglo-French military preparations in the eastern Mediterranean were conspicuously undertaken. The latter were plainly meant to convince Nasser of the value of making a concession from his insistence on purely Egyptian control of the waterway. To this end, Britain joined France and the United States in convening an international conference in London in August. Invited were all of the parties to the 1888 Convention plus other important canal users. Only Egypt and Greece did not attend, but, of those present, four (India, Ceylon, Indonesia, and the U.S.S.R.) did not accept the proposals emerging from the conference for an international Suez Canal Board, with Egyptian representation, to operate, manage, and develop the canal. Neither did Egypt accept this scheme, known as the 18-nation or 18-power proposals, when representatives from the conference subsequently visited Cairo. Nasser regarded the proposals as an infringement of Egyptian sovereignty. He was not alone in asserting this position. It was shared by the four dissenting nations at the London conference, and these included two Asian members of the Commonwealth.

The 18-nation proposals were not the last of the efforts to negotiate. A second London conference was held in September to form a Suez Canal Users Association. This organization, originally suggested by the United States, was thought by the British to provide a means to exert economic pressure on Egypt to make a favorable settlement. Its ineffectiveness for this purpose became apparent when the United States interpreted the Association's policy so as to exclude both economic pressure and shooting the West's way through the canal.

Similarly Britain was thwarted in attempting to secure international control through United Nations action. This was tried in late September and early October. The Security Council did adopt six general principles for the operation of the canal in the interests of all concerned, but the remainder of a resolution, calling for negotiation on the basis of the international control implied by the 18-nation proposals, was vetoed by Russia.[5] For the British, this seemed to eliminate the action required to make the six principles effective. In other words, the United Nations Security Council would not ask Egypt to negotiate the one thing Britain wanted to negotiate.

The likelihood of Egyptian concessions to Britain's view also declined as the weeks and months went by and the canal continued to be used effectively despite its new ownership and management. International control was bound to seem less imperative to the rest of the world as shipping continued to move through the canal under Egyptian control. The affair of the pilots drove this point home. The old canal company's pilots, mainly Western nationals, were originally ordered by Nasser's nationalization decree to remain at work. Also at this time the company itself, responding to the early British and French hopes for a favorable settlement, agreed that its employees should postpone any departure from Egypt. In mid-September, however, the company plainly welcomed the decisions of its non-Egyptian employees to leave their positions.[6] Some had already left, and many more now did so. Canal pilotage being a skilled task for experienced men, the British were no doubt encouraged to think that Nasser would now be unable to run the canal efficiently and so demonstrate Egypt's inadequacy to manage a great international waterway in the interests of world trade. But Nasser did find new pilots, some from Russia, and trained others sufficiently so that traffic was substantially unimpeded.[7] The result was to make Britain's case less convincing. Now international control had to be advocated for its value as a general principle, or as a safeguard against future Egyptian conduct at odds with the present effective Egyptian management of the canal.

Yet Britain persisted, however futilely, in its efforts to secure external control. Its arguments at the United Nations Security Council came

[5]United Nations, *Security Council Official Records*, Eleventh Year (New York), 743rd Meeting (13 October 1956), p. 18. Security Council discussion of the issue, presented by Britain and France, also took place at the 734th Meeting (26 September 1956), 735th Meeting (5 October 1956), 736th Meeting (8 October 1956), 737th Meeting (8 October 1956), 738th Meeting (9 October 1956), and 742nd Meeting (13 October 1956). The 739th, 740th, and 741st Meetings (9, 11, 12 October 1956) were private.

[6]Royal Institute of International Affairs, *Documents on International Affairs 1956* (London: Oxford University Press, 1959), pp. 115, 158, 201. Chaps. 2, 3, and 4 of this volume contain a most useful collection of documents, plus careful summary comment, on the Suez affair.

[7]As Eden later wrote, "The replacements, drawn from many lands, did their job much better than the company or we had been led to expect." *Op. cit.*, p. 468.

after Nasser's pilots were successfully on the job. At the same time, the Anglo-French military force in the eastern Mediterranean remained conspicuous. During much of this period, the British government, under Eden, also persisted in its attempts to secure American support for its strong anti-Nasser policy, although there were early indications that the United States did not share the Anglo-French zeal over the canal.[8] The story of Eden's relations with Eisenhower and Dulles from August to October is a tangled one, and it does seem possible that American policy was ambiguous enough to allow Eden to hope for strong backing that he never received.[9] Eden himself has not cited any clear-cut American promise of support for the use of force, but he was plainly disappointed by the United States at each critical juncture.[10] He wanted more American economic pressure against Nasser, plus American tolerance, at least, of Anglo-French threats to use military force. Eden tried for months to avoid acting apart from the United States, and certainly to avoid American antagonism.

Only with the disillusionment at the United Nations in mid-October was it clear that if Egyptian control of the canal was to be broken it would have to be done without the United States. This ruled out economic pressures, which could not be effective without American participation, and it left no recourse except the use of force outside the United Nations. When, therefore, Britain and France did use force, on the occasion of Israeli-Egyptian hostilities in late October, it is no wonder that much of the world believed that Britain and France had seized this occasion, if not actually arranged it, in order to serve their own anti-Nasser purpose. Eden consistently denied collusion and even any "foreknowledge that Israel would attack Egypt."[11] The most that he would admit was that his government had a "shrewd idea" of what might happen between Israel and Egypt.[12] Britain and France did seem prepared to act on 29 October, when Israeli troops entered Egypt, and to do so in a way unfavorable to Egypt.[13] The Anglo-French ultimatum, giving Egypt and Israel

[8]See the United States statement of 27 July 1956, published by the Royal Institute of International Affairs, *op. cit.*, p. 117.

[9]Eden, *op. cit.*, pp. 435, 436-37.

[10]*Ibid.*, pp. 454, 458-59.

[11]562 *H. C. Deb.* 1518 (20 December 1956).

[12]562 *H. C. Deb.* 1492 (20 December 1956).

[13]The degree of foreknowledge is probed intensively by Childers, *op. cit.*, pp. 235-61.

12 hours to cease fire and to withdraw ten miles on either side of the canal, was plainly uneven since it asked Egypt to withdraw from its own territory and Israel only from a part of Egypt which Israeli troops had not yet reached. It is hard to see how Eden, despite his stated hopes and his own desire to avoid a pro-Israeli position, could have expected Egypt to have accepted the ultimatum. Its refusal brought the Anglo-French military attack, with its air and naval bombardment and, several days later, troop landings by air and sea.[14] The troops occupied only part of the canal zone before their southward advance was halted by international pressure against Britain and France.

The effectiveness of this pressure, exerted through United Nations resolutions for a cease-fire and for an international force to replace Anglo-French occupation,[15] undoubtedly depended on American willingness to oppose Britain and France. Eden seems to have under-estimated what the United States would do to stop the military action. Even though his failure to inform the United States of the prospective Anglo-French action indicated an appreciation of likely American opposition,[16] he must have expected the opposition to be mild once Britain and France had committed themselves.[17] What Eden was not prepared for was so prompt and thoroughgoing an American effort to halt the attack before it had succeeded. Nor was he prepared for the effective American pressure, later in the fall, to force Britain and France to withdraw their troops before the canal was cleared. Before

[14]An official British description of the military operation and an explanation of why troops could not be landed earlier is contained in the Despatch by General Sir Charles F. Keightley, Commander-in-Chief, Allied Forces, published as a *Supplement to the London Gazette* of 10 September 1957, Numb. 41172 (12 September 1957).

[15]United Nations, *Security Council Official Records*, Eleventh Year (New York), 749th Meeting (30 October 1956), pp. 24-25; 751st Meeting (31 October 1956), p. 22. United Nations, *Official Records of the General Assembly*, First Emergency Special Session, 562nd Meeting (1 November 1956), pp. 34-35; 563rd Meeting (3 November 1956), pp. 71-73.

[16]558 *H. C. Deb.* 1378, 1449 (30-31 October 1956). Premier Mollet of France said candidly that the American government was not informed of the final Anglo-French decisions because the United States would have stopped them. *Debats de l'Assembleé Nationale*, III, p. 6186 (20 December 1956).

[17]Eden's Foreign Secretary, Selwyn Lloyd, has been quoted to the effect that the British government had thought that American opinion would vary from "benevolent neutrality" to "hostile neutrality." Randolph Churchill, *The Rise and Fall of Sir Anthony Eden* (London: MacGibbon & Kee, 1959), p. 293. Among the reasons suggested for this optimistic expectation were that Britain thought that Eisenhower would be preoccupied with his re-election campaign or worried about offending Jewish voters by a stand that would seem anti-Israeli as well as anti-British.

the end of December, Eden had to accept withdrawal and thus weaken any face-saving claim he was still making for the abortive invasion. His successor, Harold Macmillan, completed the liquidation of the venture when he announced in May 1957 that British ships could use the now cleared canal, under its Egyptian management.

The reasons for Eden's decision to halt and withdraw are not absolutely clear.[18] They are worth exploration at another time. Here, however, the important thing to stress is simply the failure of Eden's policy. That is the crucial datum for a discussion of the British political system during the crisis. Whatever the cause, Eden was unable to secure what he wanted from Egypt. This was plainly true of his policy in the summer and early fall, when he tried to secure American support for making Nasser yield to international control, and it was also true of the military intervention insofar as it was meant to secure such control on Anglo-French terms. And if the intervention was meant only to stop Israeli-Egyptian hostilities and safeguard the canal, as Eden unconvincingly claimed, it still seemed unsuccessful since the Egyptians blocked the canal and were able to refuse to clear it until Britain and France, plus Israel, withdrew their troops.[19] The forced withdrawal, after the forced cease-fire, undercut Britain's claim to have accomplished anything. Consequently Eden and his government had a policy that would be attacked not only as wrong but as a humiliating failure. Yet neither Eden nor his successor ever retreated from their defense of Suez policy as a useful peace-making action in behalf of a general as well as a British cause.

[18]Eden does discuss the reasons in *Full Circle*, pp. 556-57.
[19]Royal Institute of International Affairs, *op. cit.*, pp. 310-12.

Suez Log: 1956-57

	External Event	British Political Event
19 July	U.S. withdrawal of Aswan Dam offer	
26 July	Egyptian nationalization of canal company	
27 July		Eden's first parliamentary statement on nationalization
30 July		Further parliamentary statement by Eden
2 Aug		Parliamentary speeches by Eden, Gaitskell, & others
16 Aug	First London conference (22 powers)	
21 Aug	18-power proposals from London conference	
3 Sept	Menzies mission meets Nasser	
9 Sept	Rejection of 18-power proposals by Nasser	
12 Sept		Special parliamentary discussion on Suez
13 Sept		Special parliamentary discussion on Suez
19 Sept	Second London conference	
21 Sept	Users club proposals at London conference	
23 Sept	Britain and France submit case to U.N. Security Council	
1 Oct	Third London conference, re Users club	
10 Oct		Conservative party conference endorses strong Suez policy
13 Oct	U.N. Security Council adopts general principles for canal operation, but Anglo-French proposals vetoed	
16 Oct	Paris meeting of Eden, Lloyd, Mollet, & Pineau	
23 Oct	Violent Hungarian demonstration against Communist gov't	Foreign Secretary's statement to H.C. on Suez situation
24 Oct	Hungarian Communist gov't calls for Russian troops	

	External Event	British Political Event
28 Oct	New Nagy gov't in Hungary promises reforms & announces withdrawal of Russian troops from Budapest	
29 Oct	Israel attacks Egypt	
30 Oct	Anglo-French ultimatum Anglo-French veto of U.N. Security Council resolution for Israeli withdrawal Nagy announces end of Hungarian single-party system	H.C. debate on ultimatum; unexpected division
31 Oct	Anglo-French air and naval attack begins U.N. Security Council calls for emergency session of General Assembly	Labour criticism of action in H.C. & Gaitskell's announcement of party opposition
1 Nov	U.N. General Assembly debates U.S. cease-fire resolution Nagy declares Hungarian neutrality	Continued debate in H.C. & division on censure motion
2 Nov	U.N. General Assembly adopts cease-fire Nagy gov't protests new Russian troops	Labour urges, in H.C., acceptance of cease-fire. Continued questioning of Eden
3 Nov	Canal blocked by Egypt Britain & France do not accept cease-fire U.N. General Assembly continues sessions Russian troops re-enter Budapest	Saturday meeting of H.C. to debate U.N. resolution and military situation Eden broadcast
4 Nov	U.N. General Assembly adopts Canadian proposal for U.N. emergency force; again urges Anglo-French compliance U.N. General Assembly condemns Russian force in Hungary, after Russian veto of Security Council resolution	Labour mass meetings protesting Suez action Gaitskell broadcast
5 Nov	Britain & France indicate coming cease-fire but continue operations with landing of airborne troops Russia suggests joint U.S.-U.S.S.R. effort in Middle East	H.C. debate on U.N. resolution Announcement of resignation of Nutting, Minister of State for Foreign Affairs

	External Event	*British Political Event*
6 Nov	Anglo-French seaborne troops land Britain & France accept cease-fire (midnight) U.S. presidential election	H.C. debate continued after Queen's speech opening new parliamentary session
7 Nov	U.N. General Assembly establishes procedure for emergency force and calls for Anglo-French-Israeli withdrawal	H.C. debate on Queen's speech
8 Nov		H.C. debate and division on Suez action; eight Conservative abstentions
12 Nov	Nasser agrees to U.N. force	
15 Nov	First U.N. troops land in canal zone	
19 Nov		Eden ill, cancels engagements
21 Nov		Date for petrol rationing announced
23 Nov		Eden leaves for rest in Jamaica
25 Nov	Renewed U.N. call for Anglo-French-Israeli withdrawal	
3 Dec		Britain announces forthcoming withdrawal
6 Dec		H.C. debate and division on withdrawal; 15 Conservative abstentions
7 Dec	U.S. announcement of loan to Britain	
14 Dec		Eden returns from Jamaica
20 Dec		Eden denies collusion charges in H.C.
22 Dec	Anglo-French withdrawal complete	
28 Dec	U.N. salvage operations begin	
10 Jan		Eden resigns
11 Jan		Macmillan becomes Prime Minister
8 March	Last Israeli troops withdraw	
24 April	Canal fully reopened	
13 May		Macmillan announces advice to shipowners to use canal
15 May		Petrol rationing ends
16 May		Debate and division on government advice to shipowners; 14 Conservative abstentions

CHAPTER FOUR

The Staunch Imperial Position:
The Suez Group

The justification for British military intervention emerging from the previous chapter is the government's, and particularly Eden's. It was a justification drawn only in part from the tradition of Britain's imperial responsibilities. Eden did believe, along with many of his fellow countrymen, that Britain had the power and the duty, as well as the interest, to act decisively in Middle Eastern affairs. But neither he nor his governmental colleagues were ever the principal champions of the full imperial position on Suez. Rather, as already observed, Eden himself had been identified in 1954 with the nonimperial policy of withdrawal from Suez. Even his justification for re-entry in 1956 involved a peace-making claim rather than a straightforward reassertion of British authority. And he was by no means ready to act against great and overt American pressure. First, Eden thought there would be no such pressure. Then, surprised by its degree, he retreated.

On all these points, the full imperial view was different. Represented by the substantial minority of Conservative M.P.s known as the Suez group, this view involved an uninhibited commitment to the forceful assertion of British authority in the Middle East (or elsewhere). Doubts about American support were not crucial since hostility by the United States was assumed almost as a matter of course. In this as in other ways, the full imperial position of the Suez group was extremist and ordinarily untypical of the bulk of British opinion. Its importance, however, was greater than its fringe status might suggest.

This was partly because of a special appeal of imperialism to Conservative party activists—stronger than to most Conservative M.P.s— and partly because, during the Suez crisis, the full imperial position seemed a sturdier support for the government than did some of Eden's own arguments. It was the moment for the resurgence of an unadulterated imperial spirit. The essence of the old doctrine, unencumbered by the doubts and qualifications of the government, was having its day. Accordingly, it is worth looking closely at the position of the Suez group as one way of understanding support for British action at Suez. It is true that the group's high imperial theme seems out of touch with the real world, but it is a significant symptom of the crisis that this theme, no matter how unrealistic, should have been revived.

1. CANAL AND EMPIRE

Maintaining British military force in the canal zone was crucial for the Suez group, but not so much just to protect the canal as to preserve Britain's entire Middle East position. The canal zone was the principal imperial base in the Middle East, and therefore its evacuation, as promised in 1954, signaled general retreat. In this respect, it is hard to say that the Suez group did not read the signal correctly. However impractical and impolitic the long-run maintenance of the base, its evacuation did mark a retreat from a former position of strength. Cyprus, subsequently to be retreated from as well, seemed an unlikely substitute for the established facilities of Suez. The plain fact was that the surrender of the Suez base in 1954 did mark a substantial lessening in Britain's "ability to make and unmake kings and governments, to move troops and ships and aircraft as she pleased throughout the lands and waters of the Middle East and over the air space of the countries of the Middle East."[1] The only question was whether the evacuation agreement itself caused the diminution of British influence in the Middle East, or whether the agreement merely recognized an already diminished influence, in addition to an inability to derive any real use from the base in the 1950's. The Suez group refused to accept the pessimistic second alternative, and argued in 1954 that the base could and should be preserved to allow British power still to be exercised. The power, it was assumed, remained sufficient. Giving up the base was the vital step in imperial retreat as far as the Suez

[1] John Marlowe, *Arab Nationalism and British Imperialism* (New York: Praeger, 1961), p. 201.

group was concerned. The decision to evacuate could never be accepted as desirable.

The Suez group had begun to organize to defend the imperial interest in the canal zone even before 1954. It originated in 1952 just after the Egyptian military revolution, then under the nominal leadership of General Neguib, seized power and made the continued British presence in the canal zone more insecure than it had been under the Farouk regime. One of the first Conservative M.P.s to respond was Major Legge-Bourke, already known as an independent-minded critic of Britain's general imperial retreat. Almost immediately after the Egyptian revolution, Legge-Bourke suggested to Julian Amery, then a young Conservative M.P. whose imperialism was established by family background as well as by his own statements, that "some of us might be prepared to take extremely independent action"[2] if an evacuation proposal were made by the Churchill government. Shortly afterward, in the winter of 1952-53, Julian Amery called a meeting of those similarly troubled at the home of his father, L. S. Amery, the most respected of the elder imperial statesmen. The object was to exert pressure within the governing Conservative party in Parliament, and so on the Conservative cabinet itself, to stand fast against Egyptian demands for British evacuation.

When the group's effort failed and it became plain that the Conservative government of Winston Churchill, with Eden as Foreign Secretary, was agreeing in 1954 to evacuate Suez, Legge-Bourke did take the "extremely independent action" of which he had spoken. He resigned the Conservative whip—that is, he became an independent M.P. This was one step further than any of his colleagues in the Suez group were then willing to go. But they, or at least 25 of an estimated 40, did join Legge-Bourke in voting against the agreement when the government presented it to the Commons.[3] While this was an unusual break in parliamentary party discipline, the negative votes could not seriously affect the government's position since the Labour opposition, more wholeheartedly committed to evacuation than the government, could hardly vote with the Suez group. Labour simply abstained. Consequently, against the government's large majority, the Suez group was ineffective. Legge-Bourke later argued that the

[2]As recounted by Legge-Bourke in a reminiscing speech, 570 *H. C. Deb.* 629 (16 May 1957).

[3]531 *H. C. Deb.* 821-22 (29 July 1954).

group would have been more effective if it had generally followed his own more extreme action of resigning the whip. He said this in 1957 after he himself, having accepted the whip again, decided that repeated rebellion against the government's Suez policy was futile. He insisted that the die had been cast in 1954.[4] Although it is unlikely that more resignations, rather than merely negative votes, would even then have won the day, nevertheless Legge-Bourke was probably correct in thinking that the decisive act took place in 1954.

On this point, his colleagues in the Suez group did not necessarily disagree at the time even though they preferred to carry on their fight within Conservative ranks and thus to live politically to fight another day. Their apparent leader, Captain Waterhouse, was no less concerned than Legge-Bourke with the significance of British evacuation. He believed that the real reasons for withdrawal were the grievous ones of "becoming weary of our responsibilities, that our burdens are becoming too irksome for us and we are really losing our will to rule."[5] Similarly, Julian Amery struck the high note of Britain's responsibilities, but, despite his realization of the futility of the Suez group's fight on this occasion, he was more optimistic about the future than was his older colleague. When, he said, "those who now oppose or deride our efforts" do see the consequence of the agreement, they might realize that "this is not a fight in the last ditch, but perhaps the beginning of a return to that faith in Britain's imperial mission and destiny without which, in my belief, our people will never be prosperous, or safe or free."[6]

The consequences of the 1954 agreement, in the Suez group's perspective, were evident when Nasser seized the canal in 1956. Now the evident failure of a soft British policy provided an argument to reverse the 1954 decision by returning British military force to its old base. That Nasser could defy Britain and the West generally by nationalizing the canal was proof that only with the presence of military force in the area could Britain influence Middle Eastern policies and events. To maintain this influence generally, not just to reassert control of the canal, it was necessary to seize the present opportunity of reoccupying Suez. Thus the old Suez group favored a forceful policy throughout the summer and fall of 1956. It made

[4] 570 *H. C. Deb.* 633 (16 May 1957).
[5] 531 *H. C. Deb.* 743 (29 July 1954).
[6] 531 *H. C. Deb.* 782 (29 July 1954).

sense from its point of view, based as it was on the assumption that Britain could and should maintain its imperial influence. The Suez group, at least, was willing to fight in behalf of that influence. Its spokesmen understood that actual fighting might well be the consequence of their policy—advocated immediately after nationalization—that Britain and France should reoccupy the canal zone. As Julian Amery remarked in early August of 1956, ". . . one has to face the risks involved" if one is thinking in terms of armed forces going to Suez.[7] He was willing to face not only the risk of actual fighting, but also the risk of such fighting without American support. The United States, he thought, had "done us enough harm in the Middle East already. We must make it clear to them that if they will not or cannot join us, then we will go ahead without them. It will not be the first time. Our life is at stake, and we can do no other."[8] Solidarity with France was the key, Amery said. There was a "gleaming opportunity" to redeem "what has been lost and to re-establish British influence in the Middle East on firm and permanent foundations."[9] American anticolonialism was to be ignored by a revitalized imperial Britain (and France).

Specifically the Suez group wanted Eden to act immediately, in early August, without waiting for the United Nations or for any conferences. The keynote was that Nasser's unilateral nationalization presented a "momentous opportunity" which would be lost by allowing time for misgivings of other powers and for a front to be formed against Britain. Nasser had to be given an ultimatum at once, declared Lord Hinchingbrooke, a most outspoken member of the Suez group. The expiry of the ultimatum should be governed by military considerations. If Eden followed this policy, Hinchingbrooke believed, his "name and fortunes will rise to new heights of eminence among his countrymen, and the policies of his country will achieve world renown."[10] As it happened, Eden and perhaps the British military establishment were not prepared to adopt the Suez group's demand for immediate action. But even with the passage, after nationalization, of the first weeks (and probably the best weeks, in the eyes of many besides the Suez group), the group remained insistent on a strong and forceful British policy.

[7]557 *H. C. Deb.* 1700 (2 August 1956).
[8]557 *H. C. Deb.* 1701 (2 August 1956).
[9]557 *H. C. Deb.* 1701 (2 August 1956).
[10]557 *H. C. Deb.* 1641 (2 August 1956).

Their role at the Conservative party conference, in mid-October, is indicative of a continued militancy. The Suez group was still trying to press the government to take action despite the fact that the case was by no means as persuasive now that Nasser was successfully operating the canal. Anglo-French intervention no longer seemed justified as an emergency response to protect the flow of commerce. In fact, by mid-October, the occasion for intervention, if it had ever existed, seemed to have gone. The British government might well have been suspected of giving up the whole idea despite its gathering of military force and despite its failure to win any substantial concessions from Nasser via the conference route. What had been proposed at the August conference in London now seemed dead. This conclusion, however, is exactly what the Suez group did not want the government to accept. And the group was still prepared to advocate the use of force, even in less favorable international circumstances than those of the summer, as an alternative to acceptance of Nasser's terms. The extremists had not forsaken the goal of re-establishing British influence in the Middle East. Accordingly, they sought at the annual Conservative conference to commit the party, and hopefully the government as well, to a stronger line than the official one submitted by party leaders. The motion proposed by the leadership was little more than an endorsement of the government's efforts to reach "a just solution." It said nothing about military force and also nothing about the government's continued commitment to the international control of the canal which had been the "just solution" previously urged. It was this form of solution which, it was now plain, could be achieved only by force of arms against Egypt.

Nevertheless Captain Waterhouse, for the Suez group, successfully proposed an addendum to the official resolution. Obviously so popular in Conservative ranks that it had to be accepted by the leadership, the addendum put after "just solution" the words "designed to ensure international control of the canal in accordance with the proposals of the London Conference."[11] In this amended form, the motion was carried in the huge mass meeting with only one dissent. The meaning of the language of the addendum had been spelled out by its principal advocates, Waterhouse and Julian Amery. As Waterhouse said, in moving his addendum, ". . . at all costs and by all means Nasser's aggression must be resisted and defeated. For let us have no doubt

[11] *76th Annual Report of the Conservative Conference* (1956), p. 22.

at all, that at this moment Britain is at a vital cross roads in her history."[12] Let us tell the Prime Minister, he added, that if he will lead we will follow. Amery was more explicit. He told the party conference that the addendum would give the lie to "all those rumors that we are abandoning the concept of control for the concept of supervision." And if the current British appeal for control should fail in the United Nations Security Council, then "our hands are free to use any and every measure that may be necessary to achieve our ends, including, if necessary, the use of force."[13] This Britain should do, Amery declared, if necessary even against American wishes. There was not much doubt that he thought it would be necessary. Amery was saying in an only slightly less blunt way what his Suez group colleague, Lord Hinchingbrooke, had told his constituents in early October. Britain should not be afraid of using "a little bit of gunboat diplomacy."[14]

Such language was by no means the government's. Nor was the government committed by the amended resolution to any policy against its desires. Conservative governments acknowledged no conference authority to dictate policy. What the strong resolution and the fire-eating speeches did mean, however, was that the government now knew that it could count on enthusiastic rank-and-file party support for any strong action that it did decide to undertake, and that failure to secure international control of the canal without strong action would be unpopular in the party. The policy of the Suez group was clearly the policy of Conservative party activists if not of the parliamentary leadership. More precisely, the Suez group's immediate policy line with respect to the canal was accepted by party activists. Whether this also involved an acceptance of the Suez group's whole imperial perspective may be doubted. Other Conservatives may not have shared the view that the Suez crisis was principally an opportunity for a general reassertion of British imperial responsibility in the Middle East. And this meant that the party was not necessarily prepared for the consequences of such a reassertion of responsibility.

The Suez group, however, was prepared, and it supported the government's intervention, when it did come, with great fervor. Their parliamentary spokesmen expressed no doubts or reservations. They

[12]*Ibid.*, p. 31.
[13]*Ibid.*, p. 32.
[14]*Dorset Daily Echo*, 3 October 1956, p. 5.

did not seek, as did the governmental leaders, to present intervention only as a temporary police action. Instead, the government's action was possibly the beginning of "a new age in this country,"[15] as one exuberant Suez group member asserted. The new age was one in which Britain was to make its own policy, despite Commonwealth and American dissents, and to secure Commonwealth unity only after the policy was carried out and shown to be right.[16] The important thing was for Britain to re-establish its power in the Middle East. Military intervention at Suez was the great opportunity.

Understandably, then, the subsequent cessation of Anglo-French action and the eventual withdrawal were viewed as clear-cut defeats. Julian Amery, speaking only a week after the cease-fire, already reflected the Suez group's concern for the consequences of the early cessation of hostilities. Still championing the intervention, he wondered whether it should not have been carried further. Amery implied that he would have been against so early a cease-fire. He was not ready, however, to treat the campaign as a complete failure. The ignominy of withdrawal was not yet apparent. Therefore, in Amery's mind it was still an open question whether Britain could keep its "footing in the Middle East."[17] He meant to warn the nation of the consequences of failing to do so. Keeping British troops in the canal zone was crucial, and he questioned whether a United Nations police force could do the job he had in mind. The answer was plain. The kind of job Amery envisioned was to restore British influence. By definition, this could not be accomplished by a United Nations force substituting for the British force already on the spot. At the very least, British troops should be an important part, along with the French, of any United Nations force. Without that, Amery said, "the outcome will be a shambles."[18] Having to settle, as now seemed certain, for some kind of United Nations authority, he wanted it to be little more than a cover for the Anglo-French expeditionary force. This was the Suez group's last hope to salvage something from the Suez intervention by way of British influence in the Middle East. Failing in this, Amery thought, would mean the final expulsion of British influence from the area.

[15]558 *H. C. Deb.* 1468 (31 October 1956).
[16]558 *H. C. Deb.* 1545 (31 October 1956).
[17]560 *H. C. Deb.* 829 (13 November 1956).
[18]560 *H. C. Deb.* 840 (13 November 1956).

With the fading of this last hope, as Britain yielded to American pressure for withdrawal of British forces, the Suez group turned from anxious support to threatening criticism of the Conservative government. Angus Maude, the most intellectually inclined member of the group, bluntly told his constituents in late November: "If Nasser is allowed to triumph on the Canal while we go crawling to the Americans for oil, then the Conservative Party under its present leadership will be no place for me or some of my colleagues."[19] The Anglo-French withdrawal of December meant that Eden's intervention had completely failed to accomplish the only purpose which the Suez group regarded as justifying the intervention in the first place. British power, it was plain to see, was not now reasserted in the Middle East. Instead the power was withdrawn. The Suez group could derive no comfort, even argumentatively, from the government's face-saving view that Anglo-French action had been a useful and necessary preliminary to United Nations responsibility in the area. Even if the Suez group could have accepted this dubious line as an accurate account of events, the group would not have been satisfied. Bringing the United Nations into the Middle East as a substitute for Anglo-French forces could hardly be a British victory in the eyes of the Suez group. It was logical, therefore, to regard Britain as defeated, although only an extremist would say so bluntly.[20] Withdrawal could be understood otherwise only if one were to accept the official government view, still presented, that intervention had been aimed principally to stop a war.[21] But no such limited purpose had ever motivated the Suez group's support of intervention.

Certainly the group correctly understood the significance of withdrawal. Britain did thus surrender all possibility of influencing canal management policy. International control, through which British interests could be championed by British influence, was now dead. Nasser had the canal, and the United Nations force served to protect his control. Britain now had no leverage to exert against Nasser, and the Suez group, besides deploring the sorry pass to which Britain had come, could do little more than urge, in the winter of 1956-57, that Britain should refuse to use the canal after its clearance. Such

[19]*Middlesex County Times & West Middlesex Gazette*, 24 November 1956, p. 1.
[20]"We have suffered a defeat," Biggs-Davison told his constituents. *Chigwell Times & West Essex Star*, 14 December 1956, p. 1.
[21]Antony Head, 561 *H. C. Deb.* 1376 (5 December 1956).

a boycott of Nasser seemed a futile as well as a costly policy for British shipping to adopt either on its own or with French shipping. It meant that Britain should perpetuate for itself the disadvantages suffered while the canal was blocked. For the Suez group, however, this was a price worth paying. "I would rather suffer as we are suffering now," Captain Waterhouse said, "than suffer the grave dishonour of accepting unfettered control of the Canal by Egypt."[22]

When the British government, by allowing British shipping in May 1957 to use the canal, did thereby accept just this unfettered control, the Suez group made its last great protest. All hope for the government's resistance to Nasser was now obviously gone. Britain's capitulation was complete and obvious, as the Labour opposition, from its different standpoint, also stressed.[23] Thus May 1957 provided the occasion for a section of the old Suez group to restate its case most bitterly.[24] This time the group received weighty support for its position from the Marquess of Salisbury, who had only two months earlier resigned from his important place in the Conservative government in protest against Macmillan's policies, particularly on Cyprus but not without reference to general imperial questions as well. Salisbury now criticized the government for going "far too near complete capitulation to Colonel Nasser. . . ."[25] Instead of British ships being allowed to use the canal, he would have preferred a partial boycott of the canal by one or two countries. To this end, he would have had modern British tankers transport oil around the Cape instead of through Suez.[26] The cost of such a policy (which incidentally no other nation seemed likely to adopt), the Suez group, along with Salisbury, was alone in being willing to pay rather than allow Britain to lose status by surrendering to Nasser. If the canal could not be wrested from him, at least Britain should try to deprive him of the advantages of having it. The worst result was to give up entirely the effort to drive Britain's enemy from power.[27] In this perspective, a lonely

[22]566 *H. C. Deb.* 1356 (14 March 1957).

[23]The point was rubbed in by Hugh Gaitskell and by Denis Healey, 570 *H. C. Deb.* 37, 40 (13 May 1957).

[24]Chapter Five treats the parliamentary deviations of the Suez group, and Chapter Six considers the local party responses to these deviations.

[25]203 *H. L. Deb.* 637 (14 May 1957).

[26]203 *H. L. Deb.* 1155-56 (23 May 1957).

[27]The point was pungently made by Captain Waterhouse: "We have an inveterate foe in Colonel Nasser. We ought to chase him like a pest officer would chase a rat." 570 *H. C. Deb.* 450 (15 May 1957).

British boycott of the canal did not appear quixotic, but only sacrificial. Sacrifices, however, were what the Suez group was willing to make in the imperial cause.[28] Just as the group had been willing to risk a major conflict in the fall of 1956, so now in the spring of 1957 a costly boycott would have been borne instead of surrender. As Salisbury declared, ". . . a nation, if it is to be great, must always be ready to risk severe material sacrifices, if that be required, in defence of the principles in which it believes."[29]

These words, it must be stressed, are not those of a wild and irresponsible man. On the contrary, Salisbury had the very considerable status derived from his own distinguished ministerial career as well as from his family's very special record of service since the days of Queen Elizabeth I. He was one of the great figures in the Conservative party, and a big gun indeed to be added to the lesser artillery of the Suez group. He more than compensated for the loss of Julian Amery, whose extreme views were muffled in 1957 by his inclusion in the government of his father-in-law, Harold Macmillan. With or without Salisbury, however, the Suez group still had its cause even if clearly a lost one. That it could be championed so vigorously in 1957 is a tribute to the persistence of the imperial tradition as well as of its last champions. The British Empire was not forsaken by all Englishmen.

2. IMPERIAL IDEOLOGY OF THE 1950's

Continued imperial faith, of the kind exhibited by the Suez group, involved a special way of looking at Britain's place in the world. The Suez group had its own ideology of international relations. It was not, however, identical with a right-wing conservatism on domestic issues. Much of the group's following in the Conservative party may well have been right-wing on such diverse matters as economic policy and capital punishment, hence resisting postwar Tory revisionism on the domestic as on the foreign or imperial front. But the leadership of the Suez group, particularly some of its most articulate spokesmen, included M.P.s who held liberal and advanced views on domestic subjects. For example, Julian Amery, Biggs-Davison, and Lord Hinchingbrooke, all of whom have already been quoted as last-ditch

[28]Capitulation to Nasser, said Waterhouse, could only lead to "the end of the British Empire and the dissolution of the Commonwealth." 570 *H. C. Deb.* 454 (15 May 1957).

[29]203 *H. L. Deb.* 1158 (23 May 1957).

Suez men, belonged to the minority of Conservatives who had joined Labour M.P.s, on a free vote in early 1956, to favor the abolition of capital punishment. On this they were at odds with others in the Suez group and also at odds with the rank-and-file Conservative membership that subsequently supported so zealously the Suez action and, in some cases, the Suez group's view of that action. Yet men like Amery, Biggs-Davison, and Hinchingbrooke were not merely unimportant exceptions to a general coincidence of right-wing domestic politics with residual imperialism. Rather, they represented, on broader social and economic questions as well as on capital punishment, an element that had been prominent in the imperial movement of the late nineteenth and early twentieth centuries. Domestic reform and overseas expansion had often gone together. This was surely the Joseph Chamberlain tradition, over which the Amery family had assumed custody, and the notion of a Britain dynamic at home and abroad had regularly been revived.

The special quality of the Suez group's ideology was not die-hard conservatism on all fronts. It involved only a different perspective on Britain's relations with other nations, Commonwealth and foreign. It is not even clear that this much ought to be called right-wing or die-hard conservatism. Such terms might better be reserved for domestic differences. Wanting Britain to be great in some imperial sense, as late as the 1950's, would be "conservative" only in that anything which seems to belong to another age can be called conservative. The Suez group itself by no means regarded its imperial views as conservative in the sense of old-fashioned. What the Suez group said it wanted was not the restoration of the Empire of 1900, but instead the resumption of a frustrated development of that Empire into a Commonwealth of nations united under British leadership. Theirs was a fairly modernized version of the Greater Britain concept. Consequently, the Suez group deplored the loosening of ties that had accompanied the postwar multiracial Commonwealth. The important thing was not to accommodate nations, like India, which insisted on practical autonomy, but rather to develop a unity among nations, presumably English-speaking and English-settled, which wanted close ties with Britain. In order to exert leadership in such a Commonwealth, Britain itself had to maintain military strength and great-power status in such areas as the Middle East. Old-fashioned imperialism or gunboat diplomacy were only necessary means to make the Commonwealth in a British image.

Fundamentally, the Suez group thought that Britain would amount to very little in the world if it could not exert effective leadership of a larger unit. And such a fate is just what the Suez group would not accept for the British nation. Here, as much as anywhere, was where the Suez group differed from the rest of the British community. Others might see the facts in the same way, namely, that without imperial-style leadership Britain was too small for world leadership, but believe, contentedly or otherwise, that there was no hope for arresting Britain's decline. Still others might simply refuse to believe that Britain could become unimportant as a world power. What was special about the Suez group was that it saw the tendency to decline, but believed that the tendency could and should be reversed.

To this end, a vital first step was the flat assertion of an independent British power. National sovereignty, it was urged, should not be submerged into "some predicated system of international justice or some political organization—be it the United Nations, the North Atlantic Treaty Organization, or whatever it may be." Such submergence was a consequence of what the Suez group regarded as an increasing British acceptance of the "Liberal concept of the mechanistic Society of Nations, founded on a spurious morality."[30] It was abhorrent that Britain should yield its policy-making power to an international organization, like the United Nations, in which Britain could be outvoted by a majority pursuing different interests. Similarly it was abhorrent that Britain should be a partner in any alliance in which it could be dominated by its partners, whether these partners acted collectively or simply under the influence of a single dominant power like the United States. The Commonwealth, on the other hand, was acceptable, on the dubious assumption that its policies would be essentially British. Insofar as Commonwealth policies would not be British, as they surely would not be in a multiracial Commonwealth heavily influenced by India, Britain would be forced to pursue its own course—but presumably carrying at least its English-speaking partners along. Thus the kind of Commonwealth that the Suez group wanted Britain to lead really did not exist in the 1950's. The Suez group hoped to create it.

Much of the group's hope was linked to the revitalization of imperial preference. The leaders of the Suez group, notably Amery and Biggs-Davison, were also prominent in the continued though forlorn campaign to maintain and extend the system of preferential Common-

[30]Hinchingbrooke, 580 *H. C. Deb.* 804 (20 December 1957).

wealth trade. Some of the more numerous supporters of imperial preference were not in the Suez group, but there were not many Suez group members without records strongly in favor of imperial preference.[31] In any event, there was a considerable overlapping of parliamentary membership between the two Conservative groups. The imperial preference advocates who were also Suez group members saw their Commonwealth economic program as a means to unite former imperial possessions to Britain and so to provide a larger community for Britain to lead in world affairs. Their concern here was as much political as it was economic. Whatever tended to reduce or destroy imperial preference was a blow to the hope for a Greater Britain. Consequently, throughout the postwar period all programs like the General Agreement on Tariffs and Trade (GATT), with its bias against preferences, were bitterly opposed. So was any economic tie to the United States at the expense of intra-Commonwealth trade. American tariff reductions were viewed as a poor exchange for the surrender of the opportunity for increasing Commonwealth preferences.[32] The American principle of nondiscrimination, which the United States was strong enough to impose in the early postwar years, was viewed as restricting the continued development of Britain's special relations with its Commonwealth partners.

Definitely, in the eyes of the advocates of Commonwealth trade, the United States was the principal enemy of imperial preference. Biggs-Davison, for example, wrote a book on this theme, and called it *The Uncertain Ally*. Written mainly by 1953 although not published until 1957, it puts the primary responsibility for the postwar frustration of imperial preference on the unfortunate American connection. In this view, it was neither any reluctance by Commonwealth partners nor any genuinely limited possibilities in Commonwealth trade for Britain itself that caused the prewar preferential arrangements to remain unextended and so to lose their relative significance. Instead it was simply the American campaign against the British Empire. Biggs-Davison traced the roots of this campaign to the prewar Rooseveltian opposition to the Ottawa preference system, and the success of the campaign to Britain's weakened wartime and postwar con-

[31]This may be observed in the list of M.P.s signing a typical imperial preference motion during the period of the Suez controversy. House of Commons, *Notices of Motions, Questions and Orders of the Day 1955-56*, Vol. 5, pp. 5088, 5109, 5125, 5159.

[32]A good example of this postwar defense of imperial preference against American policy was provided by L. S. Amery, "Non-Discrimination and Convertibility," *World Affairs*, Vol. 2, pp. 13-22 (January 1948).

dition.[33] Taking advantage of this condition, the United States, Biggs-Davison argued, imposed its trade policies in such a way as to bring Britain and other Commonwealth countries into the American economic orbit (or American empire) instead of allowing a separate British imperial economic system to develop from its good start at Ottawa.

This sense of American-British rivalry was at the base of a good deal of the outlook of the Suez group as of the imperial preference school. The United States was regarded as the general enemy of British imperial interests. The American hand was seen in almost every British postwar overseas loss, notably in the Middle East. Suez was only the last and most serious of the American blows. It was the culmination of a deliberate American policy, not (as it was for Eden) simply an example of American naiveté or miscalculation. In the minds of the Suez group, the United States, having played a major role in pressuring Britain to agree in 1954 to evacuate the canal zone, now had an interest in preventing Britain's return to its old position of Middle Eastern strength. American oil interests, in particular, were assumed to put American policy at odds with Britain's.

For the Suez group, the crisis of late 1956 revealed to public view the long-standing Anglo-American differences in the Middle East. Certainly the crisis, with its open break between the two nations, released a storm of imperialist anti-American sentiment that had otherwise been largely suppressed in the name of North Atlantic unity. The Suez group suddenly found that its old case against the United States had become both plausible and popular. Right or wrong, it provided a coherent way to explain Middle Eastern events as a conspiracy against British interests. Such an explanation was bound to appeal, well beyond the Suez group itself, to Conservative supporters of Eden's intervention who wanted to blame somebody, other than their own government, for the failure at Suez. They might even be attracted to Julian Amery's view, stated to the Commons in mid-November, that it had been impossible "to go on much longer without a showdown with the Americans over the Middle East."[34] He noted the failure of the United States to cooperate with successive British governments over Palestine, Abadan, the Sudan, and Cyprus, as well as Suez. Trying to conciliate the Americans in any of these places, Amery argued, had led to no British advantage. In other words, open

[33] John Biggs-Davison, *The Uncertain Ally* (London: Christopher Johnson, 1957), p. 71.
[34] 560 *H. C. Deb.* 832 (13 November 1956).

disagreement with the United States was simply the inevitable result if Britain were going to pursue its own interests in the Middle East. Amery was even more direct in his castigation of the United States when he spoke to his constituents. "The United Nations," he asserted in late November 1956, "has become a cover plan for American imperialism." In this plan, Amery added, the Americans "want to take our place in the Middle East and they want to take the place of France in North Africa. They want the economic assets; they want to run the show."[35]

An attack of this kind on American imperialism also appealed outside Conservative ranks. It was significantly similar to the long-standing left-wing socialist critique of the role of the United States in world affairs. Economic determinism was basic to the Suez group's interpretation of American policy just as it was to the socialist critique. So was the desire for an independent British policy.[36] The difference, of course, was that the Suez group defended British imperialism in a way that socialists did not. Socialists, presumably, were against any-one's imperialism, even (or particularly) their own country's, but the Suez group was unabashedly the champion of British imperialism. Therefore, socialists were unlikely to echo the Suez group's attack on the United States, however much they enjoyed it, since their main target at least during the Suez crisis had to be British policy. On the other hand, there were some Labour party members of a considerably more moderate bent than the left-wing socialists who did speak of the United States in terms like those used by the Suez group. The prime example is Stanley Evans, the one Labour M.P. who broke from his party's opposition to Suez.[37] As early as August 1956, Evans argued that the history of the Middle East in the past ten years had been one of "the constant undermining of British interests, authority and prestige" by the United States.[38] This line Evans maintained throughout the crisis, and he was not alone among Labour M.P.s in doing so. At least one other Labour M.P., this one an important ex-

[35]*Lancashire Evening Post* (Preston), 24 November 1956, p. 5.

[36]Aneurin Bevan recognized the point during the crisis: "For my part, I do not even accuse the Government of taking action independent of the United States. It would be a foolish thing for me to say, as I have been advocating independent action for some time, but rather more intelligent action. I do not blame them one little bit for taking this independent action. I blame them for the action itself. It was the action that was wrong, not the independence of the action." 558 *H. C. Deb.* 1714 (1 November 1956).

[37]His case is discussed at length in Chapter Six.

[38]557 *H. C. Deb.* 1635 (2 August 1956).

minister with doubts about his party's attack on Eden, spoke of his conviction that the Americans aimed primarily to obtain Middle Eastern oil.[39]

Returning to the Suez group itself, the high point of its open antagonism to the United States came after the intervention had been halted and British withdrawal forced, evidently by American pressure. It was then, in late November and early December, that American influence seemed most evil and ubiquitous. With the canal still closed, American oil and dollars had plainly been withheld until Britain agreed to leave Suez completely and without saving face. The result led one intensely pro-Suez M.P. to ask, with grim humor, whether American consent would now be forthcoming to bring Prime Minister Eden back from his Jamaican rest holiday.[40] More seriously, another Conservative M.P. of the imperialist persuasion raised a question about the continued presence of American troops in Britain now that the United States had proved so unhelpful an ally.[41] The most significant demonstration of parliamentary anti-American views, however, was the collection of Conservative signatures on a motion tabled in late November. This motion, worded moderately to say that the attitude of the United States was "gravely endangering the Atlantic alliance," obtained at one time or another 127 different signatures.[42] Thus it included a substantial number of what might be called fellow travelers of the Suez group. These were Conservative M.P.s basically sympathetic to the imperialist case against the United States, but ordinarily unwilling to break with the public pro-American position of their party leaders. The signatories (22 of whom, incidentally, used military titles) typified the very large segment of the Conservative party essentially unreconciled to second place in an American alliance or to internationalism in general. Their impressive demonstration could not be matched by the 26 Conservative signatures obtained for a pro-American motion urging the British government to help restore active cooperation with the United States.[43]

[39]Emanuel Shinwell, 570 *H. C. Deb.* 612 (16 May 1957).

[40]Sir I. Horobin, 561 *H. C. Deb.* 891 (3 December 1956).

[41]William Teeling, 562 *H. C. Deb.* 20 (10 December 1956).

[42]There were, however, no more than 118 at any one time since some M.P.s removed their names while others added theirs. House of Commons, *Notices of Motions, Questions and Orders of the Day 1956-57*, Vol. 1, pp. 368-69, 400, 428, 1042, 1641. A comparison of this list with the list of signatories on the imperial preference motion (referred to in note 31) reveals that 25 of the 42 names on the latter motion were also on the anti-American motion.

[43]House of Commons, *ibid.*, pp. 402, 504.

No doubt the crisis and especially its immediate aftermath had aroused an otherwise latent anti-American spirit among Conservatives. What the Suez group normally represented on its own turned out to have a broader base in the party. The more extreme expressions were still left to the Suez group, which in fact became more extreme in its anti-Americanism in late 1956 than ordinarily, but a generalized resentment of the United States turned out to be characteristic of the more or less upper-class elements predominating in the Conservative party. Their resentment had qualities different from those of the better-known socialist anti-Americanism. Among many Conservatives, especially those whose own backgrounds as well as those of their families were in the imperial service, the Americans appeared to be usurpers of their positions in an almost literal sense. Old British imperial hands had seen, in the postwar years, that as American power displaced British power so did American military officers and American civilian advisers displace their British counterparts in the less developed nations of the world. In addition, educated upper-class Englishmen resented the Americanization of culture that was apparently taking place in Britain and Europe as well as elsewhere in the world.

It is true that the political expression of these resentments, as represented by the numerous signatures on the anti-American motion, did greatly diminish in early 1957. By the spring of that year, the Suez group seemed again to stand alone in its campaign against American influence. Only a die-hard man of Suez could be found still to assert that the United States "had stabbed us in the back last November."[44] The moderate anti-Americans of the winter no longer carried on the fight. Their resentments may not have vanished, but the occasion for releasing resentments was over. The dead-end cause was again left to the extremists.

3. The Lost Cause

The Suez group itself did not immediately lose the will to resist events. It was accustomed to fighting a lost cause, and most of its members were not used to having as many allies and supporters as they had had during the crisis. The problem after Suez, however, was how to develop any kind of imperial case when Britain's last great chance, as the Suez group understood it, had just been lost in

[44]Sir V. Raikes, 570 *H. C. Deb.* 540 (15 May 1957).

the fall and winter of 1956. British imperialism—indeed, the whole notion of independent British power—had now so evidently ended. Could anyone, even the most convinced member of the Suez group, have any further hope for a revived Greater Britain? Surely the crisis tended to destroy all of the bases for such a hope. The Commonwealth, even much of the English-speaking Commonwealth, had failed to follow the British lead. Britain had not been able to achieve a successful intervention, either by mounting superior force quickly enough or by persisting in a longer struggle in defiance of the United States and other international pressures. On the last point, however, the Suez group did not firmly accept the idea that Britain could not have persisted. There was still much talk of Eden's loss of nerve. But even if that point were conceded to the Suez group—namely, that British power, by persistence and sacrifice, could have been asserted successfully—surely the failure to have done so at Suez ruled out any serious likelihood of a future opportunity. This the Suez group was loathe to admit, but it did not need to face the issue as long as no occasion like Suez reoccurred.

One curious development, absorbing some of the Suez group after the crisis, was the movement for an expanded Commonwealth to include Western European nations. This was by no means the same as urging British membership in the subsequent Common Market. Such membership would have seemed to mean—as in the 1960's it did mean—virtual abandonment of imperial preference. Rather than breaking with the Commonwealth to join Western Europe, what the residual imperialist now proposed was that Western European nations join the Commonwealth or at least its system of trade preferences. The proposal was for a bloc of nations, under British leadership, that could stand politically and economically between Russia and the United States. Britain, by bridging the gap between the English-speaking overseas Commonwealth and the nations of Western Europe, would achieve a power status independent of the United States.

To avoid the American embrace was still the main objective of the residual imperialist.[45] The relatively unimportant Expanding Commonwealth idea was merely a late and nearly desperate way to try to stand apart from the United States. One is reminded of the similarly farfetched schemes for a Third Force which left-wing socialists advanced in the postwar years as alternatives to the American

[45]Patrick Maitland, *Task for Giants* (London: Longmans, Green & Co., 1957).

alliance. The Suez group was just as anxious to preserve a distinctively British influence, only the influence was of residual British imperialism rather than of British socialism. The enemy was still the United States. And in both cases, while the amount and seriousness of opposition to the alliance might diminish in response to events, the paranoic quality of the opposition could remain or even intensify. In fact, some of the extreme imperial opposition found a post-Suez home in the League of Empire Loyalists. This was a much less respectable outlet than the Suez group. It operated mainly outside of, and in open hostility to, the Conservative party. More substantial and significant as a persisting vehicle for imperial sentiments was the Beaverbrook press, long-time champion of imperial preference and, as will be amply observed in Chapter Seven, of a strong Suez stand.

Beyond the 1956-57 events, however, the full imperial position seemed too clearly removed from the real world to have the force or apparent cogency that the Suez group presented during the crisis. Even then, it ought to be observed, the cogency if not the force of the imperial case was limited. The relevance of the Suez group's arguments may always have been dubious. They seem worth attention chiefly as examples of the frustration almost necessarily felt by the defenders of the imperial tradition at a time when that tradition was especially hard pressed. The frustration, which the Suez group made so plain, was over the fact that Britain no longer played the part of a major power in world affairs. Many Englishmen might in this way have been frustrated, but, except perhaps during the Suez crisis itself, they seemed to assume that Britain was simply unable any longer to play such a part. The Suez group refused to make this assumption. On the contrary, the group thought Britain had the ability and lacked only the will. In this respect there was a general resemblance to the type of foreign policy views represented by right-wing, neo-isolationist, or nationalistic Republicans in postwar America. Not only did the Suez group, like its rough American counterpart, want the nation to go it alone, rejecting major allies and certainly United Nations auspices, but there existed also a belief in some conspiratorial force that prevented effective action in the purely national interest. For the Suez group, that force seemed to be mainly the United States.

CHAPTER FIVE

Parliamentary Conflict

The entire Suez issue was the subject of prolonged British parliamentary conflict fought mainly along partisan lines. This is a nearly unique case in the recent experience of highly developed democracies. Often as foreign policy has been the subject of partisan discussion, important international commitments have ordinarily been made only with support, or the expectation of support, from the great bulk of the political community. This has surely been the American and British pattern, labeled bipartisan, nonpartisan, or extrapartisan. We have assumed that political support extending well beyond the ranks of the party in office is essential for a successful foreign policy, especially for a substantial military venture requiring public effort and sacrifice. Even the American decision of 1950 to defend South Korea, while it was necessarily made by the Democratic administration before any apparent political consensus and while it involved the United States in an unpopular war, was never in itself a partisan policy that Republicans as a group refused to support. In contrast, Britain's Suez action of 1956 is an instance of a truly partisan foreign policy. As a significant deviant case, it provides useful insights into the process by which an alternative to the usual bipartisan arrangement is developed and conducted. Specific questions concern the cabinet's function in making the Suez intervention decision, the nature of parliamentary support for this decision, the role of party loyalty in maintaining such support, and the significance of partisan opposition.

Before attempting answers to these questions, it is useful to state briefly the parliamentary party situation just prior to the Suez action. The Conservative government of Sir Anthony Eden had been returned to office with an increased and comfortable, but not overwhelming, majority of nearly 60 in the general election of May 1955. Eden, becoming Prime Minister and party leader only shortly before the election, had been Churchill's Foreign Secretary and crown prince for an agonizingly long period. The popularity registered by Eden's election triumph did not last. Several months before Suez, Conservative fortunes declined in by-elections and in public opinion polls.[1] Economic difficulties were the likely cause. The Eden government was accused of indecisiveness, and Eden himself was subject to widely known criticism within his own party. Having as yet survived no great crisis, Eden had not established an ascendancy as Prime Minister despite his diplomatic reputation, enhanced by evident success at the Geneva summit meeting of 1955. Moreover, the imperialist wing of his own party suspected him of weakness in defending Britain's Middle Eastern interests if only because it was Eden who had been most identified with the 1954 agreement to evacuate the Suez Canal base.

The Conservative party was openly divided prior to Suez over the special issue of capital punishment. Early in 1956, the party leaders had allowed a free vote on abolition in the House of Commons, and on that occasion enough Conservatives voted with Labour M.P.s to succeed in passing the measure to eliminate the death penalty. This action was contrary to the advocacy of a majority of Conservatives in and out of Parliament. The House of Lords, with its huge Conservative majority acting in accord with government advice as well as its own convictions, rejected the bill in July 1956. The government, then, instead of facilitating repassage by the Commons of the abolitionist measure (thus overruling the Lords), decided to seek a compromise in the form of its own bill that would keep capital punishment for only specified kinds of murders. Conservative abolitionists, in the summer and early fall of 1956, were being pressured to support this compromise, and they eventually did so when the measure was presented after the Suez crisis.[2] In the meantime, however, the issue was an important source of tension in the Conservative party.

[1]See Chapter Seven.

[2]James B. Christoph, *Capital Punishment and British Politics* (London: Allen & Unwin, 1962), pp. 126-64.

Labour provided a formidable opposition in 1956. Its strength seemed, of course, to be rising as Conservative popularity declined from its May 1955 level. Furthermore, the party had settled its leadership problem, after several years of struggle, by choosing Hugh Gaitskell to succeed Clement Attlee in the fall of 1955. This, it is true, was accomplished only by open defeat of the claims of the senior Herbert Morrison and of Aneurin Bevan, who remained the favorite of the Labour left. Bevan did now join Gaitskell's shadow cabinet, and thus (with Morrison retiring from the front bench) the way seemed to be clear to consolidate the party. Gaitskell, however, was still a relatively young man, disliked for different reasons by old-guard friends of Morrison and by left-wing friends of Bevan, and he was certainly untried in meeting political crises as a party leader. Like Eden, incidentally, Gaitskell was suspected by his own militants of a softness when it came to standing up for the party's traditional ideology, be it socialism or anti-imperialism.

One other facet of the parliamentary situation deserves to be noted. We have Eden's testimony, offered after the Suez crisis, that he did not get on well with Gaitskell. Eden, in his *Memoirs*, contrasts his favorable impressions of Attlee, Ernest Bevin, and Morrison. He adds: "I was unable to establish with Mr. Gaitskell the political and personal relations which I had enjoyed with all his predecessors. This was one of my failures, but curiously enough in all my years of political life I had not met anyone with his cast of mind and approach to problems. We never seemed to get on terms."[3] How much of this view of his unhappy relations with Gaitskell was only retrospective cannot be known. The emotional clash over Suez would have deepened any dislike Eden had to begin with. Nevertheless there is no reason to doubt that Eden and Gaitskell were never "on terms," and that therefore there was in 1956 none of the easy mutual confidence in private exchange ordinarily supposed to characterize the relations of Prime Minister and opposition leader on grave matters of state.

1. EMERGENCE OF PARTISAN POLICY

The circumstances for the invasion of Egypt, namely the Israeli attack, were not anticipated during the early discussions of what Britain should do about Nasser's nationalization of the canal. Yet the partisan lines, later so sharply to divide the nation, emerged in

[3]Sir Anthony Eden, *Full Circle* (London: Cassell & Co., 1960), p. 320.

the debate of August and September over how far Britain should go in securing its desired solution of the canal issue. Only at the very first was this not the case. Then, in late July and early August, the difference over means was less evident than the nearly unanimous agreement that Nasser had acted wrongly and that Egypt's sole control of the canal was dangerous for Britain. There was no substantial dissent from the Prime Minister's statement of 30 July, repeated on 2 August, that Britain could not accept an arrangement leaving the canal in the unfettered control of a single power.[4] Nor did Labour officially object to Eden's accompanying announcement of precautionary military measures, including the call-up of reservists.

What did divide the nation largely on party lines was the suspicion, growing through August, that the government's military measures were a prelude to an Anglo-French attack on Egypt. By September, when Parliament was specially summoned, Eden was defending a publicly belligerent policy opposed by Labour. The belligerence may have been meant only as a threat to use force in order to gain Egyptian assent to British terms, but that too was further than Labour wanted to be committed. This was evident in the discussion of what Britain was to do if Egypt refused to cooperate with the recently formed Canal Users Association. The opposition reacted sharply against Eden's assertion that Britain would, in that event, be free to take steps to assert its rights even outside the United Nations.[5] Eden refused, when subsequently pressed on 13 September, to renounce entirely the threat of force without United Nations approval. The most that he would say was that the government intended, "except in an emergency," to refer to the Security Council, but he repeated meaningfully that "the Government must be the judge of the circumstances."[6] This was but limited assurance to those who had by September come to fear that the government contemplated Anglo-French military action against Nasser.

Among the critics of any such action were a few Conservatives. Unlike the Labour opposition, they did not openly accuse the government of preparing to use force. Publicly, at least, they denied that this could be the government's intention. But their parliamentary spokesman said that a nation which did use force on its own, except in self-defense, would violate the United Nations charter. This was

[4]557 *H. C. Deb.* 919, 1603 (30 July, 2 August 1956).
[5]558 *H. C. Deb.* 11 (12 September 1956).
[6]558 *H. C. Deb.* 307-8 (13 September 1956).

the point of a notable speech by Sir Lionel Heald, now a nonministerial Conservative but a former Attorney General, United Nations
delegate, and representative at the International Court.[7] Two other
Conservative back-benchers explicitly agreed with Heald, and it was
fairly assumed that he had spoken for a substantial minority of a few
dozen M.P.s. Eden thus had public notice that his own party contained an antiforce potential. At the same time, from the House of
Lords there arose an opposition from the kind of independent opinion
ordinarily supporting government foreign policy. Speaking as a highly
prestigious lawyer, Lord McNair said flatly that he was unable "to
see the legal justification of the threat or the use of armed force by
Great Britain against Egypt in order to impose a solution of this
dispute."[8] McNair's position was shared by other nonparty peers,
including churchmen, and it was plain that opposition to force went
well beyond the Labour party.

Within his own party, however, Eden's position did have strong if
not unanimous support. The muted criticism of the Heald group was
exceptional. The bulk of the Conservative party appeared to believe
in so strong an anti-Nasser stand as to risk the use of force. And Eden
did not lack for Conservative defenders, in his government or on the
back benches, during the debates of 12-13 September. Moreover,
he had behind him, even urging him on, the M.P.s who had rebelled
in 1954 against the agreement to evacuate the canal zone.[9] From the
start of the crisis, as already noted, the residual Suez rebels were
eager for action to redeem their imperial cause. On 27 July, Julian
Amery had asked Eden rhetorically: "Is my right hon. Friend aware
that he will have the overwhelming support of public opinion in this
country on whatever steps he decides to take, however grave, to repair
this injury to our honour and interests?"[10] This was probably too strong
for some Conservative M.P.s, although it was to be impressively backed
by the party's nonparliamentary activists.[11] Notwithstanding the Heald
minority, whose opposition was only potential, even the actual use of
force was likely to be popular among Conservatives. In fact, Eden risked
losing popularity in his own party if he now backed away from force
without eliminating exclusive Egyptian control of the canal.

[7]558 *H. C. Deb.* 182-87, 235-36, 273-75 (13 September 1956).
[8]199 *H. L. Deb.* 662 (12 September 1956).
[9]These M.P.s were of the Suez group, discussed in Chapter Four.
[10]557 *H. C. Deb.* 779 (26 July 1956).
[11]As indicated in the previous chapter's reference to the Conservative party conference in early October.

On the other hand, the Labour party's opposition to the use of force outside the United Nations was well established. Whatever doubts there might have been at first about Labour's position, none should have remained in mid-September. Gaitskell and his party have been accused of retreating from a stronger to a weaker anti-Nasser position, but mainly between early and mid-August. This is the burden of Eden's charge,[12] and it is also close to what Gaitskell's critics in his own party were ready to believe as they contrasted his first responses to nationalization with his subsequent stand. Even this criticism seems unfair. There might have been changes in Gaitskell's tone after he originally shared all of Eden's indignation against Nasser's take-over of the canal. But even on 2 August, when Gaitskell compared Nasser to Mussolini and Hitler and when he said there were "circumstances in which we might be compelled to use force, in self-defence or as part of some collective defence measures," he added:

I must, however, remind the House that we are members of the United Nations, that we are signatories to the United Nations Charter, and that for many years in British policy we have steadfastly avoided any international action which would be in breach of international law or, indeed, contrary to the public opinion of the world. We must not, therefore, allow ourselves to get into a position where we might be denounced in the Security Council as aggressors, or where the majority of the Assembly were against us.[13]

This reservation was repeated at the end of Gaitskell's speech. Yet there is reason to think that it received little attention at the time, partly because the bulk of the speech stressed the seriousness of Nasser's seizure of the canal. Furthermore most of the other Labour speeches, in the debate of 2 August, urged that Britain do something about the canal. In fact, there were four Labour M.P.s whose reservations about the use of force seemed less definite than Gaitskell's,[14] and among these was the semiretired Herbert Morrison, formerly Foreign Secretary and, less than a year before, defeated for the party leadership by the much younger Gaitskell. Altogether the debate of 2 August did give an impression of bipartisan agreement, and the Conservatives cannot be blamed for making much of this at the time in order to strengthen the government's hand in dealing with Egypt. However, the bipartisan picture appeared only when the question of using force outside the United Nations was not in the forefront of discussion.

[12]Eden, *op. cit.*, p. 445.
[13]557 *H. C. Deb*. 1616-17 (2 August 1956).
[14]557 *H. C. Deb*. 1658-59, 1666, 1671-72, 1713-14 (2 August 1956).

Plainly this was the question that could not be kept from the forefront once the Anglo-French forces began to gather during August. The sharp difference between the two parties as to whether to use force at all could not be concealed by Labour's claim that force, if used, should be under United Nations auspices. This was, as Eden has said, equivalent to denying Britain and France the use of force altogether.[15] There was really no chance of getting the United Nations, in the face of the Soviet veto and Asian-African opposition, to approve the use of force against Egypt. Eden may not have calculated correctly about Suez in certain respects, but he surely was right on this score. The Labour stand did amount to the advocacy of inaction. There was no point in discussing force except as an Anglo-French matter.

Here, by mid-September, Gaitskell could declare that Labour had established its opposition. Besides referring to his own statements of 2 August, Gaitskell said that even before that occasion he and his deputy leader had twice talked with Eden and that he (Gaitskell) had then warned Eden that he could not rely on Labour support if he contemplated the use of force. Moreover, Gaitskell reported that between 2 August and mid-September he had made the same point in two letters to Eden. This was in addition to a Labour parliamentary committee visit, in mid-August, with Eden and his colleagues in an unsuccessful attempt to secure a government statement renouncing the use of force outside the United Nations.[16] There could, therefore, be hardly anything new in mid-September about Gaitskell's criticism of Eden's unwillingness to renounce the use of Anglo-French force. Furthermore, there could be no doubt that Gaitskell spoke for the bulk of his party at this stage. Conservatives did not think otherwise; in fact, they argued that Gaitskell had changed his own position from early August in order to fall in line with his party, and especially with the left wing, which had been quicker than Gaitskell to criticize the government.

No matter how uncomplimentary the reasons Conservatives gave for Gaitskell's position, they had now to face the fact that the Labour party was opposed to what it regarded as a potential governmental foreign policy. The Labour leader made this explicit when he said that this was one of the circumstances in which the usual opposition restraint on an international issue was not in order. There was a

[15]Eden, *op. cit.*, p. 445.
[16]558 *H. C. Deb*. 18-20 (12 September 1956).

difference of vital importance, and it was "the duty, not only the right, of the Opposition to speak out loudly and clearly."[17] This is exactly what Labour did in the Commons on 12-13 September as it rejected the policy which the Eden government undertook a month and a half later. Gaitskell wanted Eden to accept the Dulles view against "shooting their way through the Suez Canal."[18] Repeatedly Labour speakers stated their opposition to the use of force, and specifically to its use in "what would seem to be an engineered incident,"[19] outside Britain's United Nations obligations. Not only were they against the adoption of such a policy, but they indicated that if it were adopted they would refuse to support the government in carrying it out. This promised opposition, representing about half the nation, seemed to Labour yet another reason against military action. In Labour's eyes, it appeared incredible that war could be contemplated with the support only of the majority party, and perhaps, as indicated in the September debate, not all of that.[20]

2. THE MILITARY COMMITMENT

The Israeli-Egyptian hostilities which served as justification for Britain's military action were hardly the occasion for the establishment of bipartisanship. The opposition was not consulted before the Anglo-French decision to issue the 12-hour ultimatum to Egypt on 30 October. Labour leaders were told privately of the decision after it was made and only 15 minutes before it was presented to the House of Commons.[21] In this circumstance, Gaitskell asked for time to think over Eden's announcement, although he raised almost immediately the question of what right British and French forces had to intervene before a United Nations pronouncement. In addition, he asked Eden that no further physical action be taken until either the Security Council reached a decision or the Commons had a chance to discuss the matter further. Eden said he could give no such promise,[22] thereby

[17]558 *H. C. Deb.* 16 (12 September 1956).

[18]558 *H. C. Deb.* 291 (13 September 1956).

[19]558 *H. C. Deb.* 139 (12 September 1956).

[20]Where the Liberal party stood was not clear since, in September, the five Liberal M.P.s actually voting were against the Labour motion, but were divided, three to two, in favor of the government's own motion of confidence. 558 *H. C. Deb.* 307-16 (12 September 1956).

[21]This report of the government's communication with the opposition was accepted by both parties. 558 *H. C. Deb.* 1351, 1373 (30 October 1956); 570 *H. C. Deb* 533 (15 May 1957).

[22]558 *H. C. Deb.* 1283 (30 October 1956).

making it plain that Britain was already committed to military action unless Egypt peacefully accepted occupation.

Following this brief exchange, which took place late in the after-noon, there was a more extended evening debate on 30 October, the first of several crisis debates. Gaitskell's criticism was now based on the grounds that Britain and France should not have acted inde-pendently just when the Israeli-Egyptian affair was being referred to the Security Council, that there was no legal justification for the proposed action, and that there had not been adequate consultation with the United States and the Commonwealth.[23] Since Eden refused again to defer action, Labour insisted on dividing the House by parliamentary vote. Despite a few deliberate abstentions and a generally lower-than-usual vote because of the division's unexpected-ness, the result (270 to 218) showed conclusively that Britain was launching its military action against the expressed desires of Her Majesty's Loyal Opposition.[24] Subsequently, the same partisan lines were displayed in the House of Lords, but there some non-Labour criticism was added.[25]

Although the Commons division of 30 October showed that the Prime Minister's own party supported his commitment, there is no evidence that Conservative M.P.s as a group took any part in making this particular decision. They were being asked to support the use of force in circumstances not previously discussed and to accept a justi-fication for the use of force that was entirely new. Whatever earlier Conservative parliamentary sentiment there might have been to take Suez by force was not expressed in relation to any Israeli-Egyptian hostilities in which Britain would seem to intervene on the side of Israel. Nor had it ever been clear that many Conservatives favored military action in defiance of the United States and without consulta-tion even with the Commonwealth. Still, it is not surprising, given the British practice of executive leadership, that ordinary Conservative M.P.s were uninformed of the decision until it was made. More surprising, if true, would be the alleged absence of full cabinet par-ticipation in the decision-making. The question has often been raised as to the number of Conservative leaders who were consulted by Eden before his commitment to act with France. Critics have answered

[23]558 *H. C. Deb.* 1344-51 (30 October 1956).

[24]Three Liberals, however, voted with the government. 558 *H. C. Deb.* 1377-82 (30 October 1956).

[25]199 *H. L. Deb.* 1293-97, 1304-08, 1319-21, 1365-66 (1 November 1956).

with the widely circulated, but documentarily unsubstantiated, story that "a handful of men," fewer than the whole cabinet, were involved in the decision-making stage, and that the full cabinet was informed only when it was too late to reverse Britain's commitment to join France in issuing the ultimatum.[26]

This is the version published in book form soon after the Suez crisis by Paul Johnson, a left-wing journalist, in his slashing attack on the Eden government. The background he describes for keeping much of the cabinet in late October from knowing the Anglo-French plans for intervening in an Israeli-Egyptian war was that some cabinet members had been doubtful, at least, about employing force in connection with the Users Association in mid-September, and they would presumably have been against it in October as well.[27] One of these cabinet members is supposed to have been Walter Monckton, Minister of Defence until he resigned to become Paymaster General and was replaced by Antony Head on 18 October. The official reason for the change was Monckton's ill health. But Eden's critics believe either that Monckton was removed because Eden needed an active believer in likely military action as Minister of Defence, or that Monckton voluntarily gave up his defense post because of conscientious doubts about what Eden was doing (without, however, feeling strongly enough to leave the government altogether).[28] Plausibility is given to either of these critical interpretations by the timing of the resignation, on 18 October, just two days after Eden and his Foreign Secretary, Selwyn Lloyd, had conferred with their French counterparts in Paris. It is this Paris meeting that is frequently said to have been the occasion for hatching plans for Anglo-French intervention in the projected Israeli-Egyptian hostilities. Subsequently, in Johnson's account, only Eden, Lloyd, and Head were fully informed of what was to happen. The full cabinet, he says, did not get the news until 30 October, the day after Israel had attacked and on the same day that Mollet and Pineau had visited London to draw up the Anglo-French ultimatum.

[26]Gaitskell, at a much later date, repeated this version. 602 *H. C. Deb.* 56-57 (16 March 1959).

[27]The view that the cabinet was always divided on Suez received wide circulation from Paul Johnson, *The Suez War* (London: MacGibbon & Kee, 1957), p. 72.

[28]In a profile of Monckton, published four years after Suez, it is flatly stated that he had been "appalled by the Cabinet's plans to use force" and that he had been "privately quite open about his feelings." His protest, it was noted, took an "odd and ineffectual form" of resigning as Minister of Defence but becoming Paymaster General and, as such, in charge of propaganda in the Suez operation. *Observer* (London), 23 October 1960, p. 10.

Johnson even believes that Eden told his cabinet only after meeting the French ministers that day. Then, Johnson adds, the cabinet members, particularly R. A. Butler, who had previously been against forceful intervention in Suez, were faced with the difficult choice of acquiescing or resigning. The latter course would have meant not only bringing down the government and severely injuring the Conservative party, but also the nearly unthinkable repudiation of a Prime Minister's foreign policy in mid-passage.[29]

Randolph Churchill's critical version is similar except in detail. He does extend the inner cabinet, privy to the secret policy, so that it includes Butler, Macmillan, and Salisbury as well as Eden, Lloyd, and Head. But the rest of the cabinet, Churchill says, learned of the policy only at a meeting on the morning of 30 October. In this account, however, before Eden's meeting that day with the French ministers, Eden read the cabinet the ultimatum that Britain and France were to deliver later to Egypt and Israel. Some of Eden's colleagues, Randolph Churchill reports, "were taken aback. They had not realized that war was barely sixteen hours away. They felt that it was impossible for them at such short notice to discharge their constitutional responsibilities."[30]

Eden's own account is by clear implication at odds with the Johnson and Churchill versions. Eden says there was "no friction of any kind" with his colleagues in the weeks after the canal seizure. He never knew a government more united. There were shades of opinion, but "these did not obtrude."[31] Monckton was dropped because of anxiety about his health.[32] Moreover, there is Eden's significant report that on 25 October the cabinet "discussed the specific possibility of conflict between Israel and Egypt and decided in principle how it would react if this occurred."[33] This cabinet decision, Eden specifies, did involve an ultimatum to Egypt and Israel, and a subsequent Anglo-French military intervention if either or both parties failed to comply with the projected demand for withdrawal of forces from the Suez Canal. In light of this account, then, the most that can be said about the absence of consultation with the full cabinet is that even 25 October might have been so late a date as to make it difficult to overrule a

[29]Johnson, *op. cit.*, p. 93.
[30]Randolph Churchill, *The Rise and Fall of Sir Anthony Eden* (London: MacGibbon & Kee, 1959), p. 277.
[31]Eden, *op. cit.*, p. 520.
[32]*Ibid.*, p. 519.
[33]*Ibid.*, p. 523.

governmental commitment, especially one made as early as 16 October. But it is neither certain that there was a commitment on 16 October nor clear that such a commitment, if it existed, could not still have been reversed on 25 October by cabinet decision. A reversal would have been awkward, but by no means as nearly impossible as it would have seemed on 30 October. Therefore, it is hard to escape the conclusion, unless Eden's report is flatly wrong, that the full cabinet did meaningfully agree ahead of time about what to do in the hypothetical event of Egyptian-Israeli hostilities. The accuracy of Eden's report of cabinet decision-making of 25 October is also crucial for accepting Eden's account of the subsequent cabinet action of 30 October. In his view, this represented a confirmation of the cabinet's "readiness to act as had been decided, subject to the agreement of the French Ministers who were flying to London for consultation."[34] Incidentally, this statement of the sequence of events places the cabinet meeting of 30 October earlier in the day than the meeting with Mollet and Pineau, and thus contradicts Johnson's account on this point as well as on the more significant matter of the date when the full cabinet was informed of Anglo-French intentions.

Only Eden, among members of his government, has been explicit in testimony about the timing of cabinet discussions. Other leaders have, however, asserted the solidarity of the cabinet during the crisis. For example, Harold Macmillan, in defending Suez on two occasions after he had become Prime Minister, referred to decisions that Eden took "with the full, complete and unanimous support of his Government," and insisted that Eden had "the consistent and loyal support of all his colleagues in the cabinet."[35] Of course, Macmillan himself was always assumed to have favored forceful action over Suez, at least until he found, as Chancellor of the Exchequer, that the British financial situation could not stand the strain of continuing the intervention. Thus his words could have been expected. Not so with R. A. Butler, who was often suspected of doubts if not of actual opposition to military action over Suez. He too, however, was ready, in reviewing the action, to say that "I have unhesitantly supported the Government in this venture."[36] It may be granted that Butler, like his colleagues, could not very well say the opposite, even if true, but it is possible that if the opposite were true and he had opposed the action

[34] *Ibid.*, p. 524.
[35] 570 *H. C. Deb.* 425 (15 May 1957); 602 *H. C. Deb.* 153 (16 March 1959).
[36] 561 *H. C. Deb.* 1575 (6 December 1956).

in the cabinet he would later have avoided any declarations at all. Instead Butler seemed deliberately to reiterate his support in the face of widespread stories, during and after Suez, that he was privately against the military action.

Another uncertain aspect of the Eden government's commitment concerns the purpose which military intervention was meant to serve. The Prime Minister and his colleagues presented Parliament with several different reasons for their action, and none was exactly that of the critics who claimed that Britain and France wanted, for differing reasons, to topple Nasser and to establish their own or international control over the canal. Originally, when Eden defended the Anglo-French ultimatum requiring Egyptian and Israeli withdrawals, he even claimed that his government, along with that of France, "thought that there was a fair and reasonable chance that these proposals might be accepted."[37] He urged his opponents not to impugn governmental motives. Britain and France, in this presentation, were simply intervening to stop a war and, more particularly, to keep it from the Suez Canal. But this justification could not really be made convincingly in such a narrowly pacifying context when it was well known that Britain and France had objected to Egyptian control with or without hostilities. This was not always kept in the background of government presentation. For example, just as hostilities had ended, the Minister of Defence bluntly said that "the Canal cannot and must not be solely the concern of the Egyptian Government. That is what all this has been about."[38]

No doubt this is the way Anglo-French intervention looked to the world, but it was hardly the way that it was usually presented to the House of Commons during or after the action. Instead, like Eden in his *Memoirs*, government spokesmen of 1956, when they were not claiming a strictly peace-making role as between Egypt and Israel to safeguard the canal, stated even broader, less self-interested motives. British and French forces were presented as a kind of advance guard for the United Nations, just filling in because they were ready to act before the United Nations.[39] Subsequent intervention by the United Nations was "made possible by Franco-British action."[40] This high-minded internationalism was connected to the rejection of

[37]558 *H. C. Deb.* 1344 (30 October 1956).
[38]Antony Head, 560 *H. C. Deb.* 262 (8 November 1956).
[39]Alan Lennox-Boyd, 560 *H. C. Deb.* 283 (8 November 1956).
[40]R. A. Butler, 560 *H. C. Deb.* 1943-44 (22 November 1956).

appeasement, presumably appeasement of Nasser, and to the need for action to stop a third world war.[41] A link was also made to a case for action against Russian influence in the Middle East. To intervene at Suez thus became necessary to thwart Russia and not just Nasser. As one cabinet member argued on 8 November, it was really Russian plans for a take-over of the Middle East against which Britain and France had taken arms. Nasser was Russia's instrument.[42] Anglo-French intervention had disclosed, another cabinet member later said, the extent of Russian penetration and designs.[43] This also became a theme of Foreign Secretary Lloyd in his subsequent defense of the government action. He furnished details on Russian military equipment captured from the Egyptians, and implied a degree of anti-Soviet success for the Anglo-French intervention.[44] The anti-Russian aspect of the government's case for intervention seems largely to have been presented after the fact. Therefore, it might be suspected that it was not foremost in the minds of British leaders when they made their commitment to intervene. If Russian designs had earlier been a prime concern, more would undoubtedly have been made of such a purpose in trying to convince the United States of the need for military intervention. It is true that Eden had cited Russian use of Nasser in his efforts in August to persuade President Eisenhower of the seriousness of the Suez issue,[45] but in October this did not seem to be the crux of Eden's arguments, at least publicly, for strong measures against Nasser. Certainly the Russian threat was not at all prominent in the government's parliamentary case until after the action had been taken—in fact, really until after the action had been stopped.

3. CONDUCT OF THE OPPOSITION

Whatever the government's arguments, there could have been no real hope of converting the parliamentary Labour party to support the military intervention. The only hope that government leaders might have maintained was that with actual military action the Labour party would find it expedient, or think it patriotic, to refrain from open attacks on the government's Suez policy. Labour refused

[41]Harold Macmillan, 560 *H. C. Deb.* 688 (12 November 1956).
[42]Peter Thorneycroft, 560 *H. C. Deb.* 402 (8 November 1956).
[43]Lennox-Boyd, 560 *H. C. Deb.* 767 (13 November 1956).
[44]561 *H. C. Deb.* 1261 (5 December 1956).
[45]Eden, *op. cit.*, p. 452.

thus to refrain. An all-out opposition critique of military measures being carried out by British soldiers had obvious political risks, but Gaitskell's announcement of Labour policy, on 31 October, continued and intensified the stand which the party had already taken the day before and which it had, in effect, developed over the preceding months. "I must now tell the Government and the country," Gaitskell said, "that we cannot support the action they have taken and that we shall feel bound by every constitutional means at our disposal to oppose it." He stressed the word "constitutional," and indicated that this ruled out attempts to dissuade anybody from carrying out government orders. But Labour would seek "through the influence of public opinion, to bring every pressure to bear upon the Government to withdraw from the impossible situation into which they have put us."[46] There began the most intense parliamentary attack in recent British political history. During the whole of the next week, even on a Saturday, Eden and other ministers were forced to defend their policy against a barrage of shouted interruptions and angry rhetoric.

Disuniting the nation in the face of an enemy was a charge which Labour anticipated and tried to meet. That it was tragic for Britain to be divided was granted at the outset of military action, but Labour blamed the division on the Conservative government's deviation from the established British policy of adherence to the United Nations. Opposition leaders insisted that they were "as proud and anxious for our country"[47] as were the Conservatives, and that they too disapproved of Nasser. Clearly here the Labour party was on the defensive. Probably any opposition party in such circumstances would have to defend its patriotism, but the need to do so was especially sharp for British Labour because of its still recent struggle to become respectable in the eyes of marginal voters.[48] Labour as an unreliable custodian of the national interest was an image which the party had long sought to live down, and always against the Conservatives' identification of their own party with the nation. Now Labour critics were met with epithets like "Every country but your own," "traitorous defeatist," "Nasser's little lackey," and "Nasser's party."[49] Con-

[46]558 *H. C. Deb.* 1462 (31 October 1956).

[47]560 *H. C. Deb.* 36 (6 November 1956).

[48]As explained by W. Ivor Jennings, *Parliament* (Cambridge: Cambridge University Press, 1957), pp. 179-80.

[49]558 *H. C. Deb.* 1562, 1905 (31 October, 3 November 1956); 560 *H. C. Deb.* 1370 (19 November 1956); 562 *H. C. Deb.* 1254 (19 December 1956).

spicuous patriots among Conservative M.P.s, notably a holder of the Victoria Cross and a blinded veteran who was president of the British Legion, rose to protest the damage to troop morale caused by parliamentary opposition.[50] Later some of this level of patriotic attack came to be focused on Dr. Edith Summerskill, a parliamentary Labour leader who visited Egypt in January 1957, talked with Nasser, and reported her observation that the Anglo-French attack had not only been wrong in general but heavier in its toll of Egyptian casualties than had been admitted. She seemed thereby to confirm the Conservative notion that Labour had gone over to the enemy.[51]

This, as Labour leaders must have appreciated during the crisis, would become part of a "stab-in-the-back" legend, especially if Britain were to fail in its intervention. The very words were used by a Conservative critic.[52] He was thinking of Labour opposition during the war itself, and that, of course, was the potent political point. For some, however, the Labour critique during the attack only dramatized the damage flowing from the earlier opposition to a forceful policy. The Marquess of Salisbury emphasized this earlier damage when he declared that the Labour party had done its best to ensure that government policy failed. Long before the landings in Egypt, he said, the parliamentary opposition adopted a policy, against strong measures, "which they must have known could only bolster up the morale of Colonel Nasser at the expense of their own country."[53] Salisbury's complaint here is understandable. The government would have been weakened in its appearance of firmness and toughness when the opposition indicated its unwillingness to support the use of force. Threats against Egypt would thus have lost some of their effectiveness. Nasser might have been expected to doubt that a British government would really start a war without a large measure of bipartisan support. He would not have been the only one to doubt it. The United States might have done so as well.

Nevertheless it is hard to say that Labour, for the sake of the national interest, should not have indicated its opposition to the use of force during the months when force was being threatened. To have failed so to indicate would eventually have put Labour in the position,

[50] 558 *H.C.Deb.* 1697-98 (1 November 1956); 560 *H.C.Deb.* 362 (8 November 1956)

[51] *Times* (London), 18 January 1957, p. 8; 24 January 1957, p. 5.

[52] The Earl of Airlie spoke "of people who really stabbed our troops in the back as they were going over the top into battle." 200 *H. L. Deb.* 1066 (12 December 1956). The Earl described himself as a "Backwoodsman."

[53] 203 *H. L. Deb.* 1150 (23 May 1957).

when the intervention did come, of opposing force for the first time, unless of course it is argued that Labour should still have suppressed its views for the sake of national unity. The latter would be equivalent to saying that the opposition should never oppose a foreign policy involving military action, either during its development or during its execution. Perhaps there is something in that point of view if an opposition party wants primarily to avoid seeming to help the enemies of the government. The appearance of helping Nasser, incidentally, was bolstered by the fact that Egyptian and Arab spokesmen at the United Nations quoted Labour statements in support of their own objections to the Anglo-French intervention.[54]

Hugh Gaitskell himself became the most important target for patriotic charges. He was accused of putting his own political ambitions, both to unite his party and to defeat the government, ahead of the good of his country. His "hysterical" attack on the Suez operation was even contrasted unfavorably with the more philosophic critique of Aneurin Bevan,[55] long the figure used by Conservatives to frighten marginal voters. The virulence of the attack on Gaitskell is understandable. He was intensely involved in the particular issue, and his position as the still new parliamentary party leader could cause Conservatives to believe, correctly or not, that he had stepped out of his usual moderate role in order to appeal for the first time to his earlier left-wing opponents. Moreover, Conservatives had probably expected something else of Gaitskell, perhaps on the basis of his original strong anti-Nasser speech in August and perhaps also on the basis of his middle-class, public school, and university background so similar to that of most Conservative M.P.s. Thus Gaitskell earned the special enmity reserved by Conservatives for traitors to their class and its traditions. But even without this special feature, an opposition leader criticizing a war could expect to be presented to the public as the prime nonpatriot, and to have this image used against him for years. His case was not helped by the fact that he happened to have had no military service.

[54]Both the Egyptian and the Syrian Representatives quoted Gaitskell. United Nations, *Official Records of the General Assembly*, First Emergency Special Session, 561st Meeting (1 November 1956), p. 4; 562nd Meeting (1 November 1956), p. 17. The Egyptian later cited the Archbishop of Canterbury's denunciation of the use of force. 563rd Meeting (3 November 1956), p. 46. This internationalization of Britain's internal political differences is itself a significant element in the policy-making problems of a modern democracy.

[55]As by Macmillan, 561 *H. C. Deb.* 1471 (6 December 1956).

Another opposition difficulty that seems characteristic of such a situation concerns the availability of knowledge on the conduct of foreign affairs. There is always the possibility that an opposition, cut off from confidential government sources of military and diplomatic information, may present arguments which can subsequently be destroyed when the full facts are disclosed. Although the possibility exists in any political system, it is more likely in Britain than in the United States because nonministerial M.P.s do not have the independent access to government information that American legislators enjoy through the committee system. The closest to a British counterpart is the custom of maintaining communication between former ministers, even when in opposition, and their old ministerial staffs in the civil service. But this communication, at the highest levels, tends to wither after a group of leaders have been out of office for several years. It seems likely, therefore, that Labour party leaders would in 1956 have had only as much confidential information as the government's political heads were willing to give. This would have meant no information when bipartisan consultation broke down prior to and during the Suez crisis. The political consequence of this situation was that Labour found itself attacking a policy which the government hinted could be supported by facts which had to be kept secret for the time being. No actual disclosure of such crucial facts has ever been made, but the possibility (which may still exist) was used argumentatively by the government. There is Eden's broad hint on 1 November: "We fully recognize the risks of the action we have taken, but in our full responsibility, with our full information, we believe it was the only action available to our two Governments."[56] More pointedly, at the end of the action itself, a cabinet defender of the Eden policy said that the decision had been made "in the full knowledge of all the considerations, a great many of which are not known to hon. Members opposite. . . ."[57]

Neither this factor nor any other difficulty seriously marred the unity of Labour's opposition to the Suez action. The degree of parliamentary party solidarity was impressive, and especially so when it is appreciated that Labour, like most parties, secures votes basically on domestic economic and social issues, and that there was nothing about Suez which could be assumed to rally working-class interests in automatic opposition. To be sure, the several intellectual traditions

[56]558 *H. C. Deb.* 1653 (1 November 1956).
[57]560 *H. C. Deb.* 279 (8 November 1956).

of the party were all squarely against military intervention. On this, pacifists, United Nations enthusiasts, and both liberal and socialist anti-imperialists could for once unite behind the party leadership. Furthermore, the friends of the American alliance, like Gaitskell himself, joined the onslaught against British policy with the assurance that this time it was the Conservatives who disagreed with the United States. Only two sizable elements in the parliamentary Labour party could be suspected of wavering. One consisted of an indeterminate number of older nonintellectual trade unionists, conceived as responding in purely patriotic terms. But if they did so respond, they nevertheless adhered publicly to their party's position out of habits of loyalty typical of British unionists. Here, after all, was an apparent chance to bring down the government, and it ill suited a loyal representative of the labor movement to spoil this opportunity. The second element of potential disaffection consisted of the 17 Labour M.P.s who were Jews, or at least of the several who were active and devoted Zionists. However, they too supported the Labour critique after some initial doubt and ambiguity (discussed at length in Chapter Eight). None of this group, nor any of the trade unionists, deliberately abstained in the crucial divisions of 1 and 8 November. In fact, there was only one deliberate Labour abstention on either of those dates, and that was the individual affair of Stanley Evans.[58] Aside from this case and an occasional Labour remark after the crisis, opposition M.P.s were remarkably united in public support of their leader's position that the Suez intervention was "an act of disastrous folly whose tragic consequences we shall regret for years."[59]

The six-man Liberal parliamentary party, it may be remarked parenthetically, was not so clearly united. On 1 November, in the absence of the party's newly elected leader, Jo Grimond, three Liberals voted against the government and one abstained in known dissent from his anti-Suez colleagues.[60] On Grimond's return four days later from an American trip, the party became officially anti-Suez but the one dissenting M.P. retained his own position. However, all five available to vote on 8 November did oppose the government. Some ambiguity remained in subsequent months as Grimond and other

[58]This lone Labour rebel abstained in the divisions of 30 October and 1 November. Consequent difficulties with his divisional Labour party are discussed in Chapter Six.

[59]558 *H. C. Deb.* 1454 (31 October 1956).

[60]558 *H. C. Deb.* 1691-94 (1 November 1956).

national leaders, despite their own anti-Suez stand, supported a pro-Suez Liberal candidate in a by-election.[61] At the time, this as well as any other aspect of the Liberal position was of little consequence. The Liberal political revival, even in its first stage, was yet to come.

Labour's arguments in the House of Commons were based heavily on the wrongfulness of acting outside the United Nations and finally in defiance of the United Nations. Here Labour was consistent, during the crisis, with its earlier view that Britain should refer its dispute with Egypt to the Security Council and that it should contemplate no military action without United Nations approval. Once the action was undertaken, Labour argued that it was in violation of the United Nations Charter. The opposition's motion of censure, on 1 November, was advanced on this basis.[62] In the following days, Gaitskell and his colleagues insisted that the government should accept the cease-fire resolution of the General Assembly and that it could not rightly insist on conditions for accepting the resolution. Britain, in Labour's eyes, was simply the international wrongdoer.[63] Naturally, then, when the government did accept the cease-fire, Labour was not prepared to agree with the Conservatives' face-saving position, based as it was on the claim that the Anglo-French action was responsible for the presence of United Nations troops at Suez. Any such claim, one Labour spokesman said, was "rather as though the North Koreans had boasted that they were responsible for the formation of the United Nations command in 1950."[64] The United Nations force, as Labour saw it, was started to get Britain and France out of Suez. Consequently, in November and December Labour argued that British troops should be withdrawn from Suez.[65] Like the majority in the United Nations Assembly, Labour did not think the troops should have been there in the first place. They could not now be accepted as United Nations helpers. In Labour's view, Britain had forsaken its opportunity to be part of a United Nations force when it vetoed the Security Council resolution against Israel and then proceeded to intervene militarily without United Nations authority. Labour's own policy, as Gaitskell

[61]*Liberal News*, 8 March 1957, p. 1. The reference here comes from research by Jorgen Rasmussen, *Retrenchment and Revival: A Study of the Contemporary British Liberal Party and Its Activists* (unpublished Ph.D. dissertation, University of Wisconsin, 1962).

[62]By James Griffiths, 558 *H. C. Deb.* 1635 (1 November 1956).

[63]As Gaitskell stressed, 558 *H. C. Deb.* 1753, 1858 (2-3 November 1956).

[64]Kenneth Younger, 560 *H. C. Deb.* 272 (8 November 1956).

[65]For example, Gaitskell so argued, 560 *H. C. Deb.* 1945 (22 November 1956).

stated it after the event, would have been first, before Israel's attack, to have joined France and the United States in warning Israel against aggression, and then, when and if Israel did subsequently attack, to have supported the Security Council resolution against Israel. In that situation, Gaitskell argued, Britain could have proposed an international force and offered its services as part of it.[66]

More particular criticisms were added by Labour leaders to their parliamentary case against the British military action. Much was made of the break with Commonwealth countries, as exhibited both by the absence of prior consultation and by divergent voting in the United Nations. Politically this must have seemed a more telling point than simply to stress the break with the United States. Another line was to link the Suez action with the current Russian suppression of Hungarian freedom. More than simply likening the one action to the other, Labour argued that there might have been a causal link between the two. Perhaps, it was said, the Russian action against Hungary in the first week of November was somehow influenced by the fact that Britain and France had just taken their military action. One defiance of the United Nations, it was theorized, encouraged another[67] (but subsequent Anglo-French compliance with the United Nations did not encourage Russian compliance). The tenuousness of any belief in a causal relation, however, did not preclude the acceptance of the idea that the West was so weakened and disunited by the Anglo-French action that it could not be at its maximum effectiveness (through the United Nations or otherwise) in deterring Russia from retaking Hungary, or the idea that at the very least Suez prevented the West from obtaining the largest possible propaganda value from the fact of Russian aggression. Labour, in any case, made the most of these possibilities. They had the political advantage of allowing Labour to assert its anti-Russian credentials in response to the government's claim that it was, in effect, fighting Russia when it attacked Nasser.

None of these arguments were advanced with any serious expectation that they would persuade Conservative M.P.s to desert their leaders, or that the arguments would be so difficult for the government to counter that it would irretrievably lose face with its own supporters. Nor was it likely that a line of criticism attacking the honesty and

[66]561 *H. C. Deb.* 1564 (6 December 1956).
[67]Both Gaitskell and Philip Noel-Baker made this point. 560 *H. C. Deb.* 37 (6 November 1956); 561 *H. C. Deb.* 1463 (6 December 1956).

sincerity of the government's proclaimed motives for intervention would be any more effective. Impugning the government's motives was so serious that it would almost inevitably cause Conservatives to rally to their leadership. Yet such criticism was made, since the basis for impugning the motives of Eden and his government lay in the appearance of pretext which surrounded the Israeli-Egyptian hostilities as the stated cause for intervention. A Labour leader was prompt to say on 30 October that the government was using the opportunity to regain control of the canal.[68] This was followed, after action began, with the question of why Egypt was being attacked if the object was really to force the withdrawal of troops threatening the canal.[69]

After hostilities ended, in particular, Labour went beyond the charge that Eden was using the Israeli-Egyptian hostilities as a pretext for another purpose. That would have been bad enough, but Labour also raised the question whether the pretext was not a manufactured one. In other words, the opposition brought forward the much-discussed charge of Anglo-French collusion with Israel. It was a dangerous charge to make since, despite its plausibility, there was no definitive proof of British involvement. And without such proof much of the British public might be unwilling to entertain so grave a charge against their Prime Minister. Yet Labour M.P.s hinted at collusion even during the attack itself, and these hints became most prominent in the opposition's critique in the months following. One reason for this prominence was that the suggestion of collusion was a way to keep the Suez issue alive. It provided a convenient handle for the continued discussion of an affair which, it was assumed, embarrassed the Conservatives. It also provided an outside chance of forcing a revelation damaging to the government, whether that of Eden in the few months after Suez or that of Macmillan from early 1957. That no such damage resulted was not from lack of Labour effort. Persistently Labour leaders asked for an official inquiry about the "ugly rumour of collusion,"[70] and implied that without such an inquiry the rumor was going to be widely accepted as fact. Labour pressed the government to try to prove, contrary to apparent likelihood, that it knew nothing about the Israeli plan before the attack.[71]

[68]Christopher Mayhew, 558 *H. C. Deb.* 1367 (30 October 1956).

[69]This "crucial question," frequently repeated, was emphasized by Gaitskell, 560 *H. C. Deb.* 29 (6 November 1956).

[70]The phrase was Alfred Robens', 560 *H. C. Deb.* 780 (13 November 1956).

[71]Noel-Baker, 560 *H. C. Deb.* 869 (13 November 1956).

In particular, Labour pressed for information about Anglo-French exchanges at high-level meetings on 16 and 23 October since it appeared so likely that French information about Israeli plans would have been communicated to Eden and Lloyd on those occasions. Charges to that effect had been published and they were quoted in the Commons.

The burden of Labour's collusion charge did soon shift, however, from collusion proper, in the conspiring sense, to the more moderate but still damning allegation that the British government had known about Israeli intentions and had acted accordingly. By December 1956 Bevan and Gaitskell were not suggesting that Eden had incited or helped arrange the Israeli attack, but only that he had knowledge of the impending attack when he made plans with France (which might have actually conspired with Israel) to act in the circumstances of such an attack.[72] Eden, as already noted, would admit to no more than a "shrewd idea" of Israeli intentions, not to definite knowledge, even though this "shrewd idea" was enough to justify the cabinet decision of 25 October on how to act in case of an Israeli attack. Labour used French governmental statements that appeared to indicate, on the part of Britain as well as France, a more nearly certain awareness of the Israeli plan throughout the last few weeks of October. Gaitskell quoted the French foreign secretary as saying that France and Biitain had decided together what action they would take if Israel began a preventive war.[73] This led to questions not only about whether Britain and France had agreed to military intervention in such a war, but also about whether they had agreed to veto a United Nations Security Council resolution against Israel. And if such Anglo-French agreements were made, were they communicated to Israel before the attack started?[74] The latter would be crucial in converting foreknowledge into collusion, but it was difficult to prove. Even if it could be shown that France thus communicated with Israel, British leaders might still be able successfully to claim that they themselves had not joined in such communication with Israel. Labour attempted to counter the government's professed innocence by establishing the existence of a general conspiratorial atmosphere about Anglo-French plans in the last weeks of October. A great deal was made of the fact that neither Britain nor France informed the United States of an

[72]561 *H. C. Deb.* 1276, 1564-65 (5-6 December 1956).
[73]562 *H. C. Deb.* 1487 (20 December 1956).
[4]R. H. S. Crossman, 562 *H. C. Deb.* 1496 (20 December 1956).

impending Israeli attack or of Anglo-French plans in the event of such an attack.

How effective were Labour's several lines of criticism, during and after the crisis? The ultimate desire of parliamentary opposition—overturning the government—obviously failed, despite the most strenuous effort of a virtually unanimous opposition. After trying in the first few days of the crisis itself to get Eden to change his policy, the opposition openly stated its desire to secure through the parliamentary process a new government and a new Prime Minister—presumably a coalition of some sort. This could be accomplished only by Conservative disaffection, and Labour openly appealed for help in this direction from those Conservatives known to have doubts about Eden's action. Here, in trying to overthrow the government, Labour was handicapped by the very partisanship its intense hostility had helped to create. Suez had already become a party issue when Gaitskell made his appeal to Conservative M.P.s. Furthermore, this appeal was first made while military action was still under way. However, the appeal was renewed after the cease-fire when Labour made its major effort to overthrow the Eden government on 8 November. On that occasion, Labour's motion disapproving governmental policy was moderately worded and aimed particularly at the need to convene a Commonwealth conference. Speaking for the opposition and citing his own ample experience as a rebel, Aneurin Bevan asked Conservatives to choose between what he called the welfare of the country and the claims of party. He knew that it was never easy to part from colleagues, but now, he argued, was a time when the "solid facade of the party" should be broken.[75] This appeal failed. The number of open Conservative dissenters, as will be observed, was far too small for Labour's purpose.

Whether anything short of overthrow of the government was accomplished by Labour's intense parliamentary opposition is not easily settled. At the least, the debate was nerve-racking. This was not solely because the pitch of opposition attack was so high as to cause a suspension of the parliamentary sitting on one occasion and to lead one Labour woman M.P. to say that every Conservative member "can be branded as a murderer of every working-class boy who dies."[76] It was also because the parliamentary harassment of Eden was so prolonged and nearly continuous. An important Conservative party

[75]560 *H. C. Deb.* 393 (8 November 1956).
[76]558 *H. C. Deb.* 1625, 1745 (1 November 1956).

leader went so far as to say that the strain which caused Eden to seek a Jamaica rest in late November had been "intensified by the personal and scurrilous attacks" of the opposition.[77] Eden himself reports that he had never known "such a continuous abuse of the rules of order as during the Suez debates," that the "pace was faster and the strain more intense" than at any time during World War II, and that both his sleep and his digestion were adversely affected.[78] But even if thus, through ordeal by debate, Labour contributed to the illness which in January caused Eden's resignation, it was hardly much of a parliamentary accomplishment. Its effect depended on the Prime Minister being ill to start with, and in any case it produced no immediate resignation and even subsequently its result was only the substitution of another Prime Minister (Macmillan) openly avowing support for Eden's action.

The one substantial possibility of opposition accomplishment lies in the controversial decision of the Eden government to cease hostilities in Egypt short of the desired object. At first, following the cease-fire, Labour leaders claimed a large share in forcing this decision. This was implied by Gaitskell, immediately after the decision, when he told a Labour-organized mass meeting that the cease-fire was "one of the greatest triumphs for democracy the world has ever known."[79] The credit was assigned to the protests of the British people, presumably stirred by the Labour opposition. More explicitly Gaitskell said a month later: "We have managed now to force the Government to cease fire."[80] And also in December 1956 Bevan asserted the same Labour belief in the efficacy of its opposition, although he went on to define this efficacy as making the government sensitive to United Nations demands.[81] Interestingly, however, even this reasoned claim for the opposition's role was not maintained by Labour in the years after Suez. This might have been either because belief in the parliamentary party's accomplishment was not, on sober afterthought, really convincing, or because it was simply unpopular to claim a part in stopping military action short of its goal. The Conservatives were only too willing to have Labour accept what they regarded as the blame, not the credit, for ending the Egyptian intervention. For the portion of the public which disliked the action chiefly on account of its

[77]Quoted in the *Daily Mirror* (London), 26 November 1956, p. 2.
[78]Eden, *op. cit.*, pp. 547, 549, 550.
[79]Quoted in the *Daily Telegraph* (London), 7 November 1956, p. 12.
[80]561 *H. C. Deb.* 1569 (6 December 1956).
[81]562 *H. C. Deb.* 1400 (19 December 1956).

failure, there was the politically meaningful "stab-in-the-back" legend. At any rate, in Gaitskell's 1959 restatement of his case against the Suez action, he argued that even if Labour had accepted the Conservative policy the action could not have succeeded in the face of the inevitable reactions of the United States, the United Nations, and the Soviet Union.[82]

In the absence of a consistent Labour claim and, more important, of an official government admission of the evident change in policy, there can be no certainty about the effectiveness of the parliamentary opposition. Thus Sir Ivor Jennings, in a post-Suez revision of his authoritative *Cabinet Government*, grants that the Suez case is a "more complicated and controversial" example than three other instances he cites of the principle that even a government with a large majority cannot neglect the feeling of the Commons.[83] The chief complication was that opposition pressure against continuing the Suez action coincided with United Nations resolutions, certain important Commonwealth reactions, Russian threats, international weakening of the pound sterling, and intense American efforts involving oil and dollars as well as moral suasion. Perhaps there was a consequential interaction: Labour's opposition encouraging outside pressures, and the latter strengthening Labour's case. Furthermore, it is conceivable that the government, with a more united country behind it, would have had the nerve to face the consequences of continued defiance of outside opinion, especially since those consequences would have involved both military perils and prolonged economic sacrifices difficult to require of an openly divided nation.

With so early an end to hostilities, however, the Conservative government, in succeeding years, had merely to defend itself against the attempt to exploit an already settled issue. Opposition opportunities were provided by the several steps necessary in the aftermath of military action, ranging from actual withdrawal of troops to the Anglo-Egyptian financial settlement of 1959. On such occasions, Labour might seem to indulge in recrimination. The opposition could not really avoid it. To ask Labour to do so understandably reminded Aneurin Bevan of the prisoner who, when asked what he thought of the summing up of the judge, said that he thought that there was far too much recrimination in it.[84] Bevan himself persisted, after Eden's

[82]602 *H. C. Deb.* 55 (16 March 1959).

[83]W. Ivor Jennings, *Cabinet Government* (Cambridge: Cambridge University Press, 1959), pp. 478-80.

[84]570 *H. C. Deb.* 679 (16 May 1957).

retirement, in the Labour attack on the two cabinet members, Selwyn Lloyd (still Foreign Secretary) and Macmillan (now Prime Minister), who had been most identified with the Suez policy. It was they who could be pressed for an answer to the collusion charge, even more than two years after the event. The opposition continued to ask for a committee of inquiry, as late as 1959, but there was no way for Labour to force such an inquiry on an unwilling government.[85] All that could be done was to suggest that the truth could not be known without an inquiry and that, in refusing it, the Conservative leaders (notably Eden's successor, Macmillan) were concealing their own discreditable roles. As Gaitskell said, rather melodramatically for the 1959 Commons, "I believe that the guilty men are sitting on those benches. It is time that they were brought to trial."[86] But with the passage of time and the desire of all but deeply committed partisans to consign the Suez fiasco to the past, there was little political capital to be made of the promise of an inquiry after a Labour election victory. The opposition's campaign against Suez simply dwindled away.

4. CONSERVATIVE PARTY SUPPORT

The crucial political fact about the Suez crisis was the support of the government by Conservative M.P.s, including some who never wanted to go into Egypt and some who never wanted to come out. The nearly solid party voting meant that the parliamentary system did not operate in the classical nineteenth-century manner to defeat the government on grounds of either the Suez action or its failure. Yet here, if on any occasion, M.P.s might have been expected to break with their governmental leadership. Conservatives with anti-Suez convictions did certainly exist. Sir Lionel Heald's mid-September opposition to non–United Nations force was always assumed to represent at least 25 to 40 Conservative M.P.s, whose views would not likely have been changed by the circumstances of the Israeli-Egyptian hostilities.

In this light, the paucity of open Conservative criticism is noteworthy. While hostilities were actually under way, only one Conservative M.P. indicated his opposition on the floor of the House, and he did so, not by his voting behavior, but by an unusual question

[85]The suggested lack of inquisitory power is discussed by Geoffrey Marshall and Graeme C. Moodie, *Some Problems of the Constitution* (London: Hutchinson, 1959), pp. 187-88.

[86]602 *H. C. Deb.* 58 (16 March 1959).

put to the speaker.[87] Otherwise, despite at least one heart-searching type of parliamentary speech, anti-Suez Conservatives were publicly inconspicuous during the seven days of military action. The party's normal majority did not suffer from abstentions in the censure vote of 1 November. Nor was any critical blow struck by governmental resignations. No one resigned from the cabinet. Even below this level, only two members of the government resigned. They were Anthony Nutting, a Minister of State for Foreign Affairs regarded as an Eden protégé, and Sir Edward Boyle, Economic Secretary to the Treasury.[88] The latter resignation was not publicized during the military hostilities. And Nutting, although his objections were stated in a letter to Eden while hostilities were still under way, did not undertake to lead any revolt. He withdrew individually and independently; he did not appear in the Commons at all. Damaging only in the same limited way, because it represented the disagreement of someone previously close to Eden, was the resignation of William Clark, an able and well-known young journalist who was Eden's press secretary. None of these isolated moves, springing from conscientious objections, were calculated to stop the military action or to start a group effort to overthrow the government.

Similarly after the cease-fire, when on 8 November there were two Conservative anti-Suez speeches[89] and eight deliberate abstentions, the dissenters made no concerted effort to destroy the government. On the contrary, open rebels were far too few even for psychological import. The fact that so many of the estimated 25 to 40 anti-Suez Conservatives adhered to the party line was bound to reduce the impact of the eight who abstained. The occasion amounted only to a display of especially strong personal feelings on the part of a few. It is doubtful that any of the dissenting Conservatives, including the abstainers themselves, really wanted to help Labour defeat the government. To do so would have required not only more than eight recruits, but also voting in the Labour lobby instead of simply abstaining—given the government's normal majority of 60.

Explaining why no serious Conservative rebellion took place reveals

[87]The questioner was William Yates, the government's most persistent Conservative critic. 558 *H. C. Deb.* 1716-17 (1 November 1956). His statement and his deviation are discussed in Chapter Six.

[88]On these resignations, see the *Times* (London), 5 November 1956, p. 4; 9 November 1956, p. 10.

[89]560 *H. C. Deb.* 322-24, 369-70 (8 November 1956).

a good deal about the British party system. To start with, however, the bulk of Conservative M.P.s, not just the old 1954 Suez group, must be assumed to have supported Eden from conviction, even if with varying degrees of enthusiasm. No one questions the minority status of the anti-Suez Conservatives although their number has sometimes been put as high as 50 or 60 rather than 25 to 40. And this particular minority, because it was heavily liberal intellectual in character, was removed from the main imperial traditions of the Conservative party, particularly in the constituency organizations. Open rebellion would have been by a minority, probably a permanent minority, within the party. Moreover, the anti-Suez Conservatives had no popular leader with a large potential following in the party or in the country. Both resigning ministers were too junior for this role, and none of the older ex-ministers critical of Suez was a major figure. In any case, none of these elder statesmen actually joined in the display of 8 November. Their nonabstention was subsequently the subject for critical comment in the "Political Diary" of an anti-Suez paper:

The few who have already rebelled feel a good deal of bitterness towards those elder statesmen—those incorruptible ancients—who egged them on and then retired from the fray.

"My boy," they said in effect, "I wish I could accompany you on your great adventure, but the truth is I shall do much more for the cause by keeping a watch on things at home. So over the top and good luck to you." Then, with tears in their eyes—"Poor chap, I knew his father"—they quietly disappeared from the scene.[90]

Even in the House of Lords no important former minister among the Conservatives took direct issue with the Eden government. The Earl of Halifax, once Foreign Secretary and Ambassador to the United States, did go so far, when generally defending the government on 8 November, as to indicate his anxieties about the rights and wrongs, not so much of the military action, but of the way it was taken. He was gently critical of the absence of Commonwealth and American consultations, and of the creation of a situation where Britain could have been said to flout the United Nations.[91] Halifax, however, was an unwilling and an unlikely leader of a Conservative defection.

Launching a rebellion had other problems besides the lack of prominent Conservatives to head it. The most general was the dif-

[90]*Observer* (London), 18 November 1956, p. 9.
[91]200 *H. L. Deb.* 139 (8 November 1956).

ficulty of publicly breaking with the principle of loyalty to one's leadership. This principle, characteristic of both major British parties, is plainly paramount in the Conservative code of public political behavior. It was reinforced during the seven days of military hostilities by a special argument against "letting the side down." Afterward there was pressure too, psychological as well as institutional, against deviant behavior which would help, if not Nasser, at least the socialist enemy within the gates. The fact that this enemy had openly appealed for Conservative rebel support, in a national broadcast by Gaitskell as well as in parliamentary speeches, made deviation even harder. The persuasive Conservative chief whip, Edward Heath, was now especially diligent. As Eden later wrote of Heath, "I have never known a better equipped Chief Whip."[92] But the anti-Suez Conservative risked more than offending the whip and his colleagues of the parliamentary club. The deviating M.P. would also have to face the wrath of his Conservative constituency association, surely pro-Suez and in a position, through control of party candidate selection, to react meaningfully against an M.P. disloyal to the cause.[93] To make matters still more difficult, any open criticism of the Suez action was likely to imply that Eden's reasons for military intervention were false or hypocritical. To rank-and-file Conservatives, this would seem disloyalty with a vengeance.

That Conservative parliamentary lines so generally held is not, then, very mysterious. What is harder to get at are answers to questions about the effectiveness of any nonpublic pressure exerted by anti-Suez Conservatives. Despite the obvious failure to prevent Eden from taking action in the first place, the possibility remains that privately expressed back-bench opinion contributed to the government's cease-fire decision. Of course, there is no evidence from government sources of such successful pressure. More significantly, no claim for this kind of influence has ever been made by any of the anti-Suez Conservatives, either in public or, it may be added, in the private conversations which seven of the known dissenters had with the author. Yet there is a widely circulated story, published in a sensational journalist account and repeated in a scholarly work, that it was the threat by 40 back-bench M.P.s to vote against the government which caused

[92]Eden, *op. cit.*, p. 549.

[93]This is exactly what associations did do in relation to some of the Conservative M.P.s who actually deviated. See Chapter Six.

Eden to halt the Suez attack.[94] This statement, while not necessarily incorrect, goes beyond the hard evidence on two counts. First, there is no record of anything so definite as a group threat of this sort, even though it is generally thought that the anti-Suez M.P.s did meet privately during the crisis and that some sent letters to the Prime Minister. This was in addition to criticism and doubt expressed at the usual party committee meetings, so that in one way or another the whips and the government were made aware of discontent in their ranks. But none of this necessarily amounted to a group threat. Second, even if there was such a threat, there is no proof that it affected government action. There is some suggestion to the contrary in the fact that eight assumed members of the group made their public demonstration of opposition on 8 November, after the cease-fire. If they had been responsible for changing government policy through private pressure, it would not have been sensible immediately afterward to refrain from supporting the government. The fact was that the eight rebels did have good reason to abstain despite the cease-fire since the government, far from adopting an anti-Suez position, still defended intervention despite its necessary end.

There is one other aspect of Conservative parliamentary behavior over Suez which should be described. That is the maintenance of governmental support after the crisis and during the period when Britain withdrew its troops (December 1956) from the canal zone and then agreed (May 1957) to use the canal on Egyptian terms. Naturally the anti-Suez Conservatives were content with these measures, both of which meant retreat from the Suez action's apparent goal. Now the government was straining the loyalties of its most intense pro-Suez supporters—roughly the group, also of at least 25 to 40 M.P.s, who had opposed the 1954 evacuation agreement. For them, as observed in the previous chapter, there was no attraction in the government's face-saving claim that Britain had stopped a local war and caused the United Nations to intervene. They had wanted British troops to finish the job of occupying the canal zone. However, the

[94]The journalist account is by Merry and Serge Bromberger, *Secrets of Suez,* tr. from the French by James Cameron (London: Sidgwick & Jackson, 1957), p. 147, where it is alleged that R. A. Butler led the rebellion by threatening to resign with seven other ministers unless hostilities were stopped. The Bromberger statement that 40 Conservative M.P.s were behind such a rebellion is given as a fact, with *Secrets of Suez* cited as authority, by Peter G. Richards, a British political scientist, in *Honourable Members* (London: Faber & Faber, 1959), p. 249.

pro-Suez Conservatives could hardly serve this principle by parliamentary behavior designed to destroy the government. Not only were they, like the anti-Suez Conservatives of the crisis period, subject to the internal parliamentary pressures of party loyalty, but even on the particular issue their interest could not lie in helping Labour to power. Consequently the pro-Suez Conservatives could be expected, once their private efforts to rally the majority of the parliamentary party against withdrawal had failed, to do no more than demonstrate their disagreement by abstention (and by the strong speeches described in the last chapter). This was in spite of the fact that their disagreement with the government represented, as shown by their speeches, a fundamental difference over the future British role in world affairs.

The relative harmlessness of the abstention tactic was frankly described by one of the pro-Suez Conservative leaders: "I admit that it is a clumsy way and I say straight away that if I thought that by my abstention there was any chance of putting the party opposite in power, I should no more think of abstaining than I should think of singing a song instead of making a speech in this House."[95] On this basis, 15 Conservatives abstained over the troop withdrawal in December, and, as another of them explained, this was calculated to be about the right number to display their seriousness of feeling without doing any real damage to the government.[96] How deliberately the number was calculated by the rebels is uncertain since the persuasion of the whips might also have been responsible for keeping the total abstentions well below the supposed pro-Suez maximum of 40. The government had special cause, when Prime Minister Eden was resting in Jamaica and when its popularity for this and other reasons was shaky, to present as nearly united a front as possible. That they did so well is remarkable because no one was formally in Eden's place. Butler, more or less in charge, had not been made deputy leader. Similarly, in May 1957, when the still new government of Prime Minister Macmillan had to present its proposal for renewed British use of the canal, there were undoubtedly efforts to keep down the number of abstainers although there was no chance of the pro-Suez rebels causing the government's fall. They only wanted to press for what they called a stronger line in foreign policy. For this cause, 14 abstained and eight of these M.P.s took the slightly

[95]561 *H. C. Deb.* 1302 (5 December 1956).

[96]William Teeling, quoted in *Evening Argus* (Brighton), 7 December 1956, p. 7.

more drastic, but equally futile, step of resigning the government whip to sit temporarily as Independent Conservatives.[97]

The important political consideration was that a rebellion should be so limited in numbers as to leave the government securely in office. By May 1957 this was nearly a sure thing despite the humiliation which many Conservative M.P.s, not only the Suez extremists, felt over British acceptance of Nasser's terms. Almost all could be expected to vote on the basis of the alternatives presented by the final appeal of the Prime Minister: ". . . whether the prestige and economic interests of Britain are better entrusted to a Socialist or to a Conservative Administration."[98]

5. Summary

Although the struggle over Britain's Suez policy was also carried on outside Parliament, in ways yet to be discussed, there are some general implications for the conduct of a partisan foreign policy that emerge from the strictly parliamentary experience. Not all of these implications are entirely clear because certain crucial facts, as noted, are still missing. A few tentative conclusions can nevertheless be drawn.

First, it is plain that the Suez commitment was an executive decision made without the prior approval, formal or informal, of Parliament. It may even have been a personal decision of Eden in consultation only with his closest advisers rather than with the cabinet as a whole. At any rate, before the commitment there was no consultation with the opposition, and no apparent enlistment of support from even the minority of Conservative M.P.s who had also indicated an earlier disapproval of the type of action now to be undertaken.

Second, Eden's commitment, after being made so purely as an executive matter and in defiance of partisan opposition, did receive the crucial minimum of parliamentary support. The government was not defeated in the Commons, and it may not have suffered at all because of its merely partial support in the political community. In fact, it was the very partisan nature of the division of opinion which sustained the government, and kept Conservative M.P.s who disliked Eden's action from trying to defeat their leadership. To do so would have risked either a general election, possibly bringing Labour to power on its own, or some kind of coalition dominated by Labour.

[97] *Times* (London), 14 May 1957, p. 10; 16 May 1957, p. 12. See the next chapter for more extended discussion of the pro-Suez rebels.
[98] 570 *H. C. Deb.* 698 (16 May 1957).

In such circumstances, there was not even any precedent for sub-stantial revolt in the famous action of the rebels against the Chamberlain government in 1940.[99] Then, when over 40 Conservatives voted against their party leadership and many others abstained, not only was the normal Conservative majority so large that enough remained to prevent a technical defeat, but the admittedly severe blow at the government's prestige could not, given the wartime political truce, cause a general election or even anything beyond the reconstitution of the government as a coalition under different Conservative leadership and with minority representation for the opposition parties. The Suez crisis, on the other hand, involved the more usual political demands for loyalty, now perhaps stronger anyway than in 1940, and the Conservative party, like the Labour opposition, remained cohesive in the accepted British political manner.

Third, Labour's experience in attacking the Suez action indicates definite limits on the parliamentary usefulness of partisan opposition to government foreign policy, even to one which fails. The government was not brought down during the crisis, and its public credit did not appear to have been damaged in the long run.[100] Whether it could have sustained a longer war, in the face of partisan attacks, is less certain. As matters stood, however, opposition was handicapped by its unpatriotic appearance during military hostilities, and even afterward Labour was troubled by the charge that it had caused Britain's withdrawal—although no such accomplishment could be established and Labour ceased to claim it.

[99] *Times* (London), 9 May 1940, p. 6; 10 May 1940, p. 6. 360 *H. C. Deb.* 1361-66 (8 May 1940).

[100] The government's status in public opinion surveys and in by-elections is analyzed in Chapter Seven. Eden's own political status is another matter. He may have been forced out of office by more than his illness, since other Conservatives, leaders as well as M.P.s, could have concluded that his usefulness was at an end.

CHAPTER SIX

M.P.s and Their Constituencies

The partisan conflict over Suez, so dominant in Parliament, also characterized the constituencies. It is most readily and dramatically observed in districts whose M.P.s were among the few who deviated from their parliamentary parties. Such deviations, as already noted, were mainly in the form of refusal to vote in crucial divisions, but they also include the lesser offense of publicized remarks at odds with the party's position. In response, party activists expressed their opinions in the context of the important but otherwise little-known relations between local associations and M.P.s. The result is a chance to study these relations as well as local responses to Suez. It is necessary to be cautious in generalizing from the Suez cases alone,[1] but enough information may be available at least to raise some question about the limited role ordinarily conceived for the associations. Not much recent scholarly attention has been given to the possibility that local party organizations, empowered though they are to select parliamentary candidates (subject to national advice and approval),[2] would take action, more or less on their own, to punish M.P.s for parliamentary

[1]Hopefully, there was enough caution in an earlier use of the same material by the author, "British M.P.s and Their Local Parties: The Suez Cases," *American Political Science Review*, Vol. 64, pp. 374-90 (June 1960). See especially the tentative generalizations suggested at pp. 384-89.

[2]Local parties are described by R. T. McKenzie, *British Political Parties* (London: Heinemann, 1955), *passim*. Briefly, the usual Conservative pattern is for authority to be exercised by a 40- to 70-member executive council of officers elected by the association at its annual meeting and of representatives elected by various wards and branches. A smaller finance and general purposes committee, containing most of the

deviations. No one has questioned their technical authority to refuse to readopt a candidate, even a sitting M.P., but it has often been assumed that they were unlikely to use this authority against an M.P. who took only rarely or even occasionally an independent line, as long as he maintained his standing as a member of the parliamentary party.[3]

Studying M.P.–constituency association relations requires an intrusion into business which, as one M.P. wrote in response to my inquiry, is "private, personal and confidential." Candidate selection, for example, is a closed affair at all its important stages, and the observer has much less chance to learn the political forces at work than he has even at an American nominating convention, not to mention the direct primary. Visitors are only occasionally permitted at a selection meeting, and then on the assumption that they will not publicize the proceedings. Journalists, like political scientists, usually get no more than bare announcements of resolutions and actions taken. The procedure was not basically different during the Suez crisis. But there was then enough public controversy to establish the visibility of M.P.s deviating from their parliamentary party's position, and so to direct inquiry to their constituency relations. In these cases, it has been possible to secure fairly full information from newspaper accounts, particularly local ones, and from interviews with M.P.s and occasionally with party officers. The interviews, incidentally, cannot ordinarily be annotated.

Two main questions, as already suggested, are to be raised in discussing the constituency experiences of the several deviating M.P.s. The first is the nature and the extent of the commitment of local organizations to their respective party positions on Suez. In other words, how zealously devoted were Conservative activists to a pro-Suez position, and Labour activists to an anti-Suez position? The second question concerns the actual behavior of the organized activists, in their constituency associations, toward deviations by their

important local leaders, often expresses policy. The divisional Labour party, technically not bearing the name of "association," has no annual meeting open to the entire membership, but it has a general management committee comparable in size, in elected representativeness, and in practical authority with the Conservative executive council. There is also, in the Labour case, a small and influential local executive committee elected by the general management committee.

[3]Of course, this was not M. Ostrogorski's view. In his famous alarmist study of the rise of the Liberal party "caucus," it was precisely the power of the local units of the new national party organizations that he deplored. *Democracy and the Organization of Political Parties* (London: Macmillan, 1902), Vol. 1, chaps. 4-5. Compare McKenzie *op. cit.*, p. 253.

M.P.s. How did the associations function when and if their views conflicted with those of their own elected parliamentary representatives?

Both of these questions have to be dealt with largely in terms of Conservative experiences since, with one exception, all of the important known parliamentary deviations were by Conservative M.P.s. There are two Conservative categories. The first and best-known consists of ten anti-Suez Conservatives who deviated during and just after the crisis itself. The second and very different Conservative group contains 20 militantly pro-Suez M.P.s, deriving from the old Suez group, who subsequently revolted against their government's postintervention policy of retreat in late 1956 and early 1957. Finally, there is the single case of a pro-Suez Labour M.P. deviating from his party during the crisis itself. A few other Labour M.P.s did less definitely deviate, but their different experiences are reserved for a later chapter.[4] Necessarily then, with so few cases and these almost entirely from one party, only a limited claim can be made for the representativeness of the constituencies whose politics are to be covered. The constituencies have not been selected by any sampling technique. They are merely the ones that happened to have deviating M.P.s. Therefore, even though there is no reason for believing that the constituencies as such are untypical, it is safer to say that the local politics here observed is illustrative rather than representative.

1. ANTI-SUEZ CONSERVATIVES

Limiting the anti-Suez Conservative cases to ten does understate the total number of conservative M.P.s believed to have been opposed, at one time or another, to their government's Suez action. As many as 50 or 60, noted in the last chapter, may have been at least tacit opponents of Eden's policy, and about 25 to 40 of these M.P.s constituted an informal group. Only ten, however, became publicly identified as anti-Suez critics, and thus exposed to constituency response. Getting this number even as high as ten requires counting two M.P.s who voted regularly with their party leaders but who became known as anti-Suez because of a parliamentary speech in one instance and various semipublic statements in the other. These two are added to the eight deliberate Conservative abstentions of 8 November, the high point of open intraparty opposition to Eden's intervention. This high point, it is worth stressing, came after the intervention had halted. Such was the very limited parliamentary

[4]See Chapter Eight.

rebellion to which Conservative constituency associations responded. None of the M.P.s ever voted against the government, and (with one or two possible exceptions) none deliberately abstained during the period of actual fighting. In other respects, however, the ten cases differ enough and are important enough to deserve separate treatment. It is simplest to identify each case by the name of the M.P. although it is his constituency's response on which interest is focused.

NICOLSON

In every respect, the leading case is that of Nigel Nicolson. But it is not so much what he did against the government that distinguishes him from the other anti-Suez Conservatives. He did no more than abstain on 8 November, following, it is true, a critical public speech the night before. Much more notable is what happened to him not only in the next few months but over the next two years. In the process, Nicolson's experience was widely publicized nationally as well as locally, and it became an important item for any general history of M.P.-constituency relations. Nicolson himself wrote a book covering all but the final climactic events,[5] and these, along with the earlier stages, have been most ably analyzed by a political scientist in a full-length journal article.[6] Moreover, the Nicolson case supplied an important part of the data for an earlier effort, by the author, to generalize about M.P.-constituency relations.[7] Here, therefore, many of the details of the Nicolson ordeal may be omitted in favor of concentrating on the nature of the immediate constituency response.

At least a little, however, must first be said about Nicolson. He would never have been called a typical Conservative M.P. despite an impeccably upper-class education and prestigious wartime service. The trouble was that Nicolson belonged not just to the upper class, but to an intellectual upper class. Both his parents, Sir Harold Nicolson and V. Sackville-West, were important literary figures, and Sir Harold was a most independent-minded public figure who had once even been a Labour M.P. Nigel Nicolson himself, pursuing a career as author and publisher, had been active politically only as a Conservative, but he had established a reputation as a moderate partisan and as a humanitarian liberal in his four years as the M.P. for Bournemouth East and Christchurch. He had first become M.P. in a by-

[5]Nigel Nicolson, *People and Parliament* (London: Weidenfeld & Nicolson, 1958).
[6]Laurence W. Martin, "The Bournemouth Affair: Britain's First Primary Election," *Journal of Politics*, Vol. 22, pp. 654-81 (November 1960).
[7]*Op. cit.*

election in 1952, and he had been readopted and re-elected in 1955. His moderation was revealed by a relatively kind, nonpartisan remark about Aneurin Bevan, the prime target of Conservative dislike in the late 1940's and early 1950's. His liberalism was exhibited earlier in the Suez year of 1956 by opposition to the death penalty. The latter, in particular, had already marked Nicolson, in the eyes of many of his Conservative supporters, as ideologically unreliable. Added to this as a source of potential difficulty, even before Suez, was a less-than-comradely personal relation between the intellectual M.P. and some of the most prominent local activists, especially the current chairman.

Subsequently there was a tendency to portray these local activists as mainly Colonel Blimp types. Almost certainly this involved an exaggeration. The Bournemouth constituency, a south-coast resort, did contain many retired military officers, their wives, and their widows, but they were by no means the bulk of the total population or always the only major force in local Conservative affairs. Nor were all of the retired officers Blimps. Bournemouth was a relatively modern, growing British city that attracted a large variety of the new as well as the old middle class. The constituency was overwhelmingly Conservative—almost three to one in 1955—and the Conservative association was a large and active group. Its selection of a candidate was, of course, equivalent to selecting the M.P., and Nicolson, therefore, had a safe parliamentary seat as long as the association continued the usual British practice of almost automatically readopting its M.P. as its candidate. This practice did seem likely to continue in Bournemouth, as elsewhere, despite some local restiveness over Nicolson's moderation, liberalism, and apparent intellectual superiority.

Suez changed that. Perhaps it was not alone responsible for Nicolson's trouble. His opposition to hanging might have played a part as well, but it was most unlikely, without Suez, to have cost Nicolson his seat. That his opposition to Suez should have started so much trouble may seem remarkable when it is appreciated how late and inconsequential his opposition actually was. Not only did Nicolson vote with the government during the period of military intervention itself, but he tried to present the prointerventionist case, without disputing it or overtly agreeing with it, in a speech before branches of his constituency association on 2 November. Eden's aim, Nicolson then said, was "to prick an abscess. . . ."[8] Here he was publicly at

[8]*Bournemouth Daily Echo*, 3 November 1956, p. 12.

one with his association, which telegraphed its support to the Prime Minister. But even during the intervention Nicolson privately doubted its wisdom, and by 4 November he wrote confidentially to the Conservative association chairman, Major S. G. Grant, that he no longer felt able to support the government's Middle East policy. Grant sought to dissuade Nicolson from openly opposing the government, and to this end he sought to convince the M.P. that his constituents supported the government and expected him to do likewise.

Nicolson, however, kept his peace only until the fighting stopped. Then he took the first available public forum, provided in Bournemouth on 7 November by the anti-Suez United Nations Association (of which he was a member), to attack the government. Fully reported by the local newspaper as the first open criticism of Eden's action by a Conservative back-bencher, Nicolson's speech on this occasion— to a distinctly non-Conservative audience—must have surprised almost all of his Conservative supporters except Major Grant and such few other insiders as were in his immediate confidence.[9] Nicolson had told Major Grant of the prospective speech, but he had not heeded the chairman's plea that he refrain from speaking. The association's reaction was swift. The very next night the officers of the association repudiated Nicolson's views and renewed their support of the government's policy.[10] But this was only the beginning. Backed or even pressed by strong anti-Nicolson statements from their ward units, the association's 55-member executive committee adopted, a week later, a resolution charging that Nicolson (presumably by his abstention of 8 November and by his speech of 7 November) had chosen to act so as to "a) cause embarrassment to the Prime Minister and Government; b) misrepresent the views of the vast majority of his supporters in the constituency; and c) encourage and delight the Opposition."[11] This resolution, Major Grant seems correct in asserting, represented not just the views of the 55 leaders on the executive committee, but, at the time at least, also the views of most of the several hundred most active party workers manning the branch organizations. It is harder to say the same thing for ordinary association dues-paying members, largely inactive in organizational matters, and much harder to say the same thing for ordinary Conservative voters. It was Bourne-

[9]*Ibid.*, 8 November 1956, pp. 20, 11.
[10]*Ibid.*, 9 November 1956, p. 32.
[11]*Ibid.*, 15 November 1956, p. 1.

mouth's Conservative activists who were plainly against Nicolson. He had betrayed their party cause.

Even a few weeks later, in early December, these activists strongly supported the executive committee in its anti-Nicolson commitment. The occasion was a special meeting of the whole association, which all dues-paying members were entitled to attend. Not all, or even any large portion, of the membership would ever attend such a meeting, but in this instance the number present was also limited by the size of the hall. Some members, pro- and anti-Nicolson, were turned away. But Nicolson himself did not believe the attendance to be so un-representative as to justify a postponement. The activists at the meeting heard Nicolson's plea in his own behalf, and then, 298 to 92, expressed lack of confidence in Nicolson and instructed the executive committee to begin the process of selecting a new prospective parliamentary candidate for the next general election.[12] This selection process was begun immediately, while Nicolson remained an M.P. disowned by his local party, and by early 1957 the association had its new pro-spective candidate, Major J. A. Friend. His credentials on the Suez issue were unimpeachable. "I greatly regret," Major Friend said when selected by the executive committee, "we did not occupy all the Canal."[13] In March he was adopted by the association, 569 to 176, and he reiterated his pro-Suez views: "I believe we should have gone all the way down the Canal."[14]

Major Friend's imperialism, however, was eventually his undoing. While Nicolson tried, apparently without much chance of success, to get Bournemouth Conservatives to reverse their decision, Major Friend was found, early in 1959, to have foolishly and covertly col-laborated with an extreme right-wing organization, the League of Empire Loyalists. Since the League's campaign included attacks on Prime Minister Macmillan as a traitor, Major Friend now became an embarrassment as Bournemouth's prospective Conservative candidate and M.P. Consequently he resigned, after exposure of League con-nections at first denied,[15] and Nicolson was enabled to revive his cause in circumstances that made his enemies in the association leadership seem very poor judges of candidates.[16] With no official

[12]*Ibid.*, 6 December 1956, pp. 1, 20.
[13]*Ibid.*, 12 February 1957, p. 9.
[14]*Ibid.*, 7 March 1957, p. 9.
[15]*Times* (London), 15 January 1959, p. 8.
[16]*Daily Telegraph* (London), 26 January 1959, p. 15.

candidate now in his place and with his Suez aberration over two
years old, Nicolson had an entirely fortuitous and favorable second
chance. This was not a second chance that his association, still led
by Major Grant, had wanted to give him, but there was enough
persuasion from the Conservative national office, concerned about
the adverse effect of Bournemouth on the party's reputation for
tolerance, to cause the association to allow a nearly unprecedented
postal ballot among all its members on the simple question whether
Nicolson should be readopted. Even this ballot, sent to inactive as
well as active local party members, Nicolson could not quite win.
He lost 3,762 to 3,671.[17]

Suez was not yet a dead issue among Bournemouth Conservatives
in 1959. In fact, Nicolson found it expedient to conduct his 1959
campaign for reinstatement without trying to persuade Conservatives
of the merits of his anti-Suez stand. Instead he argued that one could
vote for him in the mail ballot without thereby agreeing with him on
Suez. No one, he said, had to abandon his own view of Suez in order
to acknowledge the right of an M.P. to differ on the issue.[18] This was
Nicolson's effort to counter the argument of his opponents that "a vote
for Nicolson would mean that the Tories had ratted on Suez."[19]
Thus both sides assumed, as late as 1959, that Conservative party
members remained committed to Eden's intervention. No basis exists
for challenging this assumption, but it does seem from the closeness
of the mail ballot result that the nonactive party members—now
polled for the first time—must have been less committed or less
zealously committed than the 55 members of the executive committee,
who were still unanimously against Nicolson, or the several hundred
activists at the association meetings that had voted Nicolson out in 1956.

MEDLICOTT

The response of Central Norfolk Conservatives to the defection of
their M.P., Sir Frank Medlicott, differed in form but not in substance
from Bournemouth's response to Nicolson. The consequence was certainly the same: loss of his seat by the deviating M.P. Yet the circumstances of the constituency and of its M.P. were sharply different.
Central Norfolk was largely rural, and its divisional association,
dominated by prosperous farmers and sportsmen, was smaller and

---

[17]*Times* (London), 27 February 1959, p. 9.
[18]Speech of 17 February 1959 at Highcliff Hotel, attended by the author.
[19]John Junor, *Sunday Express* (London), 15 February 1959, p. 12.

less active than Bournemouth's urban and suburban group. Medlicott had represented roughly the same constituency since 1939. He had done so technically as a National Liberal because Central Norfolk was one of the constituencies reserved by the Conservatives, since the 1930's, for their allies among right-wing Liberals. Under this curious residual arrangement, not only was Medlicott a National Liberal, while accepting the Conservative whip, but the divisional association went by the name of "Conservative and Liberal" in order to mark the alliance. By the 1950's, however, the association had become basically Conservative in what was a fairly safe Conservative constituency. This had made for some differences with Medlicott, who preserved views derived from his own nonconformist Liberal origins, but none of the pre-Suez differences had seriously threatened Medlicott's established position as the association's candidate. Medlicott had been able to oppose blood sports, liquor, and the horse-killing Grand National, despite the convictions of his Tory landowning constituents, and he had even been able to oppose hanging without provoking his association leaders beyond disagreement. In short, Medlicott's personal relations with his association had remained amiable until the fall of 1956. It was an amiability cherished by Medlicott, an evidently sensitive man.

The M.P. inadvertently put an end to this amiability, much as he had cherished it, when he opposed the Suez intervention. But, like Nicolson, Medlicott did not publicly oppose the government until the intervention was halted. In fact, he had announced his support in a parliamentary speech of 3 November, after, to be sure, "the most desperate heart searching."[20] Only on 8 November did Medlicott abstain. Then, as his local newspaper reported, he "remained conspicuously in the side gallery and took no part" in the parliamentary division.[21] At the same time, the press carried Medlicott's letter advising the Prime Minister of his grave doubts about the rightness of the government's action.[22] These deviating acts, it seems, were enough to produce a sharply effective local reaction. Opposing Suez, even after the fact, offended Norfolk Conservatives in a way that antihanging had not. The first public reactions came from association branches, at least three of which almost immediately adopted reso-

[20]This parliamentary remark was quoted locally in the *Eastern Daily Press* (Norfolk), 5 November 1956, p. 1.

[21]*Ibid.*, 9 November 1956, p. 1.

[22]*Ibid.*, p. 10.

lutions dissociating themselves from Medlicott's position on Suez. A week later, in mid-November, the association's executive committee similarly dissociated itself in a letter addressed to the Prime Minister.[23] Now there began the process that Medlicott has aptly described, in conversation, as being "frozen out" of his constituency. It turned out to be a way for the local Conservatives to get rid of their M.P. without actually rejecting him as Bournemouth had rejected Nicolson. Medlicott's resignation was not publicly demanded. Nor was the procedure started for selecting a new candidate, despite a few hints in that direction. Mainly there was an effective political and personal unpleasantness. Medlicott was denied all of the usual Christmas recess invitations to address branch meetings. Five of the six top officers of the association spoke against his Suez views. The sixth, the chairman, wrote Medlicott suggesting that he retire so as to allow the association to unite on a new prospective candidate. Medlicott's attempt to justify his position was met by the refusal of the executive committee to let him speak when, in February, he traveled to Norwich and waited for an hour and a half outside the committee's meeting room.[24]

Medlicott, it was plain, faced a fight for readoption, and it was a fight that he could not be sure of winning. He decided in May 1957 to withdraw from consideration as a future candidate. He did so in a letter sent to a general meeting of the association at which he had been scheduled to speak (but not, it was explicit, in defense of his Suez position). The alternative, he believed, would have been to swallow his pride, gloss over his differences with the association, and give assurances about future regularity. In this way he might have secured readoption. What he could not have, however, was readoption on his own terms: association respect for his still divergent view on Suez. For the activists among Central Norfolk Conservatives, support for the lost interventionist cause was still, in the spring of 1957, a prime party credential. Medlicott could not persist in error and remain their M.P. into the next Parliament.

NUTTING

Resembling Medlicott's treatment in result, Anthony Nutting's experience at the hands of his Melton constituency in rural Leicestershire was nevertheless different in at least two vital respects. First, his defection was more serious than that of the other anti-Suez Con-

[23]*Ibid.*, 17 November 1956, p. 1.
[24]According to Medlicott's own account. *Ibid.*, 2 May 1957, p. 1.

servatives since it involved Nutting's resignation as Minister of State
for Foreign Affairs and, as it happened, publicity for this resignation
during the intervention itself. The timing of the publicity was apparently unintentional, but rumors of his opposition, prompted partly
by Nutting's absence from the Commons during the crisis debates,
led to the printing, on 5 November, of his letter of resignation as a
minister.[25] The letter left no doubt of Nutting's opposition to the
government's Middle Eastern policy and of his personal break with
Eden, whose protégé Nutting had been. The second important distinguishing feature of Nutting's case was gossip concerning an estrange-
ment from his wife and an affair with another woman. Politically,
however, Nutting had had a most successful career prior to Suez.
Entering politics early, he had represented his constituency since 1945
and had been president of the Young Conservatives. Not only was
Melton safely Conservative, but it seemed especially safe for Nutting.
He had been raised in the constituency, his family lived there, and
his father had been master of the local hunt. Nutting, therefore,
might well have been looking forward to long parliamentary service
and continued ministerial advancement. He had no reason, before
Suez, to have or to expect trouble from his constituency association.

During the Suez crisis, Nutting took some pains to avoid, or at
least to reduce, the trouble he was eventually to have. He did confidentially inform the president and the chairman of the Melton constituency association of his ministerial resignation so that they, at
least, were prepared for the news a few days before it was published.[26]
Nutting also tried to get the local officers to delay any statement in
opposition to his stand until he had a chance to meet with association
members. In this effort, however, he did not succeed. The finance
and general purposes committee of the association sent the Prime
Minister word of its unanimous support almost immediately after
Nutting's resignation was announced.[27] Thus Nutting found himself
publicly at odds with his association's leadership on a matter on which

[25] *Times* (London), 5 November 1956, p. 4. Earlier the *Times* (3 November 1956,
p. 6) had reported that Nutting's absence of 1 November was the result of asthma
and that there was no truth in reports of his resignation. Nutting's position was a
curious one since he had presented the government's apparently tough Suez views at
the party conference in early October. *76th Annual Report of the Conservative Conference*
(1956).

[26] As was granted in a subsequent statement from the association. *Melton Mowbray
Times*, 30 November 1956, p. 3.

[27] *Times* (London), 7 November 1956, p. 6.

he was much too clearly committed, because of his resignation from the Foreign Office, to think of compromising or glossing over. And whatever hope he had of securing acquiescence in or tolerance for his stand was lost now that the association was also committed. Perhaps his hope had been forlorn from the beginning. The party activists of Melton seem to have responded to Suez much as activists elsewhere. A stream of telegrams, the local press reported, assured the Prime Minister of support during the crisis.[28] It was not accidental that association officers refused Nutting's request to suspend judgment until he could give his interpretation. Even if the local chairman, with whom Nutting was in touch, had wanted to oblige Nutting, he would still have had to convince his fellow activists to delay their announcement of support for the Prime Minister. The chairman had made it clear to Nutting that it was these activists generally, not just a few officers, who wanted to repudiate their M.P.'s statement.

By mid-November, when the association did give its M.P. an opportunity to explain his position, Nutting decided against addressing a meeting whose leaders were already so firmly against his Suez views. Even in the unlikely event that he were able to convince a majority of his association, against the advice of its leaders, Nutting would almost certainly have had a split and divided association. He himself offered this explanation for his decision against appearing and for his related decision to give up his seat.[29] Nutting's explanation may be sufficient, but it is also possible that at this point his personal affairs made an open constituency fight especially difficult and awkward. Unquestionably he was faced with the fact that at least one important pro-Suez newspaper saw fit to publicize his complicated domestic situation. Between his ministerial and parliamentary resignations, the *Sunday Express*'s gossip columns displayed a picture of Nutting with his wife and three children, and another picture of Mrs. Alfred Vanderbilt. The accompanying story explained: "Since Mr. Anthony Nutting resigned, in the middle of the Suez crisis, as Minister of State for Foreign Affairs, his close friendship with Mrs. Alfred Vanderbilt—which has long been kept a fairly close secret by his family and friends—has become a subject of public rumour both here and in America."[30] However, the story continued, Mrs. Nutting

---

[28]*Melton Mowbray Times*, 9 November 1956, p. 1.
[29]*Ibid.*, 30 November 1956, p. 3.
[30]Ephraim Hardcastle, *Sunday Express* (London), 11 November 1956, p. 5.

had told the inquiring columnist that there had so far been no discussion of a divorce.

Tactics of this kind, reflecting a sturdy if unattractive journalist
tradition, could have weakened both the willingness and the effectiveness of Nutting to persuade his association to support him. As long
as he remained politically active and controversial, he would now
have to expect his domestic affairs to be used against him in his
constituency as well as nationally. Nevertheless Nutting himself insisted
that such affairs had nothing to do with his resignation. It was, he
said, "purely a matter of political principles."[31] The principles were
simply that his constituency association, notably as represented by
its leadership, had lost confidence in him as an M.P., in a way that
he could not repair, and that, therefore, his resignation, rather than
a hopeless fight, was required. It is reasonable to accept this interpretation as generally valid even if his publicized personal affairs
helped Nutting make up his mind. After all, these affairs would
probably never have been publicized if Nutting had not broken with
the government on Suez, and, publicized or not, they could not have
crucially affected Nutting's status with his association if there had been
no disagreement on Suez. There can be no doubt concerning the
nature of the response of Melton Conservatives to Nutting's deviation.
The strength of this response can be appreciated without being certain
that it would itself have forced Nutting's retirement. It is significant
enough that association leaders were so zealously pro-Suez, perhaps
because they were so zealously Conservative, as to rush their assurances
to the Prime Minister without waiting for the promised explanation
from their M.P. of over ten years' standing who had himself been
serving in the Foreign Office. For party activists in Melton no less
than for those in Bournemouth and Norfolk, their M.P. had let down
the good and righteous cause. Melton Conservatives may have felt
even more aggrieved by their representative's defection since he had
been so much a part of the government that they supported.

BANKS

Colonel Cyril Banks was the fourth of the anti-Suez Conservatives
to lose his seat as a direct result of his parliamentary deviation. His
case differed from the other three and, for that matter, from most
of the other anti-Suez Conservative cases because Banks's deviation

[31] *Yorkshire Post* (Leeds), 16 November 1956, p. 5.

was not associated with that of liberal intellectuals. Banks was a personal friend, economic adviser, and frequent visitor of Nasser, and he simply believed that Britain should come to terms with Egypt despite Nasser's seizure of the canal. His relations with Nasser constituted Banks's most unusual characteristic as an M.P. Otherwise Banks, a middle-aged businessman, was an orthodox Conservative who had represented the fairly safe Yorkshire borough of Pudsey since 1950. There is no record of serious constituency association difficulties before Suez.

Banks's Suez troubles, however, did start unusually early. He had abstained as far back as the parliamentary divisions of 13 September, when he, apparently alone among both Conservative and Labour M.P.s, deliberately refrained from voting with his party on motions concerning Eden's developing Suez policy. Pudsey Conservatives responded quickly but not yet drastically. The association's executive committee adopted two relevant resolutions in late September. One condemned Egyptian seizure of the canal and supported the government's efforts. The other resolution recognized that an M.P. was entitled to act according to his conscience and that Banks had generally rendered great service to the constituency.[32] These sentiments about Banks were later reported to have been "the subject of much argument" and to have been carried only by the chairman's casting vote.[33] In other words, Banks had already almost lost the support of his local executive, and the crisis was not yet at hand. He may not then have been given notice of an unwillingness to tolerate another Suez abstention on grounds of conscience, but he was surely informed by the first resolution that his local leaders seriously disagreed with his own position.

Banks was not deterred from acting according to his conscience. He abstained on 8 November, and he followed this immediately by an announcement of his resignation from the Conservative parliamentary party—that is, he gave up the whip. The Pudsey Conservative association took this as its opportunity to adopt a new prospective candidate even though Conservative associations elsewhere have not always so responded when their M.P.s merely resigned the whip without foreclosing a return to the fold. Plainly here it was the cause for resignation that was crucial. If Banks had not thus resigned, his association might well have, like Nicolson's Bournemouth association,

[32]*Pudsey & Stanningley News*, 27 September 1956, p. 7.
[33]*Ibid.*, 8 November 1956, p. 7.

proceeded to select a new prospective candidate anyway. Banks, after all, had twice offended by abstention, and on pro-Egyptian grounds that were peculiarly hard to defend before supporters of military action against Egypt. At any rate, while Banks remained in Parliament, now as an Independent, his local association went ahead to choose a successor. The executive committee had already, on 9 November, affirmed its confidence in the Prime Minister.[34] Later in the month, the committee, at a full meeting attended by 70 members, adopted "by an overwhelming majority" a resolution noting Banks's party resignation, backing the government, and establishing a selection committee to draw up a list of possible candidates. Just to make certain that there would be no misunderstanding about the status of the constituency's M.P., the official statement added: "The Association wishes to make it clear that Col. Banks now has no connection with the Pudsey Division Conservative Association."[35] Yet Pudsey Conservatives could not be charged with intolerance in the manner of Bournemouth Conservatives. Banks had obligingly and conveniently, if temporarily, surrendered his Conservative credentials in a way that no other anti-Suez Conservative M.P. had. Therefore, disposing of Banks as a prospective candidate was relatively painless.

Getting a new candidate, however, did accidentally turn out to take some time, but not through any shortage of pro-Suez prospects. The executive committee's first choice, in January 1957, was Major Rowland Winn, an enthusiastic supporter of intervention. But before he could be formally presented to the association, Winn succeeded to his father's title of Lord St. Oswald and so became ineligible. The next choice, also pro-Suez, was actually adopted, but he subsequently resigned for personal reasons. A third candidate was finally secured for the next general election. Significantly, however, the time that elapsed because of the loss of its two first choices did not cause the local association to reconsider Banks. Nor did Banks attempt any comeback as an Independent. In fact, he resumed the Conservative whip before the end of 1958 and completed his service as an M.P. in good standing with his parliamentary party but not with his constituency association. Suez had effectively ended his political career. But, unlike the endings of the three other parliamentary lives already described, particularly Nicolson's, what happened to Banks was not widely mourned in the national press. The difference stemmed only

[34]*Ibid.*, 15 November 1956, p. 6.
[35]*Ibid.*, 22 November 1956, p. 7.

partly from the fact that Banks had resigned the party whip before his association disposed of him. It was also relevant that the special pro-Nasser character of his deviation did not have the same appeal to the liberal conscience as did rebellion in the name of international law and order. What was significantly the same about Banks's experience, however, was the determined response of his constituency association. It seemed determined enough—although one cannot be sure—to have chosen a successor to Banks even if he had not resigned the whip.

BOYLE

Sir Edward Boyle is the first and the most significant of the ten anti-Suez Conservatives not to lose his seat as a consequence of parliamentary deviation. Yet his deviation was substantial, unequivocal, and unyielding. Boyle abstained on 8 November and resigned his prized junior ministerial post as Economic Secretary to the Treasury. His letter of resignation, dated and addressed to Eden on 5 November, was published just after his abstention. Boyle wrote, plainly enough, that he was "with that body of opinion which deeply deplores what has been done."[36] Although continuing as a Conservative M.P., he could not, he asserted, function as a minister defending government policy. Thus Boyle would seem to have jeopardized the promising parliamentary career that he had begun in 1950, when first elected at age 27 to represent the mixed working-class and middle-class Birmingham district of Handsworth. With this apparently safe Conservative constituency, Boyle could count on being an M.P. long enough to reach a fairly high ministerial level, since his parliamentary abilities were marked. Before Suez, it had not seemed at all likely that Boyle would have the kind of constituency association trouble that could even threaten his continued parliamentary candidacy. On the contrary, Boyle was especially well settled in his local party relations. Both his association chairman and party agent liked and admired him. These good relations had not been seriously disturbed by Boyle's antihanging views, which earlier in 1956 had led him to abstain instead of voting with most Conservative M.P.s for the death penalty. Many local Conservative activists did disagree with Boyle on this issue, but the disagreement led to no open movement against him.

In fact, Boyle's constituency relations were generally so good that it is testimony to the strength of pro-Suez Conservative sentiment that

[36]*Birmingham Post & Gazette*, 9 November 1956, p. 1.

he had any local trouble at all over his antigovernment stand. This may be more significant than Boyle's retention of the seat. He did have serious trouble in Handsworth even if it stopped short of depriving him of future candidacy. He could not avoid some of the same constituency association hostility that greeted other anti-Suez Conservative M.P.s. He may have been protected from the most drastic effects of this hostility only by the friendship of top local party officers. This did not mean that most of these officers were themselves anti-Suez. The chairman himself, undoubtedly one of the key figures, was strongly pro-Suez. Nevertheless Boyle had been able to meet with him, the vice-chairman and the party agent (who was most sympathetic) immediately after his resignation and abstention. Moreover, the chairman issued a statement on 9 November that seemed to commit him to defend Boyle's right to take a deviant position: "However great the regret Conservatives feel, it will be tempered by the knowledge that it demonstrates once again a fundamental principle of the party, that members are not bound by an iron discipline which prevents expression of freedom of thought and action even when times seem most beset with difficulty." [37]

The chairman's statement did not itself settle matters, but it favorably set the stage for the crucial meeting, on 16 November, of the association's 60-member executive committee—almost all of whom were known by Boyle to be pro-Suez. At this meeting Boyle did have his chance to explain his position. Until then he had avoided speaking in his constituency. The outcome of the executive committee session was in accord with the view expressed earlier by the chairman and thus with Boyle's own desire for tolerance of an admitted difference of opinion. The committee explicitly disagreed with Boyle, reaffirmed loyalty to the Prime Minister, and supported the government's Middle Eastern policy. But it recognized "the right of a Conservative member to act in accordance with his sincere convictions." [38] Later the association's general meeting took the same stand. No public recantation was requested. Indeed, Boyle made it clear that he did not regret his earlier anti-Suez decision,[39] and he even tried subsequently to explain and justify his stand to constituency activists. His main effort was at a mid-December meeting of the association's women's committee. The newspaper report of the audience's reaction is instructive:

[37]*Ibid.*
[38]*Ibid.*, 8 December 1956, p. 1.
[39]*Ibid.*, 17 November 1956, p. 7.

"They listened in silence to Sir Edward's address and there was no applause when he sat down."[40] Other signs of local Conservative hostility to Boyle's anti-Suez view were also visible in the winter of 1956-57, but Boyle survived. Of course, he did so as a Conservative M.P. pledged publicly (and, one suspects, privately as well) to support the government now that he had made his one deviant move. Surely a second break with party orthodoxy would not soon be tolerated. There was no occasion, however, for a second break by Boyle, on Suez or anything else. Consequently Boyle not only survived; he began to prosper again when Prime Minister Macmillan brought him into his new government in January 1957. Readoption in 1958 was nearly routine.

ASTOR

John Jacob Astor was another outspoken anti-Suez Conservative M.P. who did not lose his seat because of his break with the government. But his case differs from Boyle's and from those of the other survivors in that Astor, having announced his impending retirement before Suez, could not have been punished by rejection of subsequent candidacy. Unless his association had been willing to go so far as to demand his immediate resignation, which he could and probably would have refused anyway, there was no formal action possible against Astor except resolutions of disagreement. These resolutions were forthcoming, and their context and content display much the same pro-Suez devotion as that of those constituency associations which took or contemplated action against their deviant M.P.s. Moreover, the criticism of Astor's stand by his association was especially significant as a measure of pro-Suez Conservative feeling because of the special cordiality that had previously existed between the M.P. and his constituency.

The cordiality flowed both from the nature of the constituency and from Astor's own background. The constituency was the Sutton division of Plymouth, plainly urban and with a political background that was nonconformist and liberal rather than traditionally Conservative. The seat itself was marginal, having been won by Astor in 1951 after Labour had held it in 1945 and 1950. Even though his majority rose to 3,810 in 1955, after boundary revision, the constituency was by no means impossible for Labour to recapture in a

[40]*Ibid.*, 15 December 1956, p. 1.

bad Conservative year. Astor himself was most favorably situated as an M.P. for a constituency of this nature, as well as for this particular constituency. Not only was he an attractive young Conservative of moderate and liberal views, but he belonged to *the* Astor family that had long been associated politically and philanthropically with Plymouth. In fact, both his father and mother had earlier been M.P.s for the Sutton division. His mother, of course, was the famous Lady Nancy Astor, who served in the Conservative interest from 1919 to 1945 as the first woman in the British Parliament. Afterward she remained an important personage in local affairs. Her son, as M.P., also maintained more than the usual local connections although he had not been raised in Plymouth and did not maintain a full-time residence there. In addition to his substantial local advantages, Astor had the general assets, especially appropriate to a Conservative M.P., of an education at Eton and Oxford, a distinguished military record in World War II, and important connections with the national Establishment. His oldest brother, inheriting the family title, sat in the House of Lords. Another brother edited the *Observer*, one of England's two serious Sunday newspapers in the 1950's. And his uncle was chairman of the *Times* publishing company.

There is no question that Astor had enjoyed good pre-Suez relations with his association and with its leaders. His announced resignation had had nothing to do with any policy disagreement, but reflected only his personal dislike of a political career. Astor had opposed hanging, but he had been able to defend this position without great difficulty at a constituency meeting that he held for that purpose. Here he had been aided by the liberal nonconformist traditions of the West Country. Astor was not faced with organized association hostility, through resolution or otherwise, to his antihanging stand.

Suez, in this respect, was clearly different. To be sure, here the association was presented with a notably sharp deviation. Although Astor had suppressed his anti-Suez opinions as long as the fighting continued—only privately informing his local chairman what he thought and what he would eventually do—he did more than abstain from the division of 8 November. Before leaving the House that day, thus absenting himself from the vote, Astor delivered a speech in which he denounced the government's policy as "unnecessary and wrong."[41] The speech was conspicuously reported in the Plymouth

[41] *Western Evening Herald* (Plymouth), 9 November 1956, p. 9.

press. It was also noted that the M.P.'s criticism of the Eden government was part of an Astor family campaign. The eldest brother had already attacked the Suez intervention in the Lords, and David Astor's *Observer* was among the most violent newspaper opponents of Eden's campaign.

The Sutton association was as clearly committed to a pro-Eden position. The chairman, in behalf of the association, had sent Eden a telegram of support on 6 November.[42] And on 12 November, also before Astor had been able to meet with the full local leadership, the finance and general purposes committee of the association adopted a resolution dissociating itself from Astor's views and reaffirming support for Eden's Middle East policy. At the same time, the committee did grant Astor's request for a subsequent opportunity to put his views before the larger executive council.[43] There never seemed any likelihood that this opportunity would enable Astor to persuade the local leaders to change the pro-Eden position to which they were now publicly committed, but nevertheless the M.P. spent two hours on 23 November explaining why he had opposed the government. What he had principally to contend against was the charge that his parliamentary opposition to Eden was like shooting one's colonel in the back. The meeting ended with a resolution reaffirming confidence in the Prime Minister and the Conservative government.[44] Whether Astor gave any assurance of future support for the government was not revealed.

He had no subsequent cause to refuse his support on Suez or any other issue. Nor did Astor have any subsequent difficulties with his association. He was not frozen out of his constituency relations during the remaining years of his parliamentary tenure, and he was even given the honorary office of president of the association. In this manner, his substantial status in the community was still recognized. What, despite this status, Astor had not been able to accomplish was to convince his association leaders that he rather than Eden had been right over Suez. Plymouth's Conservative activists were as determined to support Suez intervention as were fellow activists elsewhere. Astor could not convince his chairman to do otherwise by private conversations before 8 November. Nor could Astor convince the rest of the leadership afterward.

[42]*Ibid.*, 13 November 1956, p. 7.
[43]*Ibid.*
[44]*Ibid.*, 24 November 1956, p. 5.

BOOTHBY

Sir Robert Boothby (later to become Lord Boothby) was in many ways an almost uniquely independent-minded M.P., but his experience over Suez can usefully be linked with Astor's since Boothby also possessed an unusual national and local prestige that proved insufficient to prevent constituency association disagreement with his anti-Suez stand. Again, however, as in Astor's case, Boothby did not lose his seat as the result of this disagreement. He left his constituency in 1958 when he became a life peer, and there was no hint that local pressure forced him to do so or even influenced his move from Commons to Lords. Pressure of that kind would have been remarkable indeed in Boothby's case. In fact, given Boothby's background and service, it was even remarkable, as evidence of the strength of association sentiment on Suez, that there was any open disagreement.

Boothby had represented the same Scottish constituency of East Aberdeenshire since 1924. It had been safely Conservative (or Unionist, to use the proper Scottish label) and especially safe for Boothby. He was always a robust and popular champion of the local herring industry. Moreover, he was a national figure as an articulate back-bencher, a journalist, and a broadcaster. In these roles, Boothby had long been known as an unorthodox Conservative. Not only were his views, as on hanging, moderate and even liberal, but he had earlier in his career been prominently identified with Winston Churchill's campaign against the appeasement policy of the Conservative government of the 1930's. This had led to brief service in Churchill's wartime coalition government, terminated by an unfortunate error of judgment causing Boothby's resignation, but mainly both before and after World War II he had built a career on the expression of views different from and more advanced than those of his party leaders. His East Aberdeenshire association must surely have been accustomed to the relative independence of their M.P., and in all probability fairly proud of it. To be sure, Boothby's unorthodoxy did not ordinarily keep him from voting with his parliamentary party.

Like the other anti-Suez Conservatives, Boothby adhered to the party during the period of military action. He abstained only on 8 November. Even this mild deviation he sought to explain away in Parliament less than a week later when he said that he would have voted with the government on 8 November if he had been able, at that time, to make a parliamentary speech about his own doubts.[45] Nevertheless, the abstention still had to be discussed with his East Aberdeenshire association executive. This he did on 23 November, making the long railway trip from London just to attend the executive's meeting, and then returning to London immediately afterward.[46] Boothby tried for an hour to convince the meeting that Eden's action had been wrong and that therefore he, Boothby, had been right to oppose Eden in the belated and moderate form of abstention after the fighting had ended. Earlier, Boothby could argue, he had supported the government's action despite his own doubts. As evidence of these early doubts Boothby produced a private letter, written six weeks before intervention, urging Eden not to use force at Suez.

According to Boothby's own account, his arguments convinced only a few of the nearly 30 executive committee members in attendance. The executive was at least three to one against him, and it produced a progovernment statement at the end of the meeting:

Sir Robert Boothby met the executive committee of the East Aberdeenshire Unionist Association this afternoon and gave a full explanation of the reasons which led him to abstain in a vote on an amendment to the Queen's speech.

The executive committee accepted his explanation and, while confirming his right to hold and to express his own views on matters of public policy, was of the opinion that his abstention on this occasion was an error of judgment.

Sir Robert accepted this opinion.[47]

The statement is quoted in its entirety as published in the local press. In this form, it not only amounted to a public rebuke, especially hard for an M.P. of 32 years' standing to accept, but it also declared that Boothby had himself admitted that his abstention, if not his actual views, involved an error of judgment. Boothby made no such admission on any other occasion, and privately he has denied that he made the admission to his local executive. In his view, all that he had accepted was an agreement to differ. He said that the statement was badly worded, so suggesting an admission that he had not made. Whatever the facts on this score, the executive's expression of disagreement and disapproval remains as a substantial indication that East Aberdeenshire Conservative (or Unionist) leaders backed Eden despite the unusual status of their deviating M.P.

[45]*Times* (London), 14 November 1956, p. 5.
[46]*Buchan Observer* (Peterhead), 27 November 1956, p. 4.
[47]*Ibid.*

YATES

Among anti-Suez Conservatives, William Yates most nearly resembles Banks in that he criticized Eden's policy even before the crisis and did so from an outspokenly pro-Arab viewpoint. On the other hand, Yates remained in the Conservative fold and definitely survived the displeasure of his constituency association (in the Wrekin, a very marginal and mixed urban-rural district of Shropshire). This survival, it has to be admitted, indicates the possibility of less acute displeasure among his local leaders than among Conservative leaders elsewhere. Certainly Yates, as much as any deviating M.P., had provided cause for adverse response by pro-Suez party activists. All that might have mitigated his offense for Conservatives was that Yates's stand was associated with a traditional pro-Arabism, once most popular in the party, and not with a liberal and intellectual internationalism. Yates, although still a young man, was simply adhering to the older Conservative view, often held by military men, that the Arabs were British allies in the Middle East. He had served in the Middle East from 1950 to 1954 as a member of the Foreign Office administration, and had returned from this duty as an outspoken friend of Arabs, their customs and their causes. As he later wrote of the Arabs, much in the spirit of T. E. Lawrence, "It was their simplicity, goodness, and integrity which interested me."[48] In addition, he was critical of Israel and Zionist influence.

Yates's pro-Arab sympathies were of little consequence in his constituency when he first became the Wrekin's Conservative candidate for the 1955 general election. It was noted that he wore Arab headgear on occasion, but much more important were his youthful attractiveness and vigor in contesting a seat that had been held by Labour since 1945. Yates won in 1955 by only 478 votes. The fact that the constituency remained marginal and uncertain must be taken into account in understanding the nature of local Conservative reaction to Yates's Suez deviation. So strong a reaction as to force Yates to retire, it might well have been calculated, could cost the Conservatives the hard-won seat in a subsequent by-election or even a general election. Perhaps this aspect of the local situation helps to explain the relatively mild response by local party leaders to their M.P.'s provocative behavior. This behavior began in early October with

[48] *Wellington Journal & Shrewsbury News*, 10 November 1956, p. 20.

statements in Cairo, of all places. After visiting Nasser, Yates declared that British policy had "made us a laughing stock from Suez to Singapore." Britain, he said, "should never have tried to bluff Egypt with the threat of force."[49] Then, in the middle of October, Yates tried to present his critique of Eden's policy to the Conservative party's annual conference. On that occasion, he was the only speaker to oppose the strong language adopted by the conference in support of an even tougher policy than it was then certain Eden was pursuing. It took an unusual kind of courage to have tried, at this stage, to persuade the Conservative conference of the usefulness of a conciliatory manner in dealing with Nasser. Yates was, in fact, booed down by the conference. His speech ended in an uproar.[50]

Yates's association leaders did not ignore these pre-Suez deviations even though they involved no formal break from parliamentary party discipline. Immediately after his Cairo statements, Yates was invited to address the association's executive council at a meeting regularly scheduled for 22 October.[51] In the meantime, Yates appeared in the constituency and insisted that he remained a good Conservative despite his dispute with the government's Suez policy. The dispute, he said, was "a minor one of policy. . . ."[52] Nevertheless, on 22 October he spent over two hours explaining his position to an exceptionally full meeting of the executive council. The result, publicly at least, was a council statement acknowledging Yates's disagreement with the government, while noting that he did "unreservedly condemn President Nasser's action in nationalizing the Suez Canal Company." The statement also noted that certain members of the council disagreed with Yates's views and thought it wrong for such views to have been expressed in Egypt. The M.P.'s work in general, however, was unanimously praised.[53] So far Yates publicly escaped with only an indication that some (probably many) of the local party leaders disagreed with his stand.

Nor did anything more serious develop as a result of Yates's action during the crisis. This was in spite of the fact that his action continued to be unorthodox. Although he voted with the government on both 30 October and 1 November, Yates abstained on 8 November. Even

[49]*Ibid.*, 6 October 1956, p. 18.

[50]*Ibid.*, 13 October 1956, p. 18. See also *76th Annual Report of the Conservative Conference* (1956).

[51]*Wellington Journal & Shrewsbury News*, 6 October 1956, p. 18.

[52]*Ibid.*, 13 October 1956, p. 18.

[53]*Ibid.*, 27 October 1956, p. 18.

more conspicuously if less seriously, he recorded his anti-Suez opinions by a bizarre intervention in the debate preceding the division of 1 November. Claiming to rise on a point of order, Yates then said: "I am a young Member of the House and I desire to have your advice, Mr. Speaker. I have been to France and I have come to the conclusion that Her Majesty's Government have been involved in an international conspiracy. . . ." Here he was interrupted, but he later resumed with a specific request for the speaker's advice: "The Government have taken this action and I want to know whether it would be considered right and patriotic for a person deliberately to try to bring down Her Majesty's Government in those circumstances?"[54] Of course, the speaker refused to consider this request as a point of order, and Yates had to decide on other grounds how he should vote. On this occasion at least, as indicated, he stayed with the government, waiting until 8 November to abstain. Whether abstention in the more heated atmosphere of 1 November would have produced more constituency association trouble is not certain. In the actual situation, his earlier agreement to disagree with his association did hold firm. The Wrekin Conservatives emerged, therefore, as the most tolerant of any local group faced with a really substantial parliamentary deviant. Still, it must be stressed that Yates's association, like the other local Conservative groups, gave no sign of anti-Suez sentiments of its own. It may even have been as pro-Suez as any other but restrained in responding to Yates because of the very small Conservative majority in the constituency.

SPEARMAN

In the case of Sir Alexander Spearman as in that of Peter Kirk (to be discussed next), the M.P. had not abstained even on 8 November but had voted consistently with the government on all critical divisions. Spearman became identified as an anti-Suez Conservative by a parliamentary speech that he gave just before the division of 8 November. It is noteworthy that this speech was enough to produce a definitely adverse response from his constituency association despite the fact that Spearman had been the constituency's representative since 1941. The district, Scarborough and Whitby, is a heavily Conservative area, partly rural and partly summer resort.

Spearman's parliamentary speech was plainly anti-Suez. He asserted that he had "always been against the use of force in this issue—alone,

[54]558 *H. C. Deb.* 1716-17 (1 November 1956).

or alone with France. In so far as the Prime Minister and the Foreign Secretary know of my existence at all, they must know that I feel that, because I have made it very clear all the way through."[55] Presumably what he meant by the last remark was that he made his anti-Suez views clear in private during the week of military action. Publicly, of course, he had then supported the government. Only after the event was Spearman announcing his disagreement, and even then he continued, in the division on the day of his speech, to vote with the government. His deviation was thus surely a mild one, having the effect of clearing his conscience without directly challenging the government. The speech itself was the only visible sign of Spearman's deviation, but it was significant in his constituency. The local daily paper reported the speech at length.[56] Spearman's views happened to be in accord with the paper's own much more outspoken anti-Suez sentiments,[57] but hardly with those of local Conservative leaders. They responded on 10 November with a telegram to the Prime Minister pledging their support for his Suez action. The association officers claimed that the telegram was not designed as a rebuff to Spearman,[58] but the disagreement was clear.

Subsequently this disagreement was aired in an executive committee meeting at which Spearman sought to explain his views. The result was a statement noting that Spearman "had consistently voted in support of the government." This appeared as a saving grace, and the statement concluded: "The committee decided to take no action, but asked their chairman to address a private letter containing their views to the member."[59] This was the last public airing of the disagreement. Spearman seems to have escaped with nothing worse than strong criticism, assumed to be in the private letter, and a certain amount of personal unpleasantness from some of the local Conservative activists.

KIRK

Peter Kirk, representing the marginal seat at Gravesend (near London), produced a sharply critical response among his constituency

[55]560 *H. C. Deb.* 369-70 (8 November 1956).

[56]*Scarborough Evening News,* 9 November 1956, p. 5.

[57]The paper was committed well before Spearman's speech. Immediately after the intervention began, an editorial declared: "Half the country, maybe more than half, will not be able to sleep easy in their beds until the Prime Minister is put under restraint—or dismissed." *Ibid.,* 1 November 1956, p. 4.

[58]*Ibid.,* 12 November 1956, p. 9.

[59]*Ibid.,* 19 November 1956, p. 5.

association activists although he neither abstained nor spoke in Parliament against the government's action. His anti-Suez opinions of the crisis period became known to his association through the circulation of an ambiguous letter from Kirk to a Labour constituent, through doubts expressed in personal conversations with constituents, and probably through private communication from the party's national leadership. National leaders, in and out of Parliament, were aware that Kirk was active among anti-Suez Conservative M.P.s in seeking to exert pressure privately against intervention, both before and during the crisis. Moreover, Kirk, although a very young and new M.P., already had a reputation for fairly independent behavior, since earlier in 1956 he had been the unofficial whip for the minority of Conservatives favoring abolition of the death penalty. The fact that Kirk did not add to this reputation by a publicly anti-Suez stand, through abstention or other action in Parliament itself, may well have been the result of local as well as national party pressure once his private doubts had been prematurely disclosed. He had, in effect, given his association an opportunity to warn him of the consequences of deviation.

Despite the absence of open parliamentary deviation, Kirk's views became matters of public controversy in his constituency. They were certain to be so after a local Labour party meeting was told, by a visiting Labour M.P., that Kirk was "one of the Conservative members of Parliament perturbed and shocked at the Middle East situation."[60] Because of the publication of his views, Kirk wanted a chance to explain to his association. He was dissuaded from doing so immediately because of the belief of the local chairman (who remained on better terms with Kirk during the crisis than did other members of the executive) that the M.P. might thus cause a rupture of his relations with the association. Therefore, Kirk waited until 17 November, when he seized the occasion of a bazaar conducted by one of his association branches to make what was less a justification of his anti-Suez position than an equivocal statement indicating almost as much sympathy as criticism. He did say, it is true, that he had been "dismayed" when the government had ordered British forces to intervene. He added: "And it seemed that initially we were out of step with the United Nations. But within a few days we came back more and more in step."[61] Kirk tended to balance his early worry with subsequent approval. The approval could be construed either as fairly general or as limited

[60]*Gravesend & Dartford Reporter*, 10 November 1956, p. 1.
[61]*Ibid.*, 24 November 1956, p. 6.

to the government's decision to halt its intervention. Kirk really believed only the latter, and he later made it clear to his association that he had regarded the original decision on Suez as a mistake.[62]

Although Kirk did not lose his association's support for subsequent candidacy and apparently did not come close to losing it, he did suffer more than merely private pressure to suppress his views. One well-known local Conservative wrote an anti-Kirk letter that became the basis for the main story in the local weekly paper. The letter writer argued that there "must be many local Conservatives who feel as I do, that Mr. Kirk has let the side down."[63] He wondered what the local Conservative executive was going to do about it. Raising such a question at all seems to be a reflection of especially strong feeling since Kirk had not offended by any formal parliamentary behavior. There was really no basis for drastic action against an M.P. who remained technically loyal to the government. Furthermore, the circumstances in the Gravesend constituency were unpropitious with respect to action against Kirk in any case. Dropping him as a candidate, or even trying to drop him, would increase the risk of losing this marginal seat which Kirk had taken from Labour in 1955, thanks in part to a split in the opposition vote between the official Labour candidate and the former Labour M.P. standing as an Independent.

2. PRO-SUEZ CONSERVATIVE EXTREMISTS

Constituency association response to the parliamentary deviations by pro-Suez Conservative extremists contrasts sharply with the treatment, just described, of the ten anti-Suez M.P.s. It will be observed that pro-Suez extremism, even when it involved a much more substantial break from Conservative parliamentary leadership than that of most of the anti-Suez M.P.s, was regularly tolerated by local party activists. To be sure, the tolerance was required only after the immediate crisis period, since the pro-Suez extremists had no occasion to revolt until December 1956 and May 1957. Earlier, as already noted, they had been enthusiastic supporters of Eden's intervention, welcoming it as a happy if belated conversion of the government to their view that the Suez base should never have been surrendered in the 1954 agreement.[64] It was when the government began to liquidate the 1956 intervention that the pro-Suez extremists became parlia-

[62]*Ibid.*, 15 December 1956, p. 11.
[63]*Ibid.*, 24 November 1956, p. 1.
[64]See Chapter Four.

mentary rebels. They did so simply by continuing to adhere to the interventionist cause. Thus the fact that they were tolerated by their constituency associations reflects a local party viewpoint entirely consistent, in one sense, with the absence of such toleration for the anti-Suez Conservative M.P.s. The two apparently contrasting sets of cases may have been produced by the same cause: strongly pro-Suez sentiments in Conservative constituency associations. This is really the main point in discussing local response to pro-Suez extremist M.P.s. Conservative associations, in a different group of constituencies from those of anti-Suez M.P.s, will be found to have displayed the same strong and durable support for the interventionist cause.

One feature of pro-Suez extremism deserves emphasis at the outset. Even when it involved parliamentary party deviations in late 1956 and in 1957, its champions could claim to be further from the Labour party's position than was the Conservative government itself. The extremists, virtually by definition, were not open to the charge that they were deserting in the partisan enemy's direction any more than in Nasser's. They were really more conventionally Conservative, in their imperialism, than their parliamentary leaders now seemed to be. Obviously this provided a basis for appealing to constituency activists. They also had some reason to expect a fairly high degree of toleration from their leaders since the growingly important leader, Harold Macmillan, was presumed to have been strongly pro-Suez himself. Furthermore, Macmillan had important personal ties with the Suez group through his son-in-law, Julian Amery, both before and after Amery was taken into Macmillan's new government in January. It is even possible that Macmillan found a limited number of rebels useful in his dealings with other nations. Their existence might have provided a diplomatic explanation for British delay in yielding to American pressure.

Nevertheless, the break of pro-Suez M.P.s from parliamentary discipline was of public significance. The break, described in the last chapter, included the 15 abstentions on 6 December 1956, on the vote on the government's withdrawal of troops from the canal zone, and the 14 abstentions (including nine repeaters from the first 15) on the vote of 16 May 1957 with respect to the government's decision to advise British shipowners to use the canal on Nasser's terms. Of the 14, in the latter instance, eight went further than abstaining and resigned the party whip in order to sit as Independent Conservatives. Altogether 20 individual M.P.s were involved: the nine repeaters plus six in December only and five in May only.[65] The vital point about this whole pro-Suez group is that not one lost his seat because of abstention, single or repeated. And in only one doubtful case can it be suspected that even going so far as to resign the whip contributed to an M.P.'s loss of his seat. This is especially noteworthy since of the eight who formed the Independent Conservative "cave," to oppose Britain's "weak foreign policy," five remained without the whip until June 1958. Despite their support for the government on other issues, these lingering Independent Conservatives posed a problem for their party, locally and nationally, as a general election was thought to be near and there was a desire to have candidates in technically good standing. No doubt there was pressure on the Independents from the constituencies, and in at least one case (Maitland's) this pressure was reported as a factor in an M.P.'s resumption of the whip.[66] Continued irregularity, even in a cause cherished by the rank and file, exposed an M.P. to attacks from local opponents, who occasionally wanted the seat for another candidate. However, to be pressured to rejoin one's parliamentary party is less significant than the fact that the local parties refrained from any more serious action during the whole year that Independent status had been maintained.

The one doubtful case is that of Lawrence Turner, M.P. for Oxford city, who counted himself an Independent Conservative until June 1958 after having abstained in both the December and May divisions. In May 1958, just before resuming the whip, Turner announced his withdrawal from consideration as a candidate for the next general election, and one might guess that this withdrawal was not entirely voluntary from the fact that his Oxford constituency association had almost simultaneously informed Turner that it was to start the process of considering candidates.[67] However, Turner's announced reason for withdrawal, namely medical advice, had a basis in fact. Furthermore,

[65]The 15 abstainers in December were Biggs-Davison, Fell, Hinchingbrooke, Patrick Maitland, Maude, Turner, Paul Williams, Hyde, McLean, Amery, T. H. Clarke, Horobin, Nabarro, Teeling, and Waterhouse. The first nine of these also abstained in May, and they were joined by Raikes, John Eden, G. Howard, Lambton, and N. Pannell. The first seven plus Raikes constituted the group resigning the whip in May. *Times* (London), 7 December 1956, p. 10; 14 May 1957, p. 10; 17 May 1957, p. 12.

[66]*Daily Telegraph* (London), 25 June 1958, pp. 1, 15. The five hold-outs were Biggs-Davison, Turner, Hinchingbrooke, Fell, and Williams. One of the Independent Conservatives, Maitland, resumed the whip late in 1957, and two others, Maude and Raikes, had left Parliament.

[67]*Times* (London), 22 May 1958, p. 4.

it was evidently Turner's own uncertainty about standing again, plus his continued delay in resuming the whip, which finally caused his association, over a year after the M.P.'s deviation, to consider other candidates. There were other reasons too for the association to reconsider Turner's situation. Over the years, since becoming Oxford's M.P. in 1950, he had deviated from his parliamentary leadership on certain economic issues, in a right-wing direction, as well as on foreign policy. These positions, plus a certain blunt businessman's outlook, tended to alienate the university element among Conservative voters. This could have been consequential even though Oxford was a pretty safe Tory seat. However, it is probable that Turner's pro-Suez extremism, while unpopular with a Conservative minority (mainly outside of active party circles), would not in itself have cost him his seat. In fact, his association executive voted Turner its full support after he addressed its meeting, in June 1957, to explain why he had abstained and joined the cave.[68]

One other pro-Suez rebel was subsequently deprived of his seat, but much more clearly than in Turner's case it was for reasons unconnected with his Suez stand. The M.P. was Montgomery Hyde, a prolific author with wide intellectual interests who represented a very safe Belfast constituency, as a Conservative-affiliated Ulster Unionist, since 1950. Without joining the cave, Hyde had abstained both in December 1956 and May 1957. But this evidence of pro-Suez extremism did Hyde no more harm than it did other M.P.s of the same group. The move against Hyde's readoption did not take place until 1959, and the list of grievances against him consisted entirely of deviations in very different directions. Specifically, Hyde was disliked in his association because he was against hanging, for a liberal approach to homosexual offenses, and for the return of a legally disputed set of pictures from a London to a Dublin gallery.[69] Besides, he was said to have too many outside interests to be a good Northern Ireland M.P. After a prolonged fight, almost rivaling Bournemouth's in interest, Hyde's association went ahead to choose another candidate.[70]

Putting aside Turner and Hyde, 18 other pro-Suez cases remain. Three of these M.P.s voluntarily retired from Parliament in the years following Suez, two of them, Waterhouse and Raikes, appropriately to business in Britain's African dependencies, and Angus Maude to

[68]*Oxford Mail*, 12 June 1957, p. 1.
[69]*Belfast Telegraph*, 9 January 1959, p. 2; 13 January 1959, p. 2.
[70]*Times* (London), 4 April 1959, p. 4.

the editorship of an Australian paper. All three may have been disgusted with Conservative politics, but in none of the three cases was there any evidence that their associations were disgusted with them. In fact, Maude, who stayed on in Parliament the longest, until mid-1958, and as a member of the cave, was treated as a hero by the local Conservatives in his safe London suburban constituency of Ealing South. On the occasion of his abstention in December 1956, his association passed a unanimous vote of confidence in Maude after he addressed the annual meeting.[71] Then in June 1957, after the M.P. had become an Independent Conservative, a special meeting (attended by 595) voted, with only 26 dissenters, that "the members of the Ealing South Conservative Association, while regretting that circumstances arose in which Mr. Maude found it necessary to resign the party Whip, affirm their continued confidence in him and express the hope that the breach between him and the Conservative Parliamentary Party will soon be happily healed."[72] Subsequently Maude's offer to resign the presidency of the local Young Conservatives was declined, and at the end of 1957 he was re-elected to that office.[73]

Similar if not always such enthusiastic support was publicly accorded at least six other pro-Suez extremists. These included, besides Maude, five more of the eight Independent Conservatives, namely Fell, Paul Williams, Patrick Maitland, Lord Hinchingbrooke, and Biggs-Davison.[74] The last M.P. of these five did, it is true, have to contend eventually with some restiveness in his new and marginal constituency of Chigwell in Essex. Significantly, however, this restiveness appears to have come from the fringes of his association, as well (of course) as from critics outside the association. The local party leadership, as represented by the top officers, the party agent, and the executive, remained loyal to Biggs-Davison. He might have strained this loyalty

---

[71]*Middlesex County Times & West Middlesex Gazette*, 8 December 1956, p. 2.

[72]*Ibid.*, 1 June 1957, p. 1.

[73]*Ibid.*, 8 June 1957, p. 12; 7 December 1957, p. 1. Maude, after leaving Parliament for Australia in 1958, sought to return in 1962 as the Conservative candidate for the Dorset seat vacated by the elevation, as Earl of Sandwich, of Hinchingbrooke, who had been one of Maude's fellow pro-Suez rebels. Maude failed to win the by-election, in part because of Hinchingbrooke's support of an independent anti–Common Market Conservative. The Labour candidate won the seat.

[74]On each of the five M.P.s, see, in order, *Eastern Daily Press* (Norfolk), 14 May 1957, p. 1; *Sunderland Echo*, 22 May 1957, p. 8; *Glasgow Herald*, 14 May 1957, p. 8; *Dorset Daily Echo*, 18 May 1957, pp. 1, 7; *Chigwell Times & West Essex Star*, 14, December 1956, p. 8; 17 May 1957, p. 1; 24 May 1957, pp. 1, 16; 6 September 1957, p. 1.

too much if he remained outside the Conservative parliamentary party beyond the middle of 1958, when the next general election became a possibility. But he survived over a year of independence and became Chigwell's Conservative candidate and M.P. again in 1959.

Only in the case of Raikes, among the M.P.s in the eight-member cave, is there an absence of a public record of local support. He seems, however, to have retained the confidence of his association. There was no open local difficulty. Indeed, the absence of an association resolution of support might simply have meant that no serious question about the M.P.'s local status was raised. This seems to have been true in the cases of the pro-Suez M.P.s who merely abstained but did not join the eight-man cave. Their deviation was not usually taken seriously enough for the question of association confidence to arise. There is a record of only one simple abstainer, John Eden, providing a cause for a public vote, and that turned out to be highly favorable to the M.P.[75]

The most convincing way to show the tolerance of a constituency association for the pro-Suez extremist is to discuss the case of Lord Hinchingbrooke. This highly individualistic, almost eccentric, son of the Earl of Sandwich functioned as leader of the Independent Conservative cave, and he abstained both in December 1956 and May 1957. The reaction of his association, after 500 local members heard Hinchingbrooke's explanation in May, was a vote of confidence, with only six dissenting votes, the singing of "For He's a Jolly Good Fellow," and the hope that "the foreign policy of Her Majesty's Government will enable him again to accept the Whip in the near future."[76] This overwhelmingly favorable outcome looks all the more significant by comparison with the other occasion, in 1952, when Hinchingbrooke, in the same fairly safe, largely rural Dorset constituency, had faced the consequences of a parliamentary deviation. Then, after Hinchingbrooke had spoken against and abstained from supporting the Conservative government's approval of German rearmament, his local executive adopted a resolution of no-confidence in its M.P. Only with much effort did Hinchingbrooke get a majority of the association, at a general meeting, to reverse this executive decision.[77] Consequently the local executive resigned, so Hinchingbrooke, it may be granted,

[75]*Times* (London), 25 May 1957, p. 4.
[76]*Dorset Daily Echo, loc. cit.*
[77]*Times* (London), 6 October 1952, p. 2; 10 October 1952, p. 3; 31 October 1952, p. 6.

triumphed in this case too. Yet there was a difference between 1952 and 1957 in the degree of difficulty for the M.P., and this difference can fairly be attributed not only to improved personal relations with a new executive, but also to the fact that Hinchingbrooke's later deviation was an essentially Conservative one, close to the imperialist nerve center of party activists, instead of one which, like his opposition to German rearmament, happened to place him in the same camp with left-wing socialists.

3. The Pro-Suez Labour Case

The Conservative party's two-way deviations over Suez had no close parallel in the parliamentary Labour party since there was no group break, in any direction, from Labour's thoroughgoing opposition to the Eden government's military intervention. Both during and after the Suez crisis, the stand taken by the party's moderate leadership was militant enough for the left-wing socialists who had, formerly as Bevanites, so often taken rebelliously independent positions on foreign and defense policies. And in more right-wing Labour circles, as well as among Jewish M.P.s, where objections to Gaitskell's zealously anti-Suez views were likelier, the established pattern of loyalty to party leadership has already been observed as generally firm through the crucial parliamentary divisions.[78] There is only the definitely separate and individual deviation of Stanley Evans to provide a Labour constituency experience comparable with what happened to several Conservative M.P.s. The comparison, of course, is primarily to the anti-Suez Conservatives because Evans, as a pro-Suez Labour M.P., stood in relation to his party as anti-Suez Conservatives did to theirs. Like them, Evans deviated toward the position of the rival party, and not away from it.

Evans had since 1945 represented the industrial constituency of Wednesbury in the Black Country of the Midlands. The seat was safely Labour's as a consequence of the trade-union strength usual in industrial areas. The local party itself contained many trade unionists, and official representatives of affiliated unions made up about half of the membership of the party's executive committee. One of the heavily represented groups was the Amalgamated Engineering Union, which had a strong but not always dominant left-wing element in its local and national leadership. This is of some importance in under-

[78]In Chapter Five. A special test of this firmness is discussed in Chapter Eight.

standing Evans' local situation because he had, even apart from Suez, expressed views generally regarded as right-wing, particularly on foreign and colonial issues. The fact was that Evans, by background as well as opinions, was an unusual Labour M.P. for almost any Labour constituency. He was neither a middle-class intellectual nor a trade unionist, but a self-made Birmingham businessman. Moreover, Evans seemed to enjoy stating his independent-minded opinions. He had in this way even achieved a brief fame in 1950 when, soon after being appointed by the Attlee government as parliamentary Secretary to the Ministry of Food, Evans referred to the government's farm subsidies as "featherbedding."[79] This refreshingly frank but politically foolish remark cost him his junior ministerial status. Because he was now unlikely to secure another leadership post, the incident may have encouraged still greater independence of expression. At any rate, in the years before the Suez crisis, Evans did frequently voice what sounded like imperialist opinions on the Middle East, where he regarded American interests as antithetical to Britain's. These opinions he delivered both to the House of Commons and directly to his constituents, especially to business groups rather than to local Labour members.

At most, however, this divergent behavior only strained, without threatening to break, the M.P.'s relations with his divisional Labour party. Before Suez, Evans was tolerated by Wednesbury's party leaders despite a feeling of neglect and even of antagonism in individual instances. There was really no issue on which differences with most trade unionists were so sharply drawn as to produce a break. Apparently there were no differences at all on domestic economic matters, chiefly of interest to his urban industrial constituents and to their union leaders. And on foreign and colonial issues, Evans had remained loyal to the party in his parliamentary voting record. Furthermore, his views on such issues, unorthodox though they were among Labour intellectuals, may well have been shared by a portion of Evans' working-class supporters. As he himself declared in justification of his prohanging stand, also at odds with the behavior of almost all Labour M.P.s in the free vote in February 1956, "I know the views of the intelligentsia on this subject, but they are not the views of my Black Country constituents."[80]

[79] *Times* (London), 17 April 1950, p. 4.
[80] *Midland Advertiser & Wednesday Borough News*, 25 February 1956, p. 1.

Even on Suez, Evans may, of course, have been in line with many of his constituents. But this time he was seriously at odds with the Labour party in a way, as it turned out, that counted in Wednesbury. His deviation, to be sure, was especially sharp and open. On 30 October, when Labour was attacking Eden's ultimatum, Evans spoke against the party leadership's decision to divide the House. He then abstained from voting in the division.[81] Again on 1 November Evans made a parliamentary speech distinguishing his position from Labour's, and abstained from voting on Labour's censure motion despite a three-line whip.[82] Although Evans returned to the fold in the division of 8 November, his actions on 30 October and particularly on 1 November had made him appear a most deliberate and conspicuous rebel. The nature of the rebellion was underlined for Evans' constituents by reports in their local paper (itself pro-Evans) that the M.P.'s speech of 1 November had been praised by a Conservative leader and frequently cheered by Conservative M.P.s.[83] Of course, Labour activists might have been expected, without this kind of evidence, to understand the significance of their M.P.'s deviation. The question was the extent to which they would tolerate it, and this in turn depended in part on how strongly anti-Suez the Labour leaders in Wednesbury happened to be. They were under no necessity of responding sharply. Nor were they under any national party pressure to do so. On the contrary, the parliamentary Labour party and the national executive committee took no disciplinary action against Evans. He himself later claimed that the PLP had "accepted" that he could not vote for the censure motion and that he was entitled to abstain under the party's standing orders.[84] This seems likely since the national Labour leaders could well afford to tolerate just one rebel and so reap favorable national publicity for relative broadmindedness.

Willingness thus to forgive, perhaps without forgetting, did not characterize the response of the Wednesbury divisional Labour party. On 17 November, after Evans explained his views to a special meeting of the general management committee (the 48-member body of delegates representing the local membership), the committee found a "deep conflict of basic principles" and voted unanimously to ask

[81]558 *H. C. Deb.* 1287 (30 October 1956).
[82]558 *H. C. Deb.* 1681-86 (1 November 1956).
[83]*Midland Advertiser & Wednesday Borough News*, 3 November 1956, p. 5.
[84]*Ibid.*, 24 November 1956, p. 5.

for Evans' resignation as an M.P.[85] The demand for resignation, it should be noted, represented a more severe reaction than that displayed publicly by any of the Conservative associations in relation to their deviating M.P.s. The severity may be explained not only by strong local anti-Suez sentiments, but also by the fact that these sentiments had been conveyed to Evans as early as September, when the general management committee discussed the impending crisis with their already dissenting M.P. In fact, the president of the divisional Labour party subsequently claimed that Evans had agreed, in September, to keep the anti-Suez views of the general management committee in mind.[86] Therefore, the demand for Evans' resignation, severe as it was, may be less surprising than the unanimity with which it passed the fairly large body of delegates. That there was not "a single dissentient" was stressed by the party's statement at the conclusion of the meeting of the general management committee. And it was also noted that the meeting itself had been called as a result of resolutions from local affiliated organizations strongly condemning Evans' action.[87] Whatever local support there was for Evans, and so against the general management committee's action, came from outside the ranks of Labour activists although, in some cases, these non-activists might have been Labour voters.

The local party's request for Evans's resignation, unlike a decision simply to look for another candidate for the next general election, was technically unenforcible. Constitutionally, meaning customarily, most M.P.s could and did resist any such demand. There was also every sign that Labour's national leadership preferred Evans to resist since his ouster involved unwelcome publicity (but no danger from a by-election to the party's hold on the safe Wednesbury seat). Yet before any effective national intervention could have taken place, Evans complied with his local party's request by announcing his resignation from the House of Commons although he remained a member of the Labour party. In leaving his seat immediately, Evans no doubt correctly anticipated his subsequent removal as a general election candidate. As he said in explaining why he chose not to stay on through his term: "A general without an army, and what is worse living on borrowed time, seldom wields much influence and lacks all

[85]*Ibid.*
[86]*Ibid.*
[87]*Ibid.*

dignity."[88] Thus Evans made it possible for the local Labour party to select a new candidate almost at once and to secure his return at an early by-election. Incidentally, this candidate, John Stonehouse, left no doubt of his own anti-Suez sentiments and, indeed, of his traditional socialist views generally. He subsequently became a well-established left-wing critic of Britain's foreign and colonial policies.

Looking back at the Evans case, it does not seem necessary to qualify in any vital way the pressingly apparent comment that a most zealous anti-Suez sentiment had to be present among Wednesbury Labour activists in order to dispose of Evans so completely and summarily. The fact that some of these activists were dissatisfied with Evans anyway does not seem crucial. They had not previously tried to purge Evans and there is no sign that they could have secured a majority to do so if it had not been for Suez. The point was confirmed, in effect, by an AEU delegate to the management committee, who, while saying that his own vote against Evans was based on more than Suez, granted that his earlier objections to Evans had not been held by a committee majority.[89]

4. GENERALIZATIONS

Generalizing about constituency party activists from the several case studies is easier with respect to the first of the two questions with which this chapter began. Certainly this is so for Conservatives. Pro-Suez commitments by Conservative associations were uniformly strong in a large enough number of constituencies to support a conclusion on this point about local Conservative leaders generally. Where the variations occurred was on the second line of inquiry about the way in which associations treated deviating M.P.s. It is useful, therefore, to separate the two sets of generalizations, and take the less complicated subject first.

NATURE OF CONSTITUENCY COMMITMENTS

That Conservative associations should have held pro-Suez views and Labour associations anti-Suez views was hardly surprising in light of the clear stands of their respective national parliamentary leaders, and, even more to the point, of their own national party conferences in the early fall. Particularly at the Conservative conference of early

---

[88]*Ibid.*

[89]*Birmingham Post & Gazette,* 24 November 1956, p. 9.

October, as already noted, the representative party activists had adopted a stronger resolution on Suez than that originally proposed by the leadership. Nevertheless the extent, fervor, and durability of constituency response during and after the crisis were striking phenomena. Mainly, of course, these phenomena were observed in the ten Conservative associations whose M.P.s were anti-Suez deviants. These ten associations, however, were in constituencies of varying sorts. Some were safe and some were marginal. Some were urban, some rural, and some mixed. They ranged geographically over much of Britain, from northeastern Scotland through Yorkshire, East Anglia, the Midlands, and suburban London to Plymouth in the southwest. There were large and active association memberships like Bournemouth's, and smaller organizations like Norfolk's. What the ten had in common was immediate and clear-cut support for the Suez position of their national leaders as opposed to that of their respective M.P.s. On this score, it did not much matter who the M.P. was—minister or back-bencher, nationally prestigious or little known, knowledgeable or nonknowledgeable in foreign affairs, experienced or inexperienced as an M.P., new or old in the constituency, previously orthodox or previously independent, personally liked or disliked. None of these factors, though varying from case to case, prevented any of the ten associations from taking pro-Suez stands, although such factors, as will be noted, may have affected the way in which M.P.s were subsequently treated.

Nothing comparable in quantity to the ten principal Conservative illustrations, bolstered by the 20 other Conservative instances of support for pro-Suez extremists, is available to show sentiment among local Labour groups. Only the Evans case in Wednesbury can be cited. Perhaps, however, it partially compensates by the clarity and convincingness of its anti-Suez evidence for the absence of other instances. The local party response was strikingly prompt and vigorous, and the nature of the constituency and the type of its Labour activists were such as to establish some claim to representativeness. At least the Wednesbury divisional Labour party could not be dismissed as middle-class intellectuals addicted to unusual excitement about Suez and other foreign policy issues. Instead, by being heavily trade unionist, the Wednesbury group was drawn from the very elements of Labour support widely supposed to be most weakly anti-Suez, if anti-Suez at all. It must be granted that these Wednesbury trade unionists were leaders and even left-wing union leaders, in some cases, rather than merely rank-and-file workers without ideological basis for anti-Suez views. Yet while the leaders may be assumed to have been more zealous than the bulk of their members, they did not necessarily lack the ability to obtain rank-and-file support for their position.

In any event, what is being discussed here, with reference to both Conservative and Labour parties at the local level, are the commitments made by the relatively small groups of leaders and activists at the core of constituency organizations. Beyond such groups of about 40 to 70 members of executive councils or general management committees, it is by no means clear that commitments on Suez were so strong or so nearly unanimous. There is some evidence to suggest a lessening of zeal from the inner core of leading activists through passively participating members to ordinary party voters. At Bournemouth, about which there happens to be the most information, the executive committee seems to have been unanimously against Nicolson, the association meeting about three to one against him, and the total association membership when polled by mail split about 50-50 (over two years later and in different circumstances, it is true). From this, it might reasonably be hypothesized that there was even less anti-Nicolson or pro-Suez sentiment among ordinary Conservative voters who held no party membership. But Conservatives of this kind do not, of course, make local party policy. Those who did make the policy (and choose the candidates) were staunchly pro-Suez. And, it must be emphasized, there were always at least a dozen leading activists involved in making the local Suez policy. The commitment was not solely the work of a limited oligarchy or of a single officer.

Since local party activists were making the commitments, it is plainly difficult to disentangle their zeal over Suez from their zeal for the national party. Surely zealous Conservative partisans, for example, meant to support their leadership generally, along with the Suez policy. Much of the strength of their response has to be understood in terms of backing any partisan cause, once declared by the national leadership and opposed by the other party. But there was genuine feeling on Suez as well. This was made plain by rougher handling of some M.P.s than desired by the national party, by local pressures on three M.P.s even before the crisis, by delegate views at a national party conference, and by the Conservative associations that supported or tolerated pro-Suez extremists who revolted against the national party after the crisis.

TREATMENT OF M.P.S

Although the treatment of deviating M.P.s did vary as between constituencies, with only five M.P.s actually losing their seats, nevertheless all of the relevant local parties took adverse action of some kind against their parliamentary representatives. At its mildest, this action involved official association statements at odds with the M.P.'s position, and requests for difficult and embarrassing explanations. More serious was the rejection of future candidacy, either by freezing out of the constituency or by formal moves to choose a successor. And most extreme was the demand for immediate resignation. All these responses, occasionally with a few special features, reflected the willingness of constituency associations, at the very least, openly to pressure their M.P.s. The pressure was based on the association's unmistakable power to refuse to readopt an M.P. as its parliamentary candidate. That power is implicit as a threat against subsequent deviation even if it is not used in a first instance. Thus open disagreements, much as semiprivate reprimands, amount to pressure for subsequent conformity. The M.P., who cannot fight back effectively from outside the party organization, is dependent on its continued good will. Any policy dispute, even one eventually patched up, may appear menacing to an M.P., who understandably fears that he cannot afford another such dispute.[90] Or, for that matter, an M.P. may well think that he cannot afford even one such dispute, and consequently curb an intended deviation. In this perspective, even the mildest of the association responses to a Suez deviant was politically significant.

In other circumstances, however, such responses might not have the same significance as they had in the Suez controversy. Constituency association pressure in October and November 1956 was in line with, even if occasionally more strenuous than, that of the national party leadership. It was not strictly local opinion against which the deviating M.P.s had offended. The anti-Suez Conservative M.P.s and the pro-Suez Labour M.P. were at odds with national party positions that happened to be zealously held by local activists. Assuredly the local organizations were not taking action, and probably could not take effective action, against M.P.s who merely disagreed with local leaders while following their national leaders. This is not to deny what is a principal point of the analysis: that association pressure on Suez was

[90]The impact of a local party's vote of no-confidence in its M.P. is vividly portrayed in the novel *No Love for Johnnie* (London: Hutchinson, 1959), written by the late Wilfred Fienburgh, himself a Labour M.P.

partly if not largely self-generated and by no means dependent on orders from the national party. The pressure was *both* self-generated and in line with the national party.

Another relevant circumstance in understanding constituency responses during the Suez crisis is that the M.P.s being reacted against were deviating in the direction of the position taken by the opposing party. They were not deviating toward an extreme position further removed from the opposition than from their own party. The anti-Suez Conservative M.P.s and the pro-Suez Labour M.P. aroused the ideological militancy of local party activists in a way that right-wing Conservative rebels or left-wing Labour rebels would not have done. Thus, as pointed out, the pro-Suez Conservative deviations of December 1956 and May 1957 did not have the same meaning for constituency associations even though these deviations were against the national party leadership. It was the coincidence of opposing both the national position and the ideology of party militants that characterized the deviating M.P.s of the crisis week. Or, put differently, during the crisis the national leaders of each party had the same positions as their respective militants. In this way, the Suez circumstances were not necessarily unique, but they were especially likely to produce sharp local responses to the deviating M.P.s.

It may be added that constituency responses in these circumstances are of special consequence to the leadership of the parliamentary parties. It is true that national leaders, in or out of Parliament, did not appear directly responsible for local actions against M.P.s deviating over Suez, and that some of these leaders may even have deplored the apparent excesses of Bournemouth and Wednesbury. Yet the constituency association pressures on deviating M.P.s, during the crisis, were in the direction of conformity to the parliamentary party position. And the pressures were exerted on those M.P.s whose type of deviation was potentially most dangerous because it was in the direction of agreeing with the opposition. Deviations of the pro-Suez extremist sort had a less troublesome potential since they could not very well be joined to an opposition effort to bring a government down or even seriously to embarrass it.

There remains the matter of trying to account for the variation that did exist in local treatment of the deviating M.P.s. Why did some but not others lose their seats? One possible explanation lies in the safeness of the seat. It does seem reasonable to hypothesize that the safer the seat the more vulnerable and the more readily dispensable the M.P. The more nearly the association can regard its candidate selection as the bestowal of a parliamentary seat, the more confident can it afford to be that it owes the M.P. little while he owes it much. In a safe seat, the association knows it can win the constituency with someone else about as easily as with the current M.P. since no particular candidate is calculated to be worth more than about 500 votes above what the party can obtain for anybody. And in a very safe seat even the intervention of a third candidate, either a Liberal or the rejected M.P. standing as an Independent, would not decisively affect the result. Nor in such a case would the association be greatly worried about a by-election brought about by its M.P.'s resignation under pressure.

Bournemouth supplies the classic example of this generalization. Here the Conservative majority was so large that the association could, and did, ignore local repercussions. Even two or three intervening candidacies by Liberals or Independents could not upset an election result. Marginal or floating voters were of no local importance even if they sympathized with the M.P. Clearly Nicolson was dispensable. So, in their safe constituencies, were Nutting, Banks, Medlicott, and Evans, the four other M.P.s whose Suez deviations cost them their seats. Nevertheless, along with this impressive fact that the five M.P.s actually forced out all came from safe seats, it has to be appreciated that some of the surviving deviants, even among the anti-Suez Conservatives, also came from safe seats. In other words, a large party majority was not in itself *sufficient* to account for the fate of M.P.s who deviated on the Suez issue. On the other hand, safeness of the seat did appear in the anti-Suez Conservative cases (plus the pro-Suez Labour case) to have been a *necessary* condition for removal of an M.P. Not only were just those with safe majorities actually purged, but the three (Yates, Astor, and Kirk) in distinctly marginal constituencies survived. Granting that their survival could be accounted for in other ways as well, it is significant that each of these three M.P.s, in personal interviews, stressed the marginal character of his constituency in explaining how he rode out his association difficulties.

Factors other than safeness of seat, however, might well have played some part in determining the survival of deviating M.P.s. One of these factors involves the extent to which the Suez deviants had committed earlier offenses against the orthodoxy of their local parties. Parliamentary opposition to the death penalty has especially been noted as a cause for local antagonism to most of the Conservative M.P.s later attacked for being anti-Suez. Perhaps there were some local critics who disliked their M.P. more for his stand on hanging than on Suez, and Suez might then have provided the opportunity for retaliation that the parliamentary free vote on hanging had not. Or it is possible that either offense could have been tolerated, but not both. In the words cruelly attributed to Bournemouth Conservatives: "Nicolson didn't want the blood of either Englishmen or Arabs. What's a Tory M.P. for?" Still, the hanging question complicates the analysis only because it was another emotional issue which had arisen at about the same time as Suez. It was important but not a prime determinant of what happened to the anti-Suez Conservatives. Some who were also against hanging survived both offenses, and some did not; and two of the anti-Suez Conservatives who had not been antihanging lost their seats. More significant is the consideration that an M.P.'s local critics, when aroused as they were in the Suez cases, could be expected to find other offenses to charge against him. If it were not the hanging issue, there would almost certainly be something else in the M.P.'s record to hold against him along with the immediate deviation. The "something else" could be his personal life, his relations with constituents, or his campaigning, as well as his parliamentary record. Another actual deviation of recent origin is the most serious way for an offense to be compounded, but it is not the only way.

This suggests that an M.P.'s personal relations with his association could have played a role in settling his political fate after Suez. On this score, Boyle and Nicolson are often compared. Boyle, one of the substantial anti-Suez Conservatives who survived association displeasure, was known to have been well liked personally by key local officers. Nicolson, on the other hand, had particularly strained relations with his local chairman, but such evidence is not persuasive even for the two cases at hand. And for the others similar information is not always available. It is necessary, therefore, to introduce here a large element of doubt with respect to the matter of explaining the differences in treatment of individual M.P.s. This is unfortunate since the differences in treatment were substantial enough so that their explanation might throw significant light on the way in which the British party system operates at the constituency level. On the other hand, it should be noted again that the differences among the cases were not of such nature as to cast doubt on generalizations about the Suez commitments of local party activists.

CHAPTER SEVEN

The Broader Public

So far the Suez issue has been presented almost entirely in terms of the conflict between the major political parties. This was true with respect both to the parliamentary conflict and to its extension to the constituencies. Thus in the constituencies it was the interparty conflict that characterized the response of local party units to any M.P.s deviating from party positions. Here as in Parliament itself (perhaps more so in the constituencies) we have been dealing with committed Conservative and Labour partisans, and only most incidentally with the less committed. What about the opinions of the rest of the community? To what extent were the ordinarily less partisan Englishmen mobilized on one side or the other? In considerable degree, this is a way of asking how successfully each party was able to mobilize its own usual voters, not just its actual dues-paying membership, to support its Suez position. But the questions also involve an inquiry into the views of opinion-makers, particularly the press, to see how the conflict was transmitted by important nonparty agencies.

There can be little doubt that the actions of political party leaders tended to extend the lines of partisan conflict to the general public. They were plainly fortified in doing so by their own zealous constituency activists. But party leaders needed and wanted to do much more than secure the support of their own usual following. For the Labour opposition, it was crucial to rally outside opinion sufficiently to cause

Conservative M.P.s to waver in their lyoalty to the government, or more feasibly to lessen the government's popularity for some future electoral occasion. Such objectives were what the partisan conflict was really about. Without projecting the conflict beyond Parliament itself, Labour could hardly hope to accomplish anything. And on their side the Conservative leadership had every incentive to seek public agreement for its policy. To this end, Prime Minister Eden broadcast an appeal to the nation during the crisis itself.[1] The opposition answered, notably in a broadcast by Gaitskell.

The major public effort, however, was Labour's "Law, Not War" campaign. Plans for this campaign were announced almost immediately after military action had begun. They were agreed upon jointly by the Labour party's national executive, the Trades Union Congress' general council, and the National Council of Labour. These agencies announced demonstrations and meetings throughout the country. While specifically excluding a general strike or any such industrial action, the trade-union leaders did thus support their party's general campaign.[2] The most publicized feature of the campaign was a mass rally at Trafalgar Square, where an estimated 30,000 heard Aneurin Bevan and from which an estimated 10,000 went on to demonstrate at Number 10 Downing Street.[3] Strong and unparliamentary language was characteristic of speech-making at some of the protest meetings, particularly outside the main London arena. In one small community, for example, a Labour M.P. (Denis Healey, later to be shadow Foreign Secretary) asked the assembled crowd: "What sort of people are you to allow a liar and a cheat to be your Prime Minister?"[4]

In exploring the extent to which this kind of partisan enthusiasm carried over to the rest of the nation, there are limited sources of information. First and most direct is the polling of opinion during and soon after the crisis, particularly in sample surveys but also in by-elections. Second, there is the press, through editorials as well as in news coverage. Third, there are unsystematically gathered statements from a variety of opinion-makers besides the press.

[1] "All my life," Eden broadcast, "I have been a man of peace, working for peace, striving for peace. I have been a League of Nations man and a United Nations man, and I am still the same man with the same convictions and the same devotion to peace." *Manchester Guardian*, 5 November 1956, p. 6.

[2] *Ibid.*, 2 November 1956, p. 1.

[3] *Daily Express* (London), 5 November 1956, pp. 1, 9.

[4] *Daily Telegraph* (London), 6 November 1956, p. 13.

1. POLLS

Fortunately a considerable amount of data on popular responses to the Suez affair was collected by the sample surveys conducted by the reliable and well-established British Institute of Public Opinion (usually known as the BIPO or the British Gallup organization). Equally fortunate, from the author's viewpoint, the Institute has generously made its data available for presentation here.[5] Much of what follows by way of analysis of sampled public opinion relies on such data. Only parenthetically is reference made to the results obtained by another poll (published in the *Daily Express*). Tables 1-3 and Figures 1-2 are all based on BIPO data, and these presentations provide the best estimates of what Englishmen thought about Suez. These estimates do have limitations, but they are most revealing on certain points.

Immediately it can be observed that the BIPO polls never showed that a majority of all voters were in favor of military action. This was true before, during, and after the action itself (Table 1 and Figure 1).[6] Even the *Daily Express* poll failed to show over 50 per cent supporting military action as it began (line 1 of Table 4), despite a spectacularly loaded question, and this source showed only barely over 50 per cent on 5-6 November favoring Eden's action generally. It is true, to return to the BIPO, that slightly over 50 per cent did, on 10-11 November 1956 and on 1-2 December 1956, agree generally with the way Eden handled the Middle East situation (Table 2). But both these polls were taken after the conclusion of military action and it is possible that a little of the agreement with Eden derived from his decision to halt. The military action itself never received the approval of half the voters polled by the BIPO. Even on 1-2 December 1956, when 51 per cent agreed generally with Eden's policy (Table 2), only 49 per cent thought Britain had been right to take military action in Egypt. It is true that two percentage points either way are not especially significant. The vital point is that there simply was not anything like a substantial majority in favor of the use of force. This seems more important than

[5] I am grateful to Dr. Henry Durant and to his staff of the BIPO both for the data and for the facilities to transcribe the data.

[6] French public opinion was more favorable to the intervention, but it was not overwhelmingly so despite the absence of much party opposition apart from that of the Communists. In a French poll taken 2-3 November 1956, 44 per cent approved the Anglo-French action, 37 per cent were against, and 19 per cent had no opinion. *Revue Française de l'Opinion Publique*, 1956, No. 4, p. 18.

Table 1. Polls by British Institute of Public Opinion on Military Action in Egypt (Per Cent)

Interview Dates and Question	Opinion	Voting Intention				
		All	*Con*	*Lab*	*Lib*	*DK*
16-24 Aug 1956. If Egypt will not accept the decision of the conference, should we take military action against her, or confine ourselves to economic and political action?	Mil. action	33	43	30	24	20
	Econ.-pol.	47	44	52	61	39
	Don't know	20	13	18	15	41
5-6 Sept 1956. If Egypt will not agree to international control of the canal, what should we do? Would you approve or disapprove if we were to give Egypt an ultimatum that unless she agrees to our proposals we will send troops to occupy the canal?	Approve	34	47	28	23	24
	Disapprove	49	41	54	55	54
	Don't know	17	12	18	22	22
1-2 Nov 1956. Do you think we were right or wrong to take military action in Egypt?	Right	37	68	16	24	23
	Wrong	44	17	67	52	44
	Don't know	19	15	17	24	33
1-2 Dec 1956. Do you think we were right or wrong to take military action in Egypt?	Right	49	81	22	30	43
	Wrong	36	10	62	49	34
	Don't know	15	9	16	21	23
27 Sept–1 Oct 1957. Looking back on Suez, do you think we were right or wrong to take military action in Egypt?	Right	48	79	30	40	33
	Wrong	32	10	51	41	23
	Don't know	20	11	19	19	44

the fact, on the other side, that there were never as many as 50 per cent clearly against military action. The "don't knows" were always numerous enough, as Table 1 makes clear, so that neither the pros nor the cons were in a clear majority on any occasion.

This much of the analysis is in accord with an earlier academic study of the polls that had been aimed particularly at contradicting

Table 2. POLLS BY BRITISH INSTITUTE OF PUBLIC OPINION ON
HANDLING OF MIDDLE EAST SITUATION (Per Cent)

Interview Dates and Question	Opinion	Voting Intention				
		All	*Con*	*Lab*	*Lib*	*DK*
7-18 Sept 1956. Do you approve or disapprove of the way the government has handled the Suez Canal incident?	Approve	42	71	21	31	36
	Disapprove	40	17	60	54	37
	Don't know	18	12	19	15	27
1-2 Nov 1956. Speaking generally, do you agree or disagree with the way Eden has handled the Middle East situation since Israel marched into Egypt?	Agree	40	76	16	25	27
	Disagree	46	16	72	55	41
	Don't know	14	8	12	20	32
10-11 Nov 1956. Speaking generally, do you agree or disagree with the way Eden has handled the Middle East situation?	Agree	53	89	20	46	50
	Disagree	32	4	63	33	24
	Don't know	15	7	17	21	26
1-2 Dec 1956. Speaking generally, do you agree or disagree with the way Eden has handled the Middle East situation?	Agree	51	85	19	46	39
	Disagree	35	9	64	31	35
	Don't know	14	6	17	23	26

the reports in the *New York Times* of a high degree of British public support for the Suez action.[7] No newspaper account of majority support could be based on the polls. Notably was this true as the military action began, since then a significantly smaller percentage of those polled thought the action right than thought it wrong (Table 2, third poll reported). Any newspaper reporter who at that time thought there was majority support for military force must have had a very different sampling method from the BIPO's—perhaps the time-honored "sampling" of taxi-drivers and customers of public houses. But if a reporter detected increasing support during and after the action he would have been decidedly in line with the trend reported by the BIPO and presented in Tables 1-2 and Figure 1.

[7]Jean Owen, "The Polls and Newspaper Appraisal of the Suez Crisis," *Public Opinion Quarterly*, Vol. 21, pp. 350-54 (Fall 1957).

Table 3. Poll by British Institute of Public Opinion on Effect of Suez on Party Voting Inclinations (Per Cent)

Interview Dates and Question	Opinion	Voting Intention				
		All	Con	Lab	Lib	DK
27 Sept–1 Oct 1957. Taking everything into account, has the way the government handled the Suez situation made you more inclined to vote Conservative, less inclined to vote for them, or hasn't it made any difference?	More	10	26	2	5	3
	Less	26	9	40	41	16
	No diff.	52	59	53	44	41
	Don't know	12	6	5	10	40

That trend is most sharply upward from 1-2 November to 1-2 December 1956, but it had also risen slightly in the earlier period (Figure 1). Probably the early rise is less striking than the fact that only about one-third of all voters favored military action in August and September. Moreover, the August result, as presented in Table 1 and Figure 1, overstates the percentage willing at that time to support military action in a circumstance approximating that which actually occurred. Specifically, the interviewees who responded to the August poll by favoring military action were also asked whether they would still want the action if America was not prepared to support it. Only 27 per cent (of all interviewees) stood for the go-it-without-America position.[8] Even with no such qualification, however, the number favoring military action before Eden made his move was markedly below the number opposing. The difference remained nearly the same as the action began, and only turned around after the action was concluded. Eden's decision, therefore, was made without evidence of even a plurality in favor. He obtained his plurality only after the event. To be sure, it might be argued that thus the public supported him retrospectively, when leadership had been exerted and the case had been made. But this is the place to recall that even after the event the plurality was not a majority. Whether it would have been a majority if the military action had plainly succeeded is in the realm of specula-

[8]The specific wording of this question, not given in Table 1, was: "If America is not prepared to support such military action, should we go ahead on our own, or not?" Four per cent answered negatively and 2 per cent answered "don't know." Thus 6 per cent of all the August interviewees shifted from an affirmative position taken in response to the first question noted in Table 1, reducing the total for military action from 33 per cent to 27 per cent.

Table 4. POLLS BY *Daily Express* ON GOVERNMENT'S ACTION IN
THE MIDDLE EAST (Per Cent)

Interview Dates and Question	Opinion	Voting Intention			
		All	Tory	Soc	Lib
30 Oct–3 Nov 1956. As a result of Israel's invasion of Egypt, Sir Anthony Eden has sent British forces to occupy the Suez Canal zone to protect British interests and to guarantee freedom of transit through the canal by British ships and ships of all nations. Do you support or oppose this action?	Support	48.5	75	28	50
	Oppose	39.0	15	60	38
	Don't know	12.5	10	12	12
5-6 Nov 1956. Do you favor or disfavor Sir Anthony Eden's Suez policy?	Favor	51.5	80	26	44
	Disfavor	36.0	11	60	32
	Don't know	12.5	9	14	24
17-21 Nov 1956. In general, are you satisfied or dissatisfied with Sir Anthony Eden as Prime Minister?	Satisf.	60.5	95	25.5	48.5
	Dissatisf.	30.5	2	60.5	40.5
	Don't know	9.0	3	14.0	11.0

tion. As far as the data go, they provide no basis for believing that Eden had a potential or incipient majority, any more than an actual majority, for military action.

A curious feature of the polls is the change in the nature as well as the degree of support for military action (Table 1 and Figure 1). In the polls of August and September, support was not nearly so closely associated with party as later. Conservative voters, it is true, did favor military action in larger numbers than Labour and other voters, but the difference was much less great than it subsequently became (and it was somewhat less in August than in September). Large numbers of Conservatives were still against military action, and large numbers of Labour voters were for it. This was the case even though party lines were more strictly followed, even in September, in response to the question of agreeing or disagreeing generally with Eden's handling of the Middle East situation (Table 2). This was likely to produce a nearly straightforward partisan response, while the military action question would not have done so in September. The government had not yet made it clear that it would really use force. When it did employ force at the end of October, however, then the question of supporting military action was converted into a partisan question. A more usual way to say the same thing is that opinion about military action became polarized around party positions. What was, in August and September, far from a straight party issue in the minds of voters became much more nearly so in November and December 1956 (and even in September-October 1957). It was most so in December 1956 when the Conservative percentage of support reached its peak and the Labour percentage of support had risen moderately from the low point of 1-2 November. Roughly the same high degree of party polarization of opinion, during and after military action, is displayed by the *Daily Express* data in Table 4.

The Conservative voters' support is really immense. Whatever doubts many of them had had earlier about military action appear to

Figure 1. POLLS BY BRITISH INSTITUTE OF PUBLIC OPINION ON MILITARY ACTION IN EGYPT

Favoring military action in Egypt (per cent)

have been dissipated, or put to one side, once their leaders took the action. Here, it seems probable, the leaders, particularly the Prime Minister, could effectively lead. What Eden did seemed right to Conservatives either simply because he did it, in collaboration with his Conservative cabinet, or because his arguments for action became persuasive. But for others, Eden's leadership appeared to produce a negative result. By taking military action, against partisan opposition, Eden may have made such action less popular with Labour voters than it was before. At least, the percentage of Labour voters favoring military action went down between August-September and November. This partisan loss, however, was not so great as Eden's partisan gain among Conservatives.

The development of opinion so much along party lines, even though less rigorously among Labour than among Conservative voters, calls into question the frequently voiced view that Labour's stand against Suez was unpopular with the party's own working-class voters. The

Figure 2. Polls by British Institute of Public Opinion on Voting Intentions

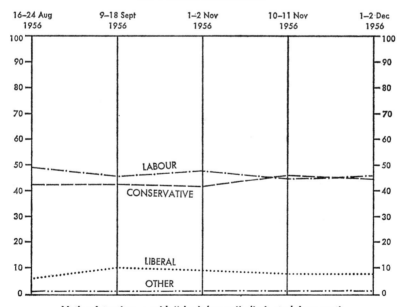

Voting intention — with "don't knows" eliminated (per cent)

supposed unpopularity was later admitted by at least one Labour M.P.,[9] and a large defection of working-class sentiment to Eden was claimed by Conservatives. The assumption was that the intellectual leaders of the Labour party were out of step with ordinary Englishmen.[10] Partly this was a matter of patriotism, and it was thought possible that Gaitskell's heavily internationalist basis for opposition, as well as opposition itself, struck the wrong note among party followers. Aneurin Bevan has been quoted to this effect. He is supposed to have said informally, during the crisis:

> If we don't take care, we shall turn the working class against us. Of course I am against Eden's crazy attempt to put the clock back. But there's no reason why, in attacking the Tories, we should commit ourselves to the view that all United Nations decisions must be accepted and that all recourse to force must be opposed as aggression.
>
> What makes the Labour Party go wrong in foreign affairs is that it takes its policies from middle-class intellectuals, devoid of antennae and with a dreadful habit of falling down and worshipping abstractions. In fact, there is only one motto worse than "My country right or wrong" and that is "The United Nations right or wrong."[11]

It was also assumed that many Englishmen felt racially superior in such a way as to applaud rather than oppose a campaign to teach the Egyptians a lesson. This attitude was supposed to be related to residual imperialism. "The contempt," it has been said, "which power breeds had been directed above all on to the Egyptians, just as in France it had been directed on to the Algerians. It is doubtful whether an attack on any other people in the world would have aroused as much enthusiasm in England as an attack on the Egyptians."[12] Also stressed was the particular contempt for Egyptians which ordinary members of the British Eighth Army had brought back from World War II. None of this can be discounted completely. It may even explain a large part

[9]R. J. Mellish said: "We do not deny that many of our supporters in the country supported the line taken by Sir Anthony Eden." 570 *H. C. Deb.* 530 (15 May 1957).

[10]Working-class Englishmen, in particular, are supposed to cherish exaggerated views of Britain's place in the world. Of these views, Richard Hoggart has written: "Those which claim superiority for Britain are not 'patriotic,' in any proper sense; they express an inherited assumption of national superiority. Though repeatedly told, especially during the last dozen years, about the change in England's international position, the majority of working-class people have no realization of it." *The Uses of Literacy* (Harmondsworth: Penguin, 1958), p. 80.

[11]The words were attributed to Bevan by R. H. S. Crossman, presumably relying on his memory of a conversation over five years earlier. *Manchester Guardian Weekly*, 28 December 1961, p. 6.

[12]A. H. Hourani, "The Middle East and the Crisis of 1956," in St. Antony's Papers No. 4, *Middle Eastern Affairs No. 1* (London: Chatto & Windus, 1958), p. 10.

of the support that Eden's military action did receive. But not much of this, as has been shown, came from Labour voters, even though most but not all of the party's voters are known to have been working class. The plain fact is that during the crisis itself relatively few Labour voters were attracted by the military action—fewer than had been willing to support it beforehand. Afterward, especially by September-October 1957, the percentage did increase. And always there were some Labour voters supporting the action. Evidently they were numerous enough to impress, perhaps to overimpress, the politicians of both parties. A good reason for this is that there were more such Labour defections in the pro-Suez direction than there were Conservative voter defections in the anti-Suez direction. Yet it must be emphasized that pro-Suez sentiment remained in a decided minority among Labour voters.

A question closely related to the degree of party polarization is one concerning the effect of the Suez affair on subsequent party fortunes. Because the military action was of very limited popularity originally and a failure ultimately, it might seem reasonable to hypothesize that the Conservative political cause would have suffered. But this does not seem to have been the case. Certainly the Conservatives did not suffer in the 1959 general election, since they improved their position over 1955. More meaningful here, however, are estimates of voter responses nearer to the Suez crisis. These estimates also do nothing to establish significant political damage to the Conservatives from Suez. Instead the BIPO polls show that Conservative fortunes took a turn for the better during the crisis itself (Figure 2). In mid-November 1956 the Conservative percentage was higher than Labour's for the first time in a year.[13] The fact was that the Conservative response had slumped below Labour's a year before Suez, and mainly stayed there until just after mid-1958.[14] The mid-November rise was exceptional and temporary. A good case might thus be made that Suez briefly helped the Conservatives regain some of their lost popularity. On the other hand, they dropped down even further by early 1957 than they had been before Suez, and it is possible that this drop was caused in part by the ignominious withdrawal from Suez and the resignation of Eden. It would be stretching matters, however, to think that the subsequent low level of Conservative standing in the BIPO poll, through the

[13]*News Chronicle* (London), 15 November 1956, p. 4.

[14]D. E. Butler and Richard Rose, *The British General Election of 1959* (London: Macmillan, 1960), p. 40.

Table 5. List of By-Elections of 1955-59 in Which Results Can
Be Compared with 1955 General Election[a]

Date	Constituency	Conservative Gain or Loss in Percentage of Poll
7 Dec 55	Gateshead West	− 1.2
8 Dec 55	Greenock	− 2.3
15 Dec 55	Torquay	− 9.4
2 Feb 56	Blaydon	− 3.4
9 Feb 56	Leeds Northeast	+ 1.8
14 Feb 56	Hereford	− 7.5
7 June 56	Tonbridge	− 8.4
27 Sept 56	Chester-le-Street	− 4.5
15 Nov 56	Chester	− 5.0 ⎤Suez
19 Dec 56	Melton	− 7.6
7 March 57	Warwick and Leamington	−12.2
7 March 57	Bristol West	− 5.1
21 March 57	Beckenham	− 6.1
21 March 57	Newcastle-on-Tyne North	− 3.6
27 June 57	Dorset North	− 7.0
28 Nov 57	Leicester Southeast	− 3.2
13 June 58	Ealing South	− 9.3
13 June 58	St. Helens	− 0.4
13 June 58	Wigan	− 5.7
8 Nov 58	Morecambe and Lonsdale	− 5.9
8 Nov 58	Chichester	+ 0.1
28 Nov 58	Shoreditch and Finsbury	− 2.5
29 Jan 59	Southend West	− 8.6
19 March 59	Harrow East	− 1.6
11 June 59	Reniston	− 1.8
18 June 59	Whitehaven	− 0.5

[a]The list includes only 26 of the 52 by-elections held between the 1955 and 1959 general elections. The other half mainly did not have candidacies politically comparable with those of 1955, usually because a third-party candidate was present to receive a substantial number of votes in one election but not the other. A few constituencies had to be excluded because of the absence of the regular party competition.

middle of 1958, was caused significantly by Suez. A likelier explanation is that a variety of domestic economic irritations against the government was responsible for the party's political slump in 1957-58 as in 1955-56.

BIPO data provide one other method of trying to estimate directly the effect of Suez on political party fortunes. Almost a year after the event, voters were asked what effect Suez had had on their party preferences. The answers, revealed in Table 3, do indicate the possi-

Table 6. THREE GROUPS OF BY-ELECTIONS OF 1955-59 IN WHICH
RESULTS CAN BE COMPARED WITH 1955 GENERAL ELECTION

Group	Ave. (mean) Conservative Loss in Percentage of Poll
Eight by-elections from 7 Dec 55 to 27 Sept 56	−4.4
Eight by-elections from 15 Nov 56 to 28 Nov 57	−6.2
Ten by-elections from 13 June 58 to 18 June 59	−3.6

bility of lessened Conservative support. No more than a possibility, however, is indicated, and that may fairly be regarded as dubious. True, significantly more voters did say that Suez had made them less inclined to vote Conservative than the number who said that Suez had made them more inclined to vote Conservative. But most of those in the first category were Labour and Liberal voters, whose existing party preferences were simply strengthened by Suez. The poll does not mean that those less inclined, as a result of Suez, to vote Conservative would ever have voted Conservative anyway.

By-elections provide another source for trying to understand the effect of Suez on voting behavior. All of the by-elections of 1955-59 that permit meaningful comparisons with the 1955 general election are listed in Table 5, and the relative Conservative gain or loss is shown. The most relevant by-elections are just before and after Suez. Here it can be seen that, as in BIPO polls, the Conservatives were doing poorly before Suez and continued doing so, at about the same level, just afterward. The sharpest slump came in March 1957, but that may have been the result of the special fact that Warwick and Leamington, then contested, was the seat from which Eden had just resigned. At any rate, from this list no case can be made that Suez directly hurt the Conservative party. Nor can anything conclusive by way of harm to the Conservative cause be drawn from the manner in which the same data are presented in Table 6. It is true that the Conservatives did do least well in the group of elections in the year after Suez, but the difference is hardly sharp. Left out of all these by-election comparisons, because of noncomparable candidacies, are the four more spectacular cases of Conservative decline sufficient to lose seats previously held by the government. But these, even if they could be compared, would not necessarily show greater decreases in Conservative voting percentages. They simply happened to be in marginal constituencies where Conservative decreases usual in the 1956-58 slump would cause loss of the seat. Certainly this seems applicable to the one Conservative loss of seat that occurred in the year after Suez. The constituency was Lewisham North, in whose by-election of 15 February 1957 the Conservative percentage dropped from 54 to 46.5, with an Independent Loyalist capturing 4 per cent (mainly, it can be assumed, former Conservative voters),[15] as against the Labour increase from 46 per cent to 49.5 per cent. If the Loyalist vote is added to the 1957 Conservative total, then the party's loss is less than usual before and after Suez. And even without thus treating the Loyalist vote, the Conservative percentage loss of 7.5 percentage points is lower than the loss in three pre-Suez by-elections. Insofar as the Lewisham North loss has been attributed to any specific issue, it was not Suez but rent control, just then being reduced by the Conservative government, that claimed the most attention.

Despite an obligatory uncertainty, it can be said that neither BIPO nor by-election data have established that the Conservative political cause suffered from Suez. Nor can it be proved that the party's cause was helped even though the polls do show that the Suez action gained in popularity in the year after the event. What is more definite and also more significant is that the Suez action became, during the crisis, a distinctively partisan issue for the voters, as it was for party activists and for M.P.s. It did not start so much that way for the voters, but it so developed and then largely remained an issue dividing voters according to their party preferences. The likelihood is that these party preferences, existing first, determined the voters' responses to Eden's military action. The available data, however, do not clearly carry this message, and it is possible that some party preferences were fixed by attitudes toward Suez rather than the other way around.[16] A heavily partisan division was the result in any case.

[15]The Loyalist candidacy represented an imperialist rebellion against the government partly because of its withdrawal from Suez, certainly not because of its earlier intervention.

[16]The high degree of coincidence between party voting and foreign policy views may be compared with American findings concerning this relationship. George Belknap and Angus Campbell, "Political Party Identification and Attitudes Toward Foreign Policy," *Public Opinion Quarterly*, Vol. 15, pp. 601-23 (Winter 1951-52), and Warren E. Miller, "The Socio-Economic Analysis of Political Behavior," *Midwest Journal of Political Science*, Vol. 2, pp. 239-55 (August 1958). The latter, in particular, appears at odds with the British data on Suez, since Miller found that foreign policy positions were not associated with partisan affiliation.

2. PRESS

How the press might have contributed to the partisan division of opinion over Suez is of major concern in reviewing the positions taken by British newspapers during the crisis. A considerable reinforcement of a reader's partisan outlook would seem likely if his favorite paper (often committed generally to his favorite party) were to have editorialized and reported on Suez from the same viewpoint as that of his party leaders. To analyze the position of the press in this respect, all of the newspapers listed in Table 7 have been examined at least for the crucial period of 29 October through 8 November 1956. The more important ones have been examined for all of October and November plus early December. Excluded from the list are certain specialized papers (notably the *Financial Times* and the *Daily Worker*) and all of the weekly and monthly magazines (some of which are discussed in the next section). In examining the newspapers, principal attention was given to editorials (in the American language), or leaders (in the British usage). But cartoons, special columns, and news stories were also studied. It must be said, however, that the line between editorializing and reporting is not so strictly drawn, or attempted to be drawn, in British as in American papers. Some papers do not even have specific editorial material; in these instances, the paper's position on Suez had to be determined, if at all, from the way it slanted its headlines and stories. More commonly this was not a problem. Rather, most papers editorialized both in their editorials proper and in their news space. This is not an unusual British practice, but its extent and intensity over Suez were especially great. It is important to observe examples of both kinds of editorializing since slanted news stories might have a particularly strong impact. Following the papers carefully in this manner has another reward. Some may be observed to have wavered even though eventually almost always adopting one position or the other.

Before relating editorial positions on Suez to generally partisan commitments, it is useful to note how much of the press was on each side of the controversy. Tables 7 and 8 contain the basic information. From these, particularly the totals for mass-circulation papers in Table 8, the press seems almost evenly divided according to circulation figures. The pro-Suez press would, however, have a more commanding lead if Sunday papers were excluded. Furthermore, the large pro-Suez lead among provincial papers suggests the possibility that the inclusion

British Politics in the Suez Crisis

Table 7. CIRCULATION AND EDITORIAL POSITION ON SUEZ OF PRINCIPAL
NEWSPAPERS IN ENGLAND AND SCOTLAND[a]

	Circulation		
Type and Name of Paper	*Pro-Suez*	*Anti-Suez*	*Doubtful*
National AM: Popular press			
Daily Express	4,042,334		
Daily Herald		1,653,997	
Daily Mail	2,071,708		
Daily Mirror		4,649,696	
Daily Sketch	1,123,855		
Daily Telegraph	1,075,460		
News Chronicle		1,441,438	
National AM: Elite press			
Manchester Guardian		163,585	
Times			220,716
National PM: Popular press			
Evening News	1,221,195		
Evening Standard	662,608		
Star		926,884	
National Sunday: Popular press			
Empire News	2,550,308		
News of the World			7,493,463
People		4,948,215	
Reynolds News		516,445	
Sunday Dispatch	2,420,159		
Sunday Express	3,331,127		
Sunday Graphic	1,190,146		
Sunday Pictorial		5,624,010	

[a]Listing of national papers includes all London papers plus the then *Manchester Guardian*. Listing of provincial papers excludes Northern Ireland. In the AM category it is selective so as to include quality papers in the larger cities, but in the popular category all provincial papers above 200,000 circulation are listed. These are evening papers except for the *Glasgow Daily Record*. Circulation figures are those reported by the Audit Bureau of Circulation for 1956 and contained in the *Newspaper Press Directory 1957* (London: Benn Brothers, 1957). The figure listed for the *Birmingham Post*, however, is out of date because it is for the paper before its merger with the *Gazette* (90,000 before its merger); no 1956 postmerger figure was available. Editorial positions are classified as doubtful either because there were no editorials (leaders), as in the instances of the *Sheffield Star* and *Newcastle Evening Chronicle*, or because of an essentially ambiguous position, as in the cases of the *Times* (London), the *News of the World*, and the *Glasgow Evening Times*. Whenever a paper's editorial tone was clearly tipped one way or the other, despite occasional wavering, the paper is classified in the pro-Suez or anti-Suez category. It is appreciated that a common ownership (Kemsley, Beaverbrook, etc.) accounts for similarity in editorial positions of many newspapers listed. Occasionally, however, newspapers owned by a single publisher did have different editorial policies on Suez.

Table 7. (*cont'd*)

Type and Name of Paper	Circulation		
	Pro-Suez	*Anti-Suez*	*Doubtful*
National Sunday: Quality press			
Observer		601,402	
Sunday Times	618,540		
Provincial AM: Quality press			
Birmingham Post	44,000		
Glasgow Herald	75,628		
Liverpool Daily Post	80,867		
Scotsman	54,269		
Yorkshire Post	118,379		
Provincial: Popular press			
Birmingham Mail	294,631		
Glasgow Daily Record		355,906	
Glasgow Evening Citizen	202,825		
Glasgow Evening Times			235,514
Liverpool Echo	381,889		
Manchester Evening Chronicle	295,729		
Manchester Evening News	340,174		
Newcastle Evening Chronicle			275,169
Sheffield Star			229,453
Yorkshire Evening Post	252,219		

of more papers in this category would have increased the margin. (Only those popular provincial papers of over 200,000 circulation are included in the tabulation.) Nevertheless, since the relative standings would not thus have been drastically changed, it can fairly be said that the anti-Suez view as well as the pro-Suez view was most substantially represented in the popular press.

Nor was the situation very different among the important papers without mass circulations. At least it was not different in the national press. The two Sunday papers of quality were on opposite sides, and of the two elite dailies the *Guardian* was anti-Suez and the *Times* vaguely neutral (a little more vague than neutral). The *Guardian*'s anti-Suez stand was at least compensated by the pro-Suez position of the *Daily Telegraph*, which, while classified in Tables 7 and 8 as a popular paper, is, despite its circulation, of quality if not of elite status. It is only in the provincial quality press that there is an imbalance, and it is unanimously on the pro-Suez side. Again this fact raises the ques-

Table 8. COMPARISON OF CIRCULATIONS OF PRO-SUEZ AND ANTI-SUEZ
NEWSPAPERS IN POPULAR PRESS CATEGORIES

| Type of Paper | Circulation | | |
	Pro-Suez	Anti-Suez	Doubtful
National AM: Popular (7 papers)	8,313,357	7,745,131	—
National PM: Popular (3 papers)	1,883,803	926,884	—
National Sunday: Popular (8 papers)	9,491,740	11,088,670	7,493,463
Provincial: Popular (10 papers)	1,767,467	355,906	740,136
Totals	21,456,367	20,116,591	8,233,599

tion of whether still more pro-Suez sentiment might not be found in the provincial press, quality or otherwise, if less well-known and smaller papers were included. Answering this only impressionistically, it can be said that an unsystematic sampling of small-town papers, dailies and weeklies, disclosed no uniformly pro-Suez sentiment but rather a considerable variety of positions.

Without any exception, all of the major newspapers with established party preferences adopted positions on Suez that conformed to those party preferences. Conservative papers were pro-Suez, and Labour and Liberal papers were anti-Suez. Classification of party preference, it may be granted, is not always clear since not all papers list such preferences in the *Newspaper Press Directory*. Many prefer "Independent," or some variation thereof, but with the national papers at least there is no doubt about the party preference whether it is listed or not. Thus the *Daily Express*, *Daily Mail*, *Daily Sketch*, *Daily Telegraph*, and *Sunday Times* were either expressly Conservative or Conservative-inclined, and they were all pro-Suez. The *Daily Herald* was a straight Labour party paper, the *Daily Mirror* almost always pro-Labour, and the *Manchester Guardian*, the *News Chronicle*, and the *Observer* all anti-Conservative and often, in their different ways, pro-Labour (as well as pro-Liberal in the first two instances); all, as noted, were anti-Suez. The significance of this kind of line-up is plain. Conservative voters were getting the same view from "their" newspapers as they were getting from their party leaders. Labour and Liberal voters were in a similar position. Partisan pressures were unidirectional from newspapers and politicians. No cross-pressures originated here, not at any rate for the citizen who had a party preference and who gave editorial attention only to those newspapers sharing his preference. An Englishman, however, who customarily read the editorials in two newspapers, say the *Daily Express* and the *Daily Mirror* or the *Observer* and the *Sunday Times*, would have had to make a choice between two radically different views of Suez. But if he always read two such papers he would usually have had a similar choice on other issues as well. The committed partisan, it can be assumed, must have made up his mind, over time, which paper (if either) to believe. Otherwise he would have had regularly to tolerate an oddly schizoid politics.

Of the pro-Suez press, the *Daily Telegraph* is most important since it provided the principal cues for Conservative activists. Although listed as "Independent Conservative," it was widely regarded as close to the Conservative Central Office and it was unquestionably devoted to the party cause even when criticizing particular Conservative leaders (like Eden, after he had become Prime Minister but before Suez). This devotion was amply demonstrated during the crisis. The *Telegraph* fully supported Eden's military action even though, beforehand, the newspaper, while favoring Britain's Suez claims, was by no means committed to military action—and certainly not in the circumstances at the end of October. Specifically, in an editorial of 30 October (after Israel's attack but before Eden's ultimatum), the *Telegraph* spoke of a disposition in Britain to rejoice at Israel's challenge to Nasser and to cheer Israel from the side lines, but then warned: "It must be remembered, however, that a full-scale Arab-Israel war would unite the whole Arab world behind Egypt."[17] Evidently the editorial writer did not foresee, any more than he advocated, British military intervention against Egypt. On the contrary, he assumed the traditional British desire to avoid lining up with Israel against the Arabs. Matters looked different the next day, after Eden's ultimatum, when "the Prime Ministers of Britain and France had no choice but to act quickly and drastically, hoping that American good sense would help them eventually through the consequences."[18] Action was justified much in Eden's terms: to prevent the risks of a large-scale Arab-Israeli war, to eliminate the threat of such a war to the canal, and to end Nasser's defiance of

[17] *Daily Telegraph* (London), 30 October 1956, p. 6.
[18] *Ibid.*, 31 October 1956, p. 6.

the United Nations on the canal as well as Israel's recent defiance. The United Nations should act against both Nasser and Israel, "but if it cannot and will not, Britain must act the policeman as best she can."[19] The "police action" theme was one which the *Telegraph* stressed regularly throughout the following week.[20] Another theme, certain to indicate the policy for true Conservatives, was criticism of the Labour opposition in the Commons.[21]

The *Telegraph*, despite its views of 30 October, can be said to have wholeheartedly defended the action once it was undertaken. The *Daily Mail* was slower to see the light. Its editorial of 31 October did accept Eden's reasons for military action, but it was obviously doubtful about his wisdom. The *Daily Mail* was unhappy about Britain and France acting without the United States, and troubled also about the existence of sufficient legal warrant for the action.[22] Subsequent editorials, however, were definite in supporting "a short, sharp, successful operation," in calling it a "police action," and in praising Eden (at the end of the week) for "sagacity and foresight."[23]

From the start the Beaverbrook press was much more decisive in favoring military action. The *Express*, like the kindred Suez group in Parliament, actually favored military action before Eden's ultimatum.[24] It is true that it did so under the mistaken impression that the Anglo-Egyptian treaty gave Britain the right to reoccupy the Suez base when Egypt was attacked, even by Israel. But the *Express* hardly retreated when its editorial writer learned, the next day, that the treaty excluded Israel from the nations whose attacks justified British reoccupation. Eden's decision was heartily welcomed. The canal was in danger, and the United Nations was "no good."[25] The *Express* approved Eden's action to "safeguard the life of the British Empire" and to "Keep Great Britain Great."[26] Its only objection to Eden was that he seemed to want the United Nations to take over the task Britain had now assumed. British withdrawal, when it did come, was regarded as a blunder.[27] All of this high and mighty British imperialism makes

[19]*Ibid.*

[20]*Ibid.*, 2 November 1956, p. 6; 3 November 1956, p. 6; 5 November 1956, p. 6.

[21]*Ibid.*, 31 October 1956, p. 6; 1 November 1956, p. 6.

[22]*Daily Mail* (London), 31 October 1956, p. 1.

[23]*Ibid.*, 1 November 1956, p. 1; 2 November 1956, p. 1; 7 November 1956, p. 1.

[24]*Daily Express* (London), 30 October 1956, p. 6.

[25]*Ibid.*, 31 October 1956, p. 6.

[26]*Ibid.*, 1 November 1956, p. 6; 2 November 1956, p. 6.

[27]*Ibid.*, 4 December 1956, p. 6.

strange reading, not only to Americans but to many Englishmen. Lord Beaverbrook's more than 4,000,000 readers were used to it. Their newspaper's position on Suez was no less than they expected.

Only a few other pro-Suez papers shared Beaverbrook's imperial enthusiasm.[28] The best that many papers could do was to support Eden's action as a tragic necessity. Mostly, like the *Daily Mail*, they expressed doubt or alarm at some stage of the crisis. For example, the *Glasgow Herald*, although consistent in its commitment, was decidedly cautious; its editorial page said originally that Britain was faced with a choice of evils, and then, on 3 November, stated that the next few days would show whether the operation was a success or failure.[29] Another pro-Conservative and pro-Suez paper, the *Yorkshire Post*, saved its doubts until near the end of the military action, when it granted that the government, knowing possible misinterpretations, had taken "a calculated risk with great courage."[30] Similarly the *Manchester Evening News*, which was pro-Suez in sharp distinction from the affiliated *Manchester Guardian*, greeted the action as a "grave step" and a "gamble," and supported it in spite of the risks.[31]

Still another kind of doubt, expressed in the pro-Suez press, involved an uncertainty about the government's reason for the unexpected military action. This meant a reluctance to take Eden's first statements as the whole story. An editorial writer with this reluctance had to assume that Eden had other reasons he could not yet disclose and that, in the meantime, one simply had to trust the Prime Minister. For example, the *Liverpool Daily Post* immediately backed the government's action, but then followed with: "Much remains obscure in the situation. Sir Anthony Eden's steadfast refusal to be stampeded into precipitate statements by ill-advised and insensitive hecklers is no doubt soundly based. If it is not he will have to answer for it later. For the present it is only fair to assume that the man at the wheel not only knows the course he is steering, but also has good reasons for not too explicitly pointing it out to us."[32] This is not quite the stuff with which to reassure newspaper readers. To be fair, however, the statement and

[28]Examples of strong support from newspapers of otherwise different qualities may be observed in the *Daily Sketch* (London), 1 November 1956, p. 1, and in the *Scotsman* (Edinburgh), 1 November 1956, p. 8.

[29]*Glasgow Herald*, 31 October 1956, p. 6; 3 November 1956, p. 4.

[30]*Yorkshire Post* (Leeds), 5 November 1956, p. 6.

[31]*Manchester Evening News*, 1 November 1956, p. 6.

[32]*Liverpool Daily Post*, 1 November 1956, p. 6.

others like it tended to be surrounded by strongly pro-government views, and even the most doubtful of Eden's editorial supporters stressed the harmfulness of the Labour opposition.

On the anti-Suez side, doubts were less prominent. They hardly seemed present at all. The anti-Suez press appeared fully confident of its cause. Absence of governmental explanation was no basis for misgiving; it only confirmed the anti-Suez newspapers in their conviction that there was no adequate explanation for what Eden was doing. The *Manchester Guardian* illustrates fully the consistency and strength of anti-Suez conviction. To begin with, it was against Israel's invasion, and immediately afterward denounced the Anglo-French ultimatum as "an act of folly." Britain's attack on Egypt was "wrong on every count— moral, military, and political."[33] This line the *Guardian* maintained throughout the week of hostilities, insisting that Britain accede to United Nations orders. Finally on 5 November the *Guardian* editorialized in favor of changing the government and urged readers to write or wire their M.P.s, a list of whom was given alphabetically by constituencies.[34] Just as strenuous, among quality papers, in its editorializing against Suez was the *Observer*. As a Sunday paper, it appeared only once during the crisis, but it compensated for this fact by devoting almost all of its editorial page to attacking the government's action. "We had not realized," the *Observer* said, "that our Government was capable of such folly and such crookedness."[35] Eden must go, and to this end the *Observer*, like the *Guardian*, urged its readers to write and lobby M.P.s, particularly the Conservatives, in whose hands Eden's future rested. Suez was "The Government's War," and the *Observer* insisted on the justice of its all-out criticism when reviewing the issue on the subsequent Sunday. It did so while reporting that three of its eight trustees had resigned in protest against the paper's editorial stand of 4 November.[36]

Most of the popular anti-Suez press shared the completely critical view of the *Guardian* and the *Observer*. Wavering took place only at the very beginning of the crisis. The tendency was to be completely critical

[33]*Manchester Guardian*, 30 October 1956, p. 6; 31 October 1956, p. 6; 1 November 1956, p. 1.

[34]*Ibid.*, 5 November 1956, p. 8.

[35]*Observer* (London), 4 November 1956, p. 8.

[36]*Ibid.*, 11 November 1956, pp. 1, 8. The *Observer*'s ownership was vested in a trust, the deed for which required that the trustees and chief officers of the paper be of the Protestant religion in the broadest sense. This provision was now, as on some other occasions, criticized by the *Observer*'s opponents.

of the government once British isolation from the United States and the United Nations had become clear. Thus the *News Chronicle* had responded on 30 October to the Israeli attack by thinking that "the rapid deployment of British power in the Canal Zone might at least give us the opportunity of holding the conflicting forces apart."[37] But the next day the paper greeted Eden's ultimatum as "A Gigantic Gamble," and expressed many doubts about "taking such a grave decision on our own— unsupported by the United Nations, the United States, or the Commonwealth." It was too early, the *News Chronicle* said, for "final judgment."[38] This apparently had to wait only one more day, for then the editor wrote that Eden's action was "folly on the grand scale" and that there could be "no further confidence in a man who has brought his country to such a dangerous state of ignominy and confusion."[39] The *News Chronicle* now joined the campaign to try to drive Eden from office. It even proclaimed that it had opposed the government's policy "from the start."[40] And it was true that the paper had very nearly done so. Only a day or so was wasted before the editorial writers saw the Eden policy in the standard Labour-Liberal fashion. They had not realized at first just how much Britain would isolate itself by using military force.

Labour's own paper, the *Daily Herald* (then still TUC-affiliated), called Eden's policy "folly" from 31 October and continued to emphasize its disastrous aspects throughout the week.[41] At least as sensational an anti-Suez campaign, and more significant because of its larger circulation, was conducted by the *Daily Mirror* and its associated *Daily Record* (of Glasgow) and *Sunday Pictorial*. The *Mirror*'s front-page editorial of 1 November labeled the Suez action "EDEN'S WAR," in large, black, and underlined capital letters,[42] and this became the theme of the paper's repeated attacks on the government. These attacks continued through and after the military action. The *Mirror* never retreated from its view that the action was disastrous, although it did grant, after two weeks, that the campaign to drive Eden from office had failed in view of the mid-November Gallup poll showing that

[37]*News Chronicle* (London), 30 October 1956, p. 4.

[38]*Ibid.*, 31 October 1956, p. 4.

[39]*Ibid.*, 1 November 1956, p. 4.

[40]*Ibid.*, 3 November 1956, p. 4.

[41]*Daily Herald* (London), 31 October 1956, p. 1. See also front-page editorial comment of 2, 3, 5, and 7 November 1956.

[42]*Daily Mirror* (London), 1 November 1956, p. 1. See also pp. 4 and 6 of the same issue, and various material in subsequent issues.

Eden now had more support than opposition.[43] It was not from want of fervor or consistency of attack that the *Mirror* and the rest of the anti-Suez press had failed to convince the public of the perils of Eden's policy.

In view of the suddenness and the uncertainty of Eden's action, it is impressive that British newspapers so promptly and fully committed themselves to editorial positions, pro or con. The occupational compulsion to offer firm opinions operated at least as strongly as usual to overcome any lack of information. The exceptions were mainly in those few papers, most conspicuously the *News of the World*, which customarily avoided controversial editorial opinions except for the publication of both sides of an issue. The *Times*, however, was an important special case. Ordinarily it does take positions and, especially on foreign policy, it is inclined to defend the government. Therefore, the absence of an all-out endorsement of Suez could be regarded as a sign of disapproval by the *Times*. Yet it is not certain that a reader would have obtained that impression from the *Times*'s editorials. Before the crisis, the *Times*, plainly sympathetic with the British government's efforts to obtain international control of the canal, had concluded that Egypt would have nothing to do with any peaceful solution on the terms which Britain and its partners declared essential for security and freedom of the canal.[44] Israel's move against Egypt, when it came, was disapproved, but with moderation. Britain's intervention, when first announced, was called "a decision of the gravest character." Fighting near the canal, the *Times* said, was a danger; it needed to be stopped somehow. "Boldness often pays. There must be every hope that it will do so now. Yet there are evident risks in the manner, and in the timing, of the Anglo-French counteraction which cannot be ignored." Reasons for disquiet were listed: the absence of American support, the request that Egypt retire from defensive positions at or near the canal, and the possibility that British action might be "misunderstood" as pro-Israel by other Arab states. Still, it was regretted that Labour had divided the House of Commons.[45]

Later also the *Times* treated opposition criticism as excessive while expressing doubts of its own, as in raising the question whether Eden had lacked candor in explaining Anglo-American consultation about

[43]*Ibid.*, 15 November 1956, p. 2.
[44]*Times* (London), 11 September 1956, p. 9.
[45]*Ibid.*, 31 October 1956, p. 9.

the Suez action.[46] Arguments both for and against action were presented even with the cease-fire, when the *Times* said: "The rashness of
the Anglo-French venture will be debated many months."[47] Five
days later, however, the need for debate seemed over as the *Times*
proclaimed that it had "never hidden its misgivings regarding the
enterprise. That it was misguided and yielded Britain no gains at all
comparable to the costs in good will and credit becomes increasingly
clear."[48] By now the *Times* could thus be said to be anti-Suez, but the
paper could not have been so classified during the period of military
action. Perhaps its editor or editorial writer was really anti-Suez all the
time but restrained by a quasi-official sense of responsibility to support
the government. Or perhaps the paper's position varied with personnel
in charge at a given time.

Not only was the *Times* exceptional in the virtual neutrality of its
editorial columns, but it was also so in the nature of its reporting of the
political crisis. Most major papers, as already remarked, carried their
editorial views into their news stories. It is this fact that makes the
policy positions of newspapers especially significant during the Suez
crisis. Readers, particularly of the popular press, would have been less
likely to miss the headlines and leads of news stories than to miss, or
avoid, editorials. On the pro-Suez side, the *Daily Sketch* provides a
leading example. Its main headline of 1 November was: "It's On—and
Eden Sticks to His Guns."[49] Two days later the opposition campaign
was reported under the headline "Labour Whips Up the Smear."[50]
And, just after action ended, the main front-page story was headed
"Russian Plot Exposed."[51] Another newspaper, operating ordinarily at
a much more respectable level, labeled its report of the first major
parliamentary debate on Suez "Mr. Gaitskell Divides Nation in
Crisis."[52] There were other less obvious ways in which news reports
reflected pro-Suez editorial opinions. The opposition campaign was
simply given less space and less prominence than it was in the anti-
Suez press. And Eden himself was fully and favorably presented.[53]

[46]*Ibid.*, 2 November 1956, p. 9.
[47]*Ibid.*, 7 November 1956, p. 11.
[48]*Ibid.*, 12 November 1956, p. 11.
[49]*Daily Sketch* (London), 1 November 1956, p. 1.
[50]*Ibid.*, 3 November 1956, p. 16.
[51]*Ibid.*, 7 November 1956, p. 1.
[52]*Scotsman* (Edinburgh), 1 November 1956, p. 9.
[53]As in the *Daily Mail* (London), 6 November 1956, p. 6.

On the other side, the same phenomenon can be amply observed. The *Daily Mirror* was entirely uninhibited. On 2 November almost the whole paper— news stories, cartoon, and columnists— was devoted to the anti-Eden cause. Bevan that day and Gaitskell the next received major attention for their speeches.[54] Any resignation from the government's ranks was treated as an important sign of growing difficulties.[55] More novel was the *Mirror*'s use of its most prominent space to continue to harry Eden after the cease-fire and during the Prime Minister's attempted recuperation in Jamaica. On 1 December it announced a contest: "We want your views, in not more than 500 words, on what the British Government should now do to regain our alliance with America, improve relationships within the Commonwealth, and restore a sense of unity in our own country."[56] The prize was a three-week holiday for two in Jamaica. The *Daily Herald* lacked any such gimmick, but its news during the crisis was nearly as devoted to the anti-Suez cause as was the *Mirror*'s. The *Herald*'s banner headline of 2 November was: "STOP THE WAR! NATION'S ANGER RISES."[57] This covered the story of Labour's "Law, Not War" campaign, which continued to have a big play in the *Herald* all week. Nor did the anti-Suez elite paper, the *Manchester Guardian*, fail to use its news columns to present its case. The style was subtler than that of the popular press. Its parliamentary report of 1 November unquestionably emphasized the strength of the case against the government. And the next day the *Guardian* reported Bevan's "penetrating attack on the Government," while calling the Prime Minister's speech "the best face he has yet put on the Government's conduct. . . ."[58] To be sure, commentary of this kind was in the settled British style of subjective parliamentary reporting. Its effect nonetheless was to strengthen the *Guardian* reader's unfavorable impression of the Suez action.

Generally, at the quality level as well as at the popular level, the bulk of British newspapers thus gave essentially partisan views of the Suez issue. These views, as noted, were partisan not only in the sense of being for or against the government on this issue, but also as a result of coinciding with the usual party preferences of the newspapers. The occasional editorial doubts were mostly submerged as party lines

[54]*Daily Mirror* (London), 2 November 1956, p. 2; 3 November 1956, p. 2.
[55]*Ibid.*, 9 November 1956, p. 1.
[56]*Ibid.*, 1 December 1956, p. 1.
[57]*Daily Herald* (London), 2 November 1956, p. 1.
[58]*Manchester Guardian*, 2 November 1956, p. 1.

sharpened. It is hard to know whether the newspapers helped to set those lines or whether they simply responded to cues given by party leaders (and picked up by ordinary voters and not just editorial writers). Probably the causation ran both ways. Anyway, it is safe to say that the newspapers tended to reinforce the partisan outlooks that readers of partisan papers were likely to have, and consequently contributed to the way the British community was divided on the Suez issue. That division, as observed in public opinion polls, seemed remarkably partisan for a foreign policy issue, but perhaps what is more remarkable, given the almost uniformly partisan line-up of newspapers as of politicians, is that public opinion was at least a little less than completely committed by party preferences on the Suez issue.

3. OTHER MEDIA

Ordinary daily and Sunday newspapers were not, in their editorial policies, the only media of opinion formation outside the political parties themselves. In addition to magazines, there was also a considerable variety of less institutionalized but nevertheless public expression of opinion about the Suez controversy. The crisis mobilized many for whom the effort directly to influence the community on public policy was only an occasional, or even a rare, performance. Many churchmen and professors, for example, now made pronouncements, and often without previous public identification with a political party. Here, then, is opinion-giving (and perhaps opinion-making) that differs from that of newspapers by virtue of its nonpartisan origin. The degree to which this was the case deserves notice because it might account for some of the minority of the public who did have Suez views at odds with their usual party preferences. Newspapers like the *Guardian* and the *Observer* might have played a similar part since they had not been clearly Labour or Conservative in previous editorial policy.

In a similar category, but even more definitely nonparty, was the most important weekly magazine (weekly newspaper, in the British language), the *Economist*. Its anti-Suez position is especially noteworthy because on most questions, and assuredly on domestic economic issues, the *Economist* was much closer to the views of the Conservative party than to those of the Labour party, although it preserved an independence in criticizing both parties much of the time. This independence the *Economist* certainly exerted in its issue of 3 November. Under the heading of "Splenetic Isolation," it editorialized that Eden had acted as "a partisan rather than a policeman." The evidence, the *Economist* said, suggested that the Anglo-French decision was aimed not at keeping peace, but at recapturing ground lost when Nasser had nationalized the canal. Even if the action were to succeed in ending the fighting, toppling Nasser, and establishing Western authority over canal traffic, "the damage still promises to be out of proportion." The *Economist* concluded: "The manner in which this crisis has been handled suggests a strange union of cynicism and hysteria in its leaders." [59] The next week the *Economist* reiterated its opposition to the now halted action, and urged that Eden should leave office. [60]

Less clear-cut in its anti-Suez views yet mainly critical of Eden's policy was the *Spectator*, another independent weekly journal. Much lighter and more general than the *Economist*, the *Spectator* was in this period tipped slightly to the right in British politics. Its first reaction, of 2 November, began with the view that it was reasonable in the circumstances for Britain to want to throw a protective screen between the opposing Egyptian and Israeli forces. But the editorial stated that the action taken was actually inappropriate and untimely. The ultimatum had given an impression of a put-up job. [61] A similar tone was sounded in the *Spectator*'s next issue. [62] More predictable, and therefore less important in this context, were the weekly journals with established partisan viewpoints. The pro-Labour *New Statesman* was unequivocally critical of Eden's military action as it had been of his threatened action in previous months. [63] And *Time and Tide*, then occupying an extreme right-wing position, was entirely in favor of the use of British force. [64]

The impression to be gathered from the policies of the *Economist* and the *Spectator*, when taken along with those of the *Guardian* and the *Observer*, is that opinion of what might be called the liberal, humanitarian sub-Establishment was anti-Suez. Such an impression is largely sustained by glimpses of other opinion-givers. One of the most interesting is that of churchmen. Although Britain had ceased to be as heavily a churchgoing and church-supporting nation as was contemporary America, religious leaders still commanded attention. Moreover, the

[59]*Economist*, Vol. 181, p. 393 (3 November 1956).
[60]*Ibid.*, pp. 481-82 (10 November 1956).
[61]*Spectator*, Vol. 197, pp. 595-96 (2 November 1956).
[62]*Ibid.*, pp. 627-29 (9 November 1956).
[63]*New Statesman and Nation*, Vol. 52, p. 533 (3 November 1956).
[64]*Time and Tide*, Vol. 37, pp. 1315-16 (3 November 1956).

principal leaders, especially of the Church of England, were public figures expected to make pronouncements on general if not political issues. A notable few were even active political controversialists. Unfortunately there was no ready systematic survey of the expressed views of churchmen during the Suez crisis. No doubt there existed a considerable diversity of responses among individual ministers, who must be assumed to have had diverse partisan convictions along with religious principles. The few active political controversialists, who happened to seem more left than right especially on military policy, may well be unrepresentative of the ministry as a whole. And what was said, if anything, about Suez in most British churches is not known.

What can be reported about churchmen consists of but a few high-level pronouncements. These were broadly anti-Suez. Most fully developed was the stand of the ordinarily moderate Archbishop of Canterbury, then Geoffrey Fisher, whose criticism of Eden's action carried the authority of the head of the Church of England. The Archbishop, admittedly mild compared to the usual opposition critic, stated his view in the House of Lords just after the announcement of military action. "Are we doing the right thing," he asked, "by the highest and wisest standard that we, as a nation, know?" Most of the world, he declared, was against Britain. "The point to which the Christian conscience must acutely address itself is whether or no we are standing to the spirit of the United Nations Charter." The Archbishop added that Christian opinion was "terribly uneasy and unhappy."[65] Clearly he was uneasy himself since he urged the government even now to reverse its policy and not go into Egypt. Later the same day, 1 November, the Archbishop continued to press his view by intervening eight times during the Lord Chancellor's defense of government policy. The Archbishop pressed the question of who was making the attack when the Lord Chancellor spoke of Britain acting in self-defense.[66] Nor was this the end of the Archbishop's effort to exert his considerable influence. On 3 November he headed a three-man delegation of the interdenominational British Council of Churches, representing all Protestants, to urge the government, through the Lord Chancellor substituting for the Prime Minister, to arrange a cease-fire.[67] The Council had condemned the government's action in Egypt, lending the weight of representative authority to the opposition by the religious leadership.

[65]199 *H. L. Deb.* 1296 (1 November 1956).
[66]199 *H. L. Deb.* 1352-54 (1 November 1956).
[67]*Manchester Guardian*, 5 November 1956, p. 9.

Academic opinion was expressed more individually than church opinion. The closest that academics came to a collective expression was usually in lists of names gathered on petitions or letters. This name-gathering became a popular form of competitive political activism at major British universities. Anti-Suez lists, widely publicized, were countered by pro-Suez lists. Each side enlisted dons as well as important nonacademic men of letters and other public figures. Again the anti-Suez side had most of the liberal sub-Establishment— that is, the professorial and other authors previously known for their identification with public-spirited liberal causes, not necessarily of a left-wing character. One conspicuous exception was Gilbert Murray, the grand old man of international causes, who was pro-Suez. Another less surprising, because less identifiable, pro-Suez academic publicist was Max Beloff. Otherwise the pro-Suez names tended to be mainly those of the right, moderate or extreme. It is hard, however, to generalize about the usual political opinions of all those who took stands on Suez. So many had never made their politics a matter of public record. It is a significant characteristic of the intense feelings about Suez that such men, particularly dons, were now motivated in large numbers to declare themselves for or against the government's action.

The Suez fever affected in this way much of the British community. Virtually everyone with anything like a public status felt compelled to try persuading his fellow countymen of the rights or wrongs of Eden's policy. Understandably this included Sir Winston Churchill, still a Conservative M.P. but since his retirement as Prime Minister in early 1955 much more a national monument than a party politician. He lent his weight to Eden's cause by writing a widely publicized letter to his constituency association chairman in behalf of "the Government's resolute action."[68] Former military officers as well as elder statesmen joined the lists. Mostly they were pro-Suez, but even here opinion was not monolithic. An important special case was Lord Tedder, Marshall of the Royal Air Force, who held his fire until over a month after the crisis but then criticized the government vigorously. He said that while bound to silence while troops were engaged he had regarded the action as a "tragic mistake" in the beginning. It was, he thought, "the wrong action at the wrong time and in the wrong place." Despite his background, Tedder rejected the view that he should now be bound by the maxim "My country, right or wrong." This, he said in words

[68]*Daily Express* (London), 5 November 1956, p. 9.

attributed to Chesterton, was "like saying 'my mother, drunk or sober.' "[69] Tedder's lengthy critique of Eden's policy is referred to here despite the fact that it was given only after the immediate crisis had ended, because it is a leading example of the extent to which anti-Suez views were held by nonparty persons concerned with British foreign and military policy. "Informed London opinion," meaning particularly the views derived from Middle Eastern specialists in the Foreign Office and elsewhere, has usually been estimated as largely unfavorable to the government. Like Lord Tedder, many of these informed persons felt bound to public silence during the crisis, and many of them afterward as well. The extent of anti-Suez views in this quarter must remain a guess, or (more accurately) a well-circulated rumor. What adds to its credibility is the established reputation of British Middle Eastern experts for a pro-Arab policy plainly at odds with military action against Egypt.

The great bulk of British citizens were unrestrained in publicizing their opinions during the crisis. How much they argued with each other in small groups (at work, at play, or at home) is unrecorded, but a very large amount of such informal but crucial exchange can be guessed from the flow of individual letters to newspapers in the first weeks of November. Letters to the *Times*, as always, constituted a major opinion-giving medium. Now, however, all newspapers were flooded with letters of opinion on Suez. This held for the mass press as well as the quality papers, and particularly for the small-town and suburban dailies and weeklies ordinarily less concerned with international questions. These local letters, mentioned in the earlier discussion of constituency politics, were vigorous and often emotional. Both viewpoints were fully expressed. Editors could not publish all of their mail, and some finally had to call a halt in order to have room for other material. The *Observer* published a count of its Suez mail. While probably it was unusually high because of the intensity of the paper's own attack and because of the articulateness of its readership, it gives some idea of the dimension of active interest. On 11 November the *Observer* reported that it had received 866 letters attacking the paper for its anti-Suez editorial of the previous week, 302 supporting the editorial, and 59 general comments on Suez. The next week it reported 1,851 new letters favoring the paper's stand, 619 new complaints, and 143 new general comments.[70]

[69]200 *H. L. Deb.* 1081-87 (12 December 1956).
[70]*Observer* (London), 11 November 1956, p. 2; 18 November 1956, p. 8.

Except for the widespread participation in opinion-giving, as illustrated especially by the number of letters, what emerges from this discussion of opinion media other than newspapers and parties is not entirely conclusive. The churches and the liberal sub-Establishment, it is true, appear mainly on the anti-Suez side. This added some non-party sentiment to an otherwise largely Labour line-up, but a large number of respectable and well-known figures without regular Conservative identification publicly supported the government. Here too the community was divided, and in such a way as not seriously to blur the party division. Rather, the tendency of the line-up of nonparty public figures was, with some exceptions, to reinforce the party division even though neither the liberal intellectuals nor their opponents among public figures were taking party stands, in the usual sense, when they adopted anti-Suez or pro-Suez positions. Their respective intellectual predispositions tended to lead them to take the side of the party sharing such predispositions— that is, liberal internationalism on the one side and imperial traditionalism on the other.

4. The Divided Community

The partisan division of opinion on Suez, first observed in parliamentary debate and then in the constituencies, was certainly maintained in the broader public sectors of the British community. Both the polls and the press confirm this general observation, although the polls, in particular, do not present as complete a correspondence of party and Suez views as was found in parliamentary voting. The correspondence, however, is high. It follows from this division of the larger community that there was roughly as much opposition to British military action in the country as a whole as there was in the Commons. The views of the parliamentary Labour party were representative of about half the nation. Eden did lack clear majority support for his campaign against Egypt. This has been established plainly enough from the polls. The best that Eden had was a plurality in favor of military action, and he did not clearly have that until after the action had ended. The greater popularity of the Suez campaign after the fact is itself an interesting phenomenon. This occurred despite the gross failure marked by ignominious forced withdrawal and despite the unpleasant domestic aftermath marked by petrol rationing.[71] A

[71]Petrol rationing measures were announced by the Minister of Fuel and Power, 560 *H. C. Deb.* 1557-58 (20 November 1956).

possible reason for the action's rising popularity lies in the fact that at least the danger of serious war, if not of economic hardships, had passed once the cease-fire was accepted. This suggests, speculatively of course, that many Englishmen were not originally so much troubled about the moral or legal offensiveness of Britain's action, or even about its likely failure, as they were about the sheer physical consequences of a war that might spread or be prolonged.

Perhaps the rising popularity of the Suez campaign, after the event, is a nearly sufficient explanation of the apparent absence of political damage to the Conservative cause. The governing party did not clearly suffer from Suez either in public opinion polls or in electoral contests. Its short-run ups and downs seem to have been largely independent of Suez, and its generally upward trend in the 1950's did not seem to be halted by its support of unsuccessful military action. It might be argued that the Conservatives would have done even better in the late 1950's if it had not been for Suez, but such a view is most difficult to sustain in light of the surprisingly large Conservative victory in the 1959 general election (with only a slight decline in percentage of the total vote). By that time, the Labour party could make only very limited use of the Suez issue, not just because opposition had turned out to be unpopular or unpatriotic but because it was suspected that many Englishmen regarded it as unpleasant to be reminded of their nation's failure or to be told that they should have guilty consciences about what had been done three years before. The Labour manifesto did attack the Conservatives on Suez, repeating that the action had been "a crime" and also "an act of folly," mainly to illustrate how unfit Suez defenders, like Prime Minister Macmillan and Foreign Secretary Selwyn Lloyd, were to represent Britain at a summit conference and to work with the United Nations and Asian-African nations.[72] Aneurin Bevan made the same point in his speeches, but generally the Suez issue was not prominent in the 1959 campaign. In fact, the Nuffield study of the campaign states that Suez "was rarely brought up."[73] Only very minor mention of the issue is contained in Nuffield reports on four individual constituencies during the campaign. Conservatives had no incentive to discuss Suez, and they did not mention it at all in their party manifesto.

One place where Suez was advanced as a major 1959 campaign issue was in the *Observer*. Here, where the crisis had been especially traumatic, the newspaper used Suez as a principal cause for abandoning its

[72]Butler and Rose, *op. cit.*, pp. 276-77.
[73]*Ibid.*, p. 64.

17-year policy of political neutrality to express a preference for the Labour and Liberal parties. The Conservatives, the *Observer* said, "have not yet adjusted their thinking to the facts of the modern world and to the part which Britain can successfully play in it."[74] The *Observer* argued that the clearest evidence of the Conservative failure to adjust was Suez. But to have attached so much significance to Suez in determining a 1959 voting decision seems decidedly exceptional. Not many Englishmen previously uncommitted to the Labour or Liberal parties were likely to have felt so strongly against Suez, three years after the event, as to let their votes thus be decisively influenced. Certainly the election results showed no such movement of opinion. If there was any movement against the Conservatives because of Suez it must have been largely balanced by the addition of new Conservatives because of other issues or even because of pro-Suez sentiments.

What seems likelier is that very few British citizens permanently shifted party because of Suez. Rather, the effect of Suez was more often to intensify existing partisan commitments— to give activists in particular, but ordinary voters as well, an additional reason for their identification. It would be too simple, however, to say that Englishmen did no more than follow the cues of their respective party leaders. After all, voters were accustomed to look at issues in much the same way as their parties. That is why they identified with parties in the first place. There was a perception of foreign as well as domestic issues which party leaders and followers had in common. More clearly was this the case among Conservatives, whose increasing solidarity on Suez has been emphasized. The somewhat lesser, though still notable, Labour voter solidarity on Suez may well reflect a party mobilization primarily around domestic issues. Labour's internationalist, anti-imperialist, and quasi-pacifist traditions may not have been so widely shared by its electorate as the Conservative party's patriotic, military, and imperialist traditions were with its electorate. The latter traditions, it seems, appealed also to some Labour voters. A straight "national" perspective thus could have cut across party perspective, but it must be emphasized that any such cutting affected only a minority of the ordinary Labour-voting public. The community remained divided on largely partisan lines. Exceptions from this division were interesting and significant *because* they were deviant cases. They deserve attention as deviant cases always do, but they should not conceal the basically partisan division characterizing the Suez controversy.

[74]*Observer* (London), 4 October 1959, p. 16.

CHAPTER EIGHT

An Example of Cross-Pressure

Having already demonstrated the strongly partisan alignment in Parliament, the constituencies, the press, and (to a lesser extent) the community at large, it may seem unnecessary to explore this phenomenon from yet one more angle. But it is worth inquiring into the way in which the demonstrable party cohesiveness, on Suez, was related to any intraparty group resistance. Clearly the cohesiveness would look still more significant in the face of such group resistance, as distinct from the objections of independent-minded individual M.P.s. What would be most useful for the proposed inquiry is a fairly well-defined group, in a major party, that was influenced on Suez by non-party considerations in a direction opposite to the position taken by the party. Was there, in other words, a significant instance of cross-pressure, and, if so, can it be studied so as to provide a broader understanding of the patterns of British opinion, illustrated in the Suez crisis, and at the same time help in comprehending the process by which party cohesiveness was achieved?

Certain cases, insufficiently clear-cut for the present purpose, have already been noted. Individual M.P.s in both parties did suffer from cross-pressure in the sense that their own convictions (liberal internationalist in the instance of Conservatives and nationalist in the instance of Labour M.P.s) were at odds with their parties' positions. A few of these M.P.s acted on their convictions, with the interesting results described in Chapter Six, but most of them stayed in line with their party. In any event, however, these examples do not represent a group response to a well-defined pressure. The same can be said of individuals, hypothesized in the last chapter as subscribers to two newspapers each presenting a radically different view of Suez. Similarly there must have been many Englishmen, politically active or inactive, whose opinions were subject to influence from more than one direction. It was not unknown even for families to be divided on the issue. None of these cases, however, are available for study. They are too personal or too ill-defined, or both.

The case that comes closest to fulfilling the definition of cross-pressure involves the Labour M.P.s with significant ties to the pro-Israeli sentiments of the Jewish population of Britain. These M.P.s were plainly subject to cross-pressure, since sympathy for Israel called for a less critical view of Britain's action, if not for outright advocacy, than that which was implied by the Labour party's all-out opposition to Eden. To some extent, this cross-pressure could have been felt by pro-Israel but non-Jewish Labour M.P.s, but there is no substantial evidence of their ambivalence, if it existed. For some of the Jewish M.P.s[1] in the Labour party, on the other hand, such evidence certainly exists. There are even indications that these M.P.s were subject to a group pressure against the Labour party position. Such pressure, when overt and external, is interesting in itself as well as for the light it throws on parliamentary behavior. Still, it is not necessarily the most important element in the case. Here, as in other examples of political cross-pressure, the affected individuals suffer a conflict between two different viewpoints of their own, not just of groups to which they may belong. A Labour M.P. of Jewish background might have had trouble making up his mind where to stand on Suez simply because his own beliefs included the Labour party's anti-imperialism and the Jewish community's sympathy for Israel. Neither the party nor the ethnic group would have had openly to pressure him in order for his decision to be difficult. Cross-pressure, in other words, is internal as well as external. What the external influences mainly contribute to this case is an exhibit, which might not otherwise have come to light, of the cross-pressure that did exist.

The choice of Jewish M.P.s for analysis here, it must be stressed, does *not* indicate a belief that they or the Jewish community exerted any special influence in British policy-making or even in British politics during the crisis. The choice is not made because of any importance of

[1] "Jewish M.P.s" should be understood as a shorthand way of saying "M.P.s with Jewish backgrounds."

the group, but because of its unique visibility for the limited purpose at hand. It should be added that many other British groups—bankers, shipping companies, oil companies, and civil servants, for example— would more clearly require treatment on the grounds of interest in and potential influence on Britain's Suez policy. But these are not the grounds for selecting a parliamentary example of cross-pressure in relation to party pressure.

1. BACKGROUND

Only a few of the events of the Suez crisis need to be noted again to provide the background for the opinions of M.P.s with Jewish ties. The Israeli attack on Egypt, it will be recalled, occurred on 29 October, and it was the next day that Britain and France vetoed the United Nations Security Council resolution demanding Israel's withdrawal and issued their own ultimatum to Egypt and Israel. Also on 30 October the first crisis debate, with its unscheduled division, took place in the House of Commons, preceding by one day the actual attack by Anglo-French forces. The problem for a pro-Israeli Labour M.P. was thus initially acute, on 30 October, and in some ways especially difficult then because the issue seemed to revolve heavily about the rightness of what amounted to Britain's pro-Israeli veto in the United Nations. This aspect loomed less large in the following week of controversy, but by no means disappeared. By attacking Egypt, Britain, with France, did become the enemy of Israel's enemy.

These previously recounted events, however, provide only part of the background for this particular case study. Several other matters served to complicate any straightforward notion of identifying British action with a pro-Israeli policy. To begin with, there was nothing in the record of the Conservative government to cause one to expect a pro-Israeli policy. Eden, in particular, was widely regarded as committed to the Foreign Office's tradition of pursuing British interests by placating the Arabs, if necessary at Israel's expense. Eden himself had seemed to propose just such an arrangement a year before in a well-known Guildhall speech that alarmed Zionists. He had suggested that the Arab-Israeli boundary dispute be settled by compromising the rival claims in such a way as to cause Israel to withdraw from territories which, while not originally assigned to Israel, had been populated and developed since 1948 by Israel. These territories, already regarded by Israelis as theirs, Eden had referred to ominously as "the present territories which they occupy." Furthermore, he had proposed his settlement in the familiar context of Britain's "long tradition of friendship with the Middle East."[2] Zionists understood this tradition only as friendship with Arab nations, now more than ever important to British interests because of their oil or their control of oil shipments.

To the same effect, as concerns the Zionist view of British policy in the 1950's, was the refusal of the Conservative government to do anything about Egypt's refusal to let Israeli shipping (including non-Israeli ships dealing with Israel) use the Suez Canal even at a time when British forces still occupied the canal zone. On this as on other aspects of Middle Eastern policy, Eden and his ministers had been unyielding in response to criticisms from pro-Israeli parliamentary questioners in the Labour party. Consequently it was Labour that had been able to assume a pro-Israeli posture in the years immediately preceding the Suez crisis. This was true even though in the late 1940's, before and during the creation of Israel, the Labour government's Foreign Secretary, Ernest Bevin, had been the *bête noire* of Zionists everywhere. Apart from Bevin and the actual performance of the Labour government on Palestinian questions while he was Foreign Secretary, there was considerable precedent in Labour experience for the pro-Israeli sentiments of the 1950's. Historically the Labour party, particularly its intellectuals, had been receptive on humanitarian grounds to the establishment of a Jewish national home and, in the 1930's, critical of the Chamberlain government's limits on Jewish entry to Palestine. This favorable view was reinforced after the establishment of Israel by the emphasis in the new state on democratic socialist forms of economic organization. Certain non-Jewish Labour leaders, notably Hugh Dalton, Hugh Gaitskell, and Anthony Greenwood, proclaimed their sympathy and concern for the new state. The Labour party was for this reason, and because of the presence of Jewish members who championed Zionism, much more nearly identified with the Israeli cause than the Conservatives.

Despite Churchill's known sympathy, and Balfour's much earlier, the Conservative party generally stood aloof, at the very least, from Zionism. Moreover, the Conservative party contained some members with records of hostility to Zionist aspirations, and a few previously regarded as hostile to Jews in general. Their support for British action at Suez was hardly likely to be treated as pro-Israeli. To cite an extreme instance, a Conservative M.P. who had once been an admirer of

[2]*Times* (London), 10 November 1955, p. 10.

the British Union of Fascists had his championship of British military action greeted by the derisive dry, from a Jewish Labour M.P., "Another friend of the Jews! Up the Blackshirts!"[3] This kind of case is not important in itself, since the Conservative involved was a minor figure and so were any other M.P.s with similar records. It did, however, symbolize an awkwardness for pro-Israeli Jews in finding allies on the extreme right. And it happened, of course, that much of the right wing of the Conservative party was most enthusiastic about Britain's military action at Suez. On the other hand, some Conservatives, with liberal pro-Israeli records, were critical of the government; Boothby and Nicolson were good examples.

Most important, the Conservative government, as already noted, did not justify its intervention in anything like pro-Israeli terms. Eden was particularly careful to avoid a verbal identification and so were other government leaders. They adhered to the view, however strange it sounded, that Anglo-French intervention was meant to separate the combatants. R. A. Butler, for example, stressed the government's concern that the Israeli attack might, with success, have produced circumstances preventing free transit through the Suez Canal. Thus Israel was made to seem the immediate agent causing intervention although, at the same time, the Israeli attack was regarded sympathetically as a response to Arab pressure. As Butler said, the government should not "do anything to condone Israeli action." Rather, it was "a fact with which the Government had to deal."[4] Conservative back-benchers were more blunt in their separation of Britain's action from Israel's. Vice-Admiral Hughes-Hallett, for instance, spoke of Anglo-French intervention as a means of checking "the headlong advance of the Israeli armies."[5] Still another Conservative M.P. and an old Suez grouper, Major Legge-Bourke, explicitly responded to a pro-Israeli speech by a Jewish Labour M.P. by stressing the "danger of assuming, as he has apparently assumed, that in light of what has happened in the United Nations the Government have reoriented their policy and come down definitely in favour of Israel."[6] That,

[3]The Conservative was Sir Thomas Moore, and the Jewish Labour M.P. was Maurice Orbach. 558 *H. C. Deb.* 167 (1 November 1956). Moore's "blackshirt" reputation had been advertised by a widely circulated attack on prewar Conservatism by Simon Haxey, *Tory M.P.* (London: Gollancz, 1939), who cited Moore as a member of the Council of Anglo-German Fellowship and as a public admirer in 1934 of the British Union of Fascists. Pp. 207-8, 234-35.

[4]558 *H. C. Deb.* 1723 (1 November 1956).
[5]558 *H. C. Deb.* 1688 (1 November 1956).
[6]558 *H. C. Deb.* 1497 (31 October 1956).

he added, was not so, since the meaning of the Prime Minister's speech in defense of the British veto was only, as Legge-Bourke spelled it out, to indicate that the government had not been ready to condemn only one side in the Arab-Israeli dispute.

These Conservative remarks, more subtly made by government spokesmen than by back-benchers, gave public notice to Jewish M.P.s in the very days of the crisis that British intervention was not intended to reverse the government's policy of aloofness toward Israel. The effect might be pro-Israel, but not the intent. Eden would be aligned with Israel at most incidentally and temporarily. The point was driven home to Jewish M.P.s in the Labour party by one of their non-Jewish colleagues. Emphasizing that the government's action was not related to any tenderness for Israel, he warned Jews against choosing Tory allies. "The Israel situation is simply something available at the moment to cover or make decent the plans which the Government have had all along."[7] This, presumably, a pro-Israeli Jewish M.P. would grant along with his fellow Labour members. The canal and not Israel, he well knew, was what concerned the Eden government. Still, might he not welcome, besides the British veto of United Nations condemnation of Israel, also military intervention against Israel's foe?

Here is the crucial question. The answer depended largely on a calculation as to the advantages of the Anglo-French intervention to the Israeli cause. Such a calculation was difficult because the official Israeli attitude toward the intervention was not necessarily clear. The Israelis must have welcomed even temporary friends, but they may not have wanted the intervention to take the form it did. Subsequently, the Israelis let it be understood that the Anglo-French action had deprived them of what could have been their own military triumph, or at least the reputation for such a triumph, in the David-against-Goliath pattern.[8] The presence of Western troops enabled Nasser to pass off the Israeli victory as a piece in a broad imperialist campaign against Egypt, and perhaps to save his regime from ignominy and consequent overthrow. Moreover, but again after the event, the Israelis could well have believed that it was British and French forces that caused the threat of really large-scale hostilities in the Middle

[7]Wilfred Fienburgh, 558 *H. C. Deb.* 1514 (31 October 1956).

[8]This view is reflected by Robert Henriques, writing of the military operation from Israeli sources in *100 Hours to Suez* (New York: Viking Press, 1957), when he said: ". . . Israel would be in a better position now if the British and French had kept out of the active operations." P. 30.

East and thereby produced the pressure for an early cease-fire.[9] Before and during the crisis, however, both Israel and its friends may not have had the same critical view of Anglo-French intervention. At the very least, it can be assumed that help of some kind was wanted from Britain and especially France. Perhaps it was mainly air cover for Israeli cities, or other forms of aid short of an actual assault on Egypt by British and French troops. But Israel, obviously unable unilaterally to determine the form of Anglo-French help, might still have welcomed help in the form actually given if that was the best that could be obtained. Israeli misgivings afterward do not eliminate the possibility of willing acceptance at the time.

Nor do such misgivings expressed at the conclusion of the Sinai victory necessarily indicate that that victory could actually have been achieved, or achieved so readily, without Anglo-French intervention. Not only might the delivery of French fighter aircraft (some rumored to have included French pilots) have been essential to support the Israeli attack and to protect the homeland, but it is also possible that both the Anglo-French threat of intervention and then the intervention itself caused Nasser to reserve forces to protect Suez that might otherwise have been committed to the Sinai campaign.[10] Regardless, however, of whether Anglo-French intervention did thus in fact turn out to be crucial to quick Israeli success, there seems little doubt that, during the crisis, the impression existed in London that Israel willingly accepted action by Britain and France as in some way helpful. Such an impression was almost bound to develop since France was by now overtly pro-Israel, and Britain seemed to be acting with France.

The Israeli government's own calculation of the advantages of British intervention, while of importance to Israel's supporters in Britain, cannot be assumed to have determined the views even of Zionists who were also M.P.s. Besides their opinions as Labour members and British subjects, they might also as Zionists have made a different

[9]Walter Eytan, who was the Israeli Foreign Ministry's Director General, specifically took this position. *The First Ten Years* (London: Weidenfeld & Nicolson, 1958), p. 141.

[10]That the Anglo-French military force did thus indirectly but substantially help Israel's quick success is stated by Edgar O'Ballance, *The Sinai Campaign of 1956* (London: Faber & Faber, 1959), pp. 190-91, in a work generally sympathetic to Israel. Erskine B. Childers seems to go further in arguing that the Anglo-French threat and actual intervention were necessary for Israel's success. *The Road to Suez* (London: MacGibbon & Kee, 1962), chap. 12. He seems also to believe that Israel wanted Anglo-French intervention, but not, of course, in such a way as to deprive Israel of its own victory over Egypt. P. 185.

estimate from Ben-Gurion's of what was in the Israeli interest. British Zionists, decidedly less numerous and less rich than American Zionists, would have been troubled about Britain "helping" Israel in opposition to the United States. Not only would the United States have long been regarded as more friendly to Israel than the British government, but its help was of much greater consequence to Israel's future than Britain's even if the British government were genuinely to have become friendly to Israel. Britain as an Israeli ally, along with France, would not represent a net gain for Israel if the United States were to be estranged.

What can be concluded from these various considerations is that a pro-Israeli British Jew would, if in that role alone, have been subject to less than a completely straightforward pressure to identify himself with British intervention. At the very least, he could have rationalized an anti-Eden position as not entirely incompatible with the long-run advantage of Israel, despite the likelihood of current Israeli views to the contrary. Having said this, it is nevertheless essential to note again that the emotions of Zionists in Britain as elsewhere were understandably turned to favor the action of Eden's government as the new enemy of Israel's enemy.

2. Jews in Britain and in Parliament

It is necessary to say something explicit about British Jews and about the Labour M.P.s of 1956 who happened to be Jewish. The starting point must be the important observation that by no means all Jews, particularly if the group is broadly defined by ethnic background, were Zionist or pro-Zionist, or even pro-Israel. There was nevertheless a tendency for many Jews to be at least pro-Israel, and the same tendency was evident among some but not all Jewish M.P.s. Certainly the degree of pro-Israeli sympathy on the part of British Jews varied, often in response to the degree and the nature of identification with the Anglo-Jewish community generally.

The Jewish community in Britain is an old one that can claim continuity from the famous Cromwellian resettlement, the tercentenary of which was being celebrated in 1956. Not many Jews, however, are able to trace their British nationality to any such early time or even to a date before the end of the nineteenth century. Only a small aristocracy is descended from the Jews who, in the seventeenth and eighteenth centuries, came from Spain and Holland, and not so many more are descended from German immigrants of the early nineteenth century. The large influx was the later one from Eastern Europe. Nevertheless the older Jewish families long maintained positions of influence and leadership in the enlarged community. They were important, for instance, in the long nineteenth-century struggle for equal rights under British law. They helped to secure the provision of 1826 for naturalization without the Anglican communion, the abolition in 1846 of the technical illegality of Judaism under a sixteenth-century statute suppressing non-Anglican rites, the House of Commons resolution of 1859 allowing a Jew (Rothschild) to sit as an M.P. without taking an oath "upon the true faith of a Christian," and the parliamentary act of 1866 expressly abandoning the old language for the M.P.s' oath of office. These achievements were victories for Jews long established in Britain but who, unlike Disraeli, maintained their religious faith. They thus obtained official status, even as M.P.s, on their own terms, and they did so before the arrival of the large Jewish population from Eastern Europe. The significant impact of this new immigration, while of course smaller than the comparable American immigration, may be observed in the increase of Britain's Jewish population from 60,000 in 1880 to 250,000 in 1914.[11]

By the 1950's the number had increased to about 450,000, or to just less than 1 per cent of Britain's total population. This proportion of Jews was well below the contemporary American figure of about 3 per cent. About 280,000 of Britain's Jews lived in Greater London, but this too was a good deal smaller proportion than the Jewish percentage of New York's population. In consequence, there could be very few parliamentary constituencies dominated by Jews, although there was a concentration of Jewish population in certain sections of London (lately in Hendon, Finchley, and Stoke Newington as well as in the older declining areas of Bethnal Green, Hackney, and Stepney).[12] The same holds even more clearly outside of London. Only Manchester and Leeds, each with about 25,000 to 28,000 Jews, would have had large enough proportions to make for a really important "Jewish vote" if the Jews also happened to be concentrated in particular constituencies

[11]Israel Finestein, *A Short History of Anglo-Jewry* (London: Lincolns-Prager, 1957).

[12]Howard M. Brotz, "The Outlines of Jewish Society in London," in *A Minority in Britain*, ed. by Maurice Freedman (London: Vallentine Mitchell, 1955), pp. 139, 141.

within the respective metropolitan areas.[13] These cases would have been decidedly exceptional since for the most part the Jewish population simply was not large enough to have an important electoral influence even if Jews were to vote primarily as Jews.

A distinctive feature of the Anglo-Jewish community, from an American viewpoint, is the existence of the Board of Deputies of British Jews. The Board has had an official status since 1760 to represent the Anglo-Jewish community, and it has had explicit statutory recognition since the Marriage Act and Registration Act of 1836. Synagogues, certain friendly societies, and other groups provide the basis for election of the deputies.[14] As the Board's early start indicates, it was originally an agency of the older Jewish community. The Board long remained under the guidance of the established community leadership, even as it absorbed the new Jewish population in the late nineteenth and early twentieth centuries, but a decisive change was marked in 1943 when Zionists won a majority on the Board of Deputies for a Jewish state.[15] The older leadership was not necessarily anti-Zionist, but it had been slow to champion Palestine as more than a home for refugee Jews. The 1943 victory for the Zionists was to some extent, therefore, a triumph over the older elite. But the triumph had itself been made more likely by a previous tendency, which now became stronger, for the old elite to withdraw from the Board of Deputies in favor of activity in the more assimilationist Anglo-Jewish Association (dating from 1871). The Board, on the other hand, tended, as before, to maintain the separate identity of Jews, especially of those adhering to Orthodox Judaism. Very largely this now meant Jews of Eastern European backgrounds. That many of them should be Zionists is understandable. The leadership of the Board overlapped that of the British Zionist organization. The Board, however, continued its broader functions in behalf of the Anglo-Jewish community. A good example of such functions was the Trades Advisory Council created by the Board in order to reduce tensions among businessmen over charges of price-cutting by Jews.[16] Altogether the Board, by maintaining itself and its activities, gave the Anglo-Jewish community an appearance of cohesion despite some religious backsliding. The cohesion tended to be reinforced by the

[13]Major Jewish population centers outside of London are listed in the *Jewish Year Book 1961* (London: Jewish Chronicle Publications, 1961), pp. 192-93.

[14]*Ibid.*, pp. 48-49.

[15]Finestein, *op. cit.*, p. 166; Brotz, *op. cit.*, pp. 158-59.

[16]Maurice Freedman, "Jews in the Society of Britain," in *A Minority in Britain*, p. 213.

continued existence, in flourishing condition, of the London *Jewish Chronicle* as *the* national (although unofficial and privately owned) newspaper of the Anglo-Jewish community.

Not all of the 450,000 British subjects officially counted as Jews can be said to belong to the Jewish community in the sense of being members of synagogues or of other groups represented by the Board of Deputies. Nor, of course, would all belong in the sense of reading the *Jewish Chronicle*. Many have been counted as Jews simply because of their descent and despite the absence of current formal identification. The point is that this is the usual and socially realistic way of defining Jewishness. It takes into account the hard truth that a Jewish family background alone is likely to make one a Jew in the eyes of the rest of the community, Jewish and non-Jewish, and do so in one's own eyes as well. The exceptions tend to be only the very few who have (probably some time ago) passed into the Christian community by an acceptance of the Christian religion or who have otherwise deliberately cut their ties. The much larger number who have only given up religious observances do remain Jews in an important social sense, in Britain as in the United States. They too are members of the Jewish community although they might be regarded as "freeloaders" since they are not usually formal members or active participants. They may very well contribute to Jewish charities and to Zionist causes, while allowing the hard core of formally affiliated Jews to do the collecting and the administering.

Willingness to join or contribute to Zionist causes is one useful measure of Jewish identification that is broader than formal organizational membership and yet not quite so broad as the definition based on the visibility of the Jewish background. Thirty per cent of British Jews, it has been estimated, were directly connected with Zionism in the 1950's, either as contributors or in some other way. Even this substantial number, the estimator believes, understates the importance of Zionist opinion and interest in the Jewish community.[17] Perhaps it is too much to say that all British Jews, when the broadest definition is used, became sympathetic to Israel once it was established, but "almost all" would not seem to be an exaggeration if being pro-Israel is not exactly the same as being Zionist. A minority of Jews, it must be said, carried into the postwar period an older non-Zionist or even anti-Zionist attitude toward the establishment of a Jewish state. This

[17]*Ibid.*, p. 236.

minority was very small and probably diminishing at least as an anti-Zionist force. Since some of its members were among the highly assimilated and successful elite, whatever importance the minority had was greater outside the Jewish community than within it.

So far, from this presentation, British Jews would seem to resemble American Jews both in the manner of their identification as Jews and in their attitudes toward Israel. Yet there is an important difference at least on the second point. Pro-Israeli sentiment was at a relative disadvantage in Britain. This derives not merely from the fact that Jews have been a smaller portion of the total population in Britain and, for this reason as well as because of a less fragmented political system, were not in as strong a position as American Jews to exert pressure on governmental policy. The disadvantage also derives significantly from the more hostile British attitudes engendered during the Palestinian mandate and particularly toward its end, when British soldiers were being killed by Zionist terrorists. Then, in 1947-48, a British Jew might seem to have a divided loyalty in a way that an American Jew need never have felt, since the United States kept itself removed from any direct responsibility during the mandate. It was not easy for a Jew in Britain to champion the prospective establishment of a Jewish national state at a time when Zionists were killing Englishmen as part of a campaign to obtain such a state. This immediate problem accented the difficulty flowing from the view that Jews were not "Englishmen" anyway, but an ethnically alien group that happened to be British subjects. Accordingly, even in the 1950's, when being pro-Israel or even Zionist did not involve the same direct conflict with British policy as it had in 1947-48, overtones of the earlier difficulty remained. To be sure, their significance was a little different in 1956, when Britain seemed on the side of Israel, but even then the responsible leaders of the Anglo-Jewish community could well fear the domestic consequences of a war in which British blood might seem to be shed on behalf of Jews. Any such uneasiness could muffle, if not entirely suppress, a straightforward desire of Jews to welcome British action against Nasser.

All of these complexities must be taken into account in understanding any pro-Israeli pressure on Jewish M.P.s in the Labour party. So must we consider that such pressure would not be felt uniformly. Some Jewish M.P.s were undoubtedly more Jewish than others. And certainly some were more Zionist or pro-Zionist than others. These differences relate to group membership or simply to individual conviction, or to both. A brief accounting of the 17 Labour M.P.s identifiable as Jews—

in the broad social sense previously used—will give an idea of the variety.[18] Notable, in the first place, is that only two represented constituencies whose Jewish populations were large enough to be politically dominant or near dominant. One of these was in Manchester, and the other was the London constituency of Stoke Newington and Hackney North, where the M.P., David Weitzman, was exposed to some open pressure. A third Jewish M.P., Orbach, represented a marginal constituency (Willesden East) in which even a minority of Jews might affect the result.

With the possible exception of these constituencies, especially Stoke Newington and Hackney North, any pro-Israeli pressure on Jewish M.P.s did not come primarily from their own parliamentary electorates. Much more consequential was Jewish group identification in a larger sense. The leading case of such pressure was undoubtedly provided by Barnett Janner, M.P. for Leicester North-West. His Jewish constituents in Leicester were insignificant in numbers and in influence. But he very definitely represented the Anglo-Jewish community in another capacity. He was indeed a major figure in Jewish affairs. Janner was president of the Board of Deputies and president of the Zionist Federation of Great Britain and Ireland. In these posts he was a spokesman on Jewish affairs generally and also particularly in the House of Commons. The latter is in accord with the accepted British parliamentary practice of M.P.s openly acting for interests like the British Legion, coal miners, the textile industry, or various other equally legitimate groups. In fact, their legitimacy was marked by having M.P.s who were often officers of the group and occasionally on the group organization's payroll. Janner was clearly a special kind of

[18]The 17 Jewish M.P.s in the Labour party were Austen Albu, Frank Allaun, Maurice Edelman, Barnett Janner, George Jeger, Harold Lever, Leslie Lever, Marcus Lipton, Ian Mikardo, Maurice Orbach, Emanuel Shinwell, Julius Silverman, Sydney Silverman, George Strauss, Barnett Stross, Moss Turner-Samuels, and David Weitzman. Two other Jewish M.P.s were Conservatives: Sir Henry d'Avigdor-Goldsmid and Sir Keith Joseph. Both of the Conservatives came from high strata of the Anglo-Jewish community and, for that matter, of British society generally. D'Avigdor-Goldsmid bears one of the oldest and most famous of Anglo-Jewish names. As Conservatives, they could obviously support their party without being in conflict with any Jewish pressure. Interestingly, however, Sir Keith Joseph, then a new liberal-minded Conservative M.P., was rumored to have expressed doubts about his party's stand on grounds similar to those of the other moderate Conservatives, some of whom rebelled openly. If so, his situation would have been interesting not only because, as a Jew, he might have been expected to have an additional reason for supporting his party's stand, but also because he represented a Leeds constituency with a large Jewish population.

group representative, and not in the category of paid agent. He did not owe his parliamentary presence to the Jewish community. On the contrary, he owed it to the willingness of a non-Jewish local Labour party in a non-Jewish Labour constituency to adopt him as its candidate. Yet he did also represent, openly and frankly, a national constituency of British Jews. His public importance rested heavily on this representative function. Otherwise, Janner, a prosperous London solicitor in private life, was not an especially conspicuous back-bench M.P. He had never been in a Labour government although his tenure as a Labour M.P. dated from 1945 (after being a Liberal M.P., 1931-35). Nor was Janner identified as a leading figure in any party faction. He seemed a moderate, or even a right-winger, who regularly supported the party leadership.

No one else among the 17 Jews in the parliamentary Labour party had Jewish organizational connections that were nearly as significant as Janner's. Actually only seven others listed any kind of Jewish group membership either in *Who's Who* or in the *Jewish Year Book* (whose biographies were fuller on this score).[19] Of these seven, the most significant connections seemed to be David Weitzman's as president of the North London Lodge of B'nai B'rith, Leslie Lever's as a member of the Board of Deputies and of a number of other Jewish organizations, Maurice Orbach's as general secretary of the Trades Advisory Council (created by the Board of Deputies), Marcus Lipton's as a member of the Board of Deputies and as an officer in the Jewish Ex-Service Association, and Sydney Silverman's as an officer of Zionist organizations. The other two of the seven had organizational connections of a different nature. Barnett Stross simply listed his membership among the Friends of the Art Museums of Israel, and Maurice Edelman his membership on the Council of the Friends of the Hebrew University (in Jerusalem) and of the Council of the assimilationist Anglo-Jewish Association. Neither was regarded as active in the usual Anglo-Jewish affairs. In fact, of the seven only Weitzman and Leslie Lever were likely to be counted along with Janner as very much identified with such affairs.

Nevertheless, the others, including at least some of the nine with no listed Jewish organizational connections, cannot necessarily be said to be without significant Jewish identification. Almost all of the whole

[19]Biographical data here are from 1961 sources except for Turner-Samuels, who died in 1957 and for whom 1956 sources are, therefore, used. The *Jewish Year Book 1961* contains a most useful "Jewish Who's Who" of its own.

group of 17 had backgrounds which were not notably assimilationist in character. While most were born in Britain, they appear usually to be sons of immigrant parents or, at any rate, of parents who, while born in Britain, had not themselves entered the ranks of the privileged, the educated, and the powerful. These M.P.s were likely, in other words, to have been raised as Jews, socially and perhaps religiously, and to have risen markedly, as members of their own generation, in business, professional, or public life. Two almost certain exceptions were George Strauss and Austen Albu, both of whom had gone to the expensive boarding schools which the English call "public schools." Strauss, who had gone to Rugby, had married Patricia O'Flynn, and had been a Labour minister, was the more conspicuous exception. Several of the others had university degrees and subsequent professional careers, but these achievements appeared to be strictly of their own generation and to be compatible with fairly nonassimilationist family backgrounds.

Of considerable import in understanding the cross-pressure situation of the Jewish M.P.s are their respective positions in the factional and ideological conflict within the Labour party during the 1950's. The 17 M.P.s had no position as a Jewish group; indeed, they were not in this sense a group at all. As individuals they ranged from a regular supporter and even a member of the party's moderate leadership, like George Strauss, to extreme left-wing M.P.s, like Ian Mikardo or Sydney Silverman. And there were various degrees of left-wing and right-wing positions between these extremes. Despite the variety, it is true that a substantial number—larger in proportion than was the case for non-Jewish Labour M.P.s—were on the left. This is measured simply enough since 16 of the 17 Jewish M.P.s were in the House during the Bevanite revolt. Of these 16, six were among the 57 Labour M.P.s (out of a total of 295 in the PLP) who openly joined Aneurin Bevan in voting against defense policy in a parliamentary division of March 1952.[20] Later left-wing revolts indicate a similar pattern, as in December 1960, when seven of the 15 Jewish M.P.s (from the group of 17 still in the House) were among the 72 abstainers on a crucial defense issue.[21] The significance of such a tendency, in the Suez context, derives from the likelihood that a left-wing M.P. would have been subject to even stronger partisan ideological influence to oppose Suez than would an ordinary Labour M.P., and thus would have been

[20]497 *H. C. Deb.* 559-60 (5 March 1952).
[21]632 *H. C. Deb.* 351 (13 December 1960). The 72 abstainers are listed in the *Daily Herald* (London), 13 December 1960.

particularly unlikely to be influenced in the opposite direction by any Jewish identification.

Generally, the M.P.s with the strongest identification with Jewish affairs were not the left-wingers. Neither Janner nor Leslie Lever were of the left, and David Weitzman, the third of the group of most prominent activists in the Jewish community, was not regularly or importantly a left-winger. On the other hand, the clearly left-wing M.P.s, Sydney Silverman and Ian Mikardo, were not so conspicuous in Anglo-Jewish affairs although both had been outspokenly favorable to Israel. In addition, Sydney Silverman had a record as an officer in Zionist organizations. Their situations during the Suez crisis do, therefore, have a special interest. So, for another reason, does Emanuel Shinwell's. By 1956, Shinwell was no longer of the PLP leadership, but he had been in the party's front rank for many years. He had been the first Jew to be a Labour M.P., and his service included cabinet posts in Labour governments. Now over 70 but still vigorous, Shinwell had by no means resigned himself to a benign elder statesman role in the PLP. On the contrary, he stood outside the party's new middle-class intellectual leadership, and he was capable of opposing the leadership, although not exactly from the left-wing viewpoint. Shinwell's background did not include Jewish organizational activity, but rather the trade-union and socialist activism usual in his generation of Labour leaders who had risen with the party. He had been assimilated as a Labour activist if not as an upper-class Englishman. Nevertheless, Shinwell was plainly sympathetic with Israel, and in many respects prepared to assume an independent position.

3. PARLIAMENTARY BEHAVIOR AND ITS CONSEQUENCES

There can be little suspense about the actual behavior of the Jewish M.P.s in the Suez crisis. It is evident, from an earlier chapter, that the Jews, like virtually all of their PLP colleagues, stayed in line with Labour policy. What remains, then, is to discuss certain minor and halting deviations and, more important, to explain how the Jewish M.P.s justified their adherence to the anti-Suez line when cross-pressure did exist. Jewish M.P.s responded without exception to the three-line whip in the divisions of 1 and 8 November. All 17 voted on 1 November, and all but one (Shinwell, by then traveling abroad) voted on 8 November. Only in the unexpected division of 30 October could there have been deliberate abstentions. On that occasion, when failure to vote would not necessarily have meant a clear-cut violation of party discipline, seven of the 17 Jews were unrecorded. Of these seven, Shinwell and Harold Lever made it clear, by their presence or their statements, that they had deliberately abstained. At least one other is alleged to have thus abstained, and this seems probable since among those not voting were two M.P.s, Janner and Weitzman, with records of activism in Jewish affairs.[22] It was easy, on 30 October, for a Jewish M.P. to resolve his doubts, or to meet any cross-pressure, simply by not talking and not voting. Shinwell and Harold Lever went further by speaking in such a way as to indicate that their nonvoting was deliberate abstention.

The situation on 30 October was, as already noted, especially likely to present cross-pressure in an acute form. Not only was the parliamentary division unexpected and therefore less clearly disciplined, but it took place just after the British veto had been used on the side of Israel in the United Nations but just before British military forces were actually engaged. The Egyptian-Israeli war was still the major event. In this circumstance, opinion with respect to British action was more fluid than it became during the first week of November. It was then, at the beginning of the crisis, that individual views might more readily be expressed within the Labour party. Some of these views persisted, however, throughout the subsequent week.

Shinwell provides a special example. Before abstaining on 30 October from voting for Labour's motion against the government, he attacked the Conservatives for having failed earlier to counter Arab threats and aggression against Israel. He found Eden's present ultimatum ambiguous.[23] He opposed the subsequent British military action at least by his vote on 1 November. But still later, during Commonwealth travels that accounted for his absence from the House on 8 November and afterward, Shinwell made statements in support of Eden's action and in defiance of Labour's continued critique of the Suez campaign. From Singapore, Shinwell was quoted as saying that Anglo-French intervention was "justified because of the United Nations delay in taking prompt decisions and action."[24] He added that his vote with his party (presumably on 1 November) did not necessarily mean that he disagreed with everything the government did. From Australia, several days later, Shinwell took an even more definitely

[22]The seven unrecorded Jewish Labour M.P.s were Albu, Janner, H. Lever, L. Lever, Shinwell, Turner-Samuels, and Weitzman. The other ten Jewish Labour M.P.s voted for the Labour motion. 558 *H. C. Deb.* 1377-82 (30 October 1956).

[23]558 *H. C. Deb.* 1278-81 (30 October 1956).

[24]*Times* (London), 10 November 1956, p. 5.

progovernment position. Now he spoke proudly of his abstention, presumably on 30 October, and specifically championed Israel while expressing contempt for "those Jews, including British M.P.s, who, though professed Zionists, claim to see in Israel's action an offence against international law."[25] As might have been expected, these statements by an ex-minister were well publicized in the British press. Taken together with the proud display of his 30 October abstention, the statements made Shinwell the nearest thing to a rebel of any Jewish M.P. in the Suez crisis. In fact, it is hard to reconcile his remarks in Singapore and Australia with his vote in the Labour lobby on 1 November. The most that could be said in behalf of Shinwell's consistency in this respect is that the Labour motion of 1 November deplored only Britain's and not Israel's action.

Harold Lever, the other known deliberate abstainer of 30 October,[26] made a different kind of Suez record from Shinwell's. Lever, while he began by stating an especially open pro-Israeli case, did not publicly dissent from his party's position after 30-31 October. Lever voted in the divisions of 1 and 8 November. Yet he could be suspected of continued party disloyalty on the basis of his parliamentary speech of 31 October, following his abstention of the day before. This speech is notable for its exposition of the difficulty and ambiguity of the position of a Jewish Labour M.P. who wanted to support both Israel and his party. Lever explicitly denied that Israel was an aggressor, and consequently he applauded Britain's use of the veto in the United Nations and generally the apparent alignment of Britain with Israel.[27] This put him at odds with his party on at least one score, but admittedly not now the major one. For Lever hedged on whether to support Britain's own military action. He said that he would welcome it "if it could be properly supported as being within our other obligations under the United Nations."[28] Claiming doubt on the last point, Lever stated that he could not support the government's action. He made it abundantly clear, however, that he appreciated the action even though he could not support it. Lever was glad that the "identity of British interest with the State of Israel has at last belatedly been recognized."[29]

[25]*Jewish Chronicle* (London), 16 November 1956, p. 1.

[26]Lever was later quoted: "I deliberately abstained because I could not by a vote unequivocally support some of the statements made from my side of the House." *Glasgow Herald*, 31 October 1956, p. 7.

[27]558 *H. C. Deb.* 1487 (31 October 1956).

[28]558 *H. C. Deb.* 1493 (31 October 1956).

[29]558 *H. C. Deb.* 1493 (31 October 1956).

That there was such an identity was, incidentally, Lever's defense in response to a Labour colleague's accusing question as to whether Lever was "here speaking as an Israeli nationalist first, foremost, and all the time?"[30] This was but one kind of argument brought to bear within the Labour party against a wavering pro-Israeli M.P. The other argument, but this one itself pro-Israel, was that the Eden government was a poor and untrustworthy ally for Israel.

The two Jewish M.P.s furthest to the left did not seem to waver despite their pro-Israeli views. Both Sydney Silverman and Ian Mikardo voted against the government in all three divisions. They did find it necessary on 30 October to explain their positions by rather special lines of reasoning. Silverman referred specifically to his own sympathy for Israel's position, but said that the general interest was better served by peace in the Middle East.[31] Mikardo had a more ingenious argument. Israel, he said, was not moving to the Suez Canal but only across the Sinai Peninsula to try to demilitarize it.[32] Therefore, Eden was not helping Israel or even doing anything to stop the fighting by moving British troops to the canal zone. All Eden was doing, Mikardo implied, was to carry out his own plan with respect to the canal. If he wanted to help Israel and really contribute to peace in the Middle East, Eden should add his influence to a guarantee of demilitarization of the Sinai Peninsula.[33]

Distinguishing the British government's actions and motives from those of Israel was plainly necessary for any pro-Israeli M.P. who supported his party's position. This is what Barnett Janner did most carefully and fully on 6 November. It was he more than any other M.P. who was addressing British Jews as well as Labour colleagues and followers. His task was not an easy one. While he could surely say, as he did, that the Anglo-French action was not undertaken purely in the interests of Israel, he could hardly deny that "in the result the position was that there was not some help to Israel." In fact, this much he had to admit specifically in response to a Conservative statement about the benefits to Israel which resulted from the Anglo-French destruction of the Egyptian air force. "No one," Janner granted, "would be foolish enough to say that the circumstances, wrong as they

[30]558 *H. C. Deb.* 1488 (31 October 1956).

[31]558 *H. C. Deb.* 1285-86 (30 October 1956).

[32]This interpretation was by no means improbable. O'Ballance's later account is similar. *Op. cit.*, p. 79.

[33]558 *H. C. Deb.* 1359-60 (30 October 1956).

were in which this action was taken, did not give some kind of assistance."[34] Yet his principal point was that it was unfortunate that the Israeli action had been mixed up with the Anglo-French movement to the canal zone. He specifically rejected the collusion charge that some Labour M.P.s were making. Israel, he declared, had never wanted British soldiers to risk their lives for Israel. All that Israel had wanted from Britain as from America were the necessary defensive arms. Accordingly, Britain's United Nations veto was appreciated as right enough since the Israeli attack was assumed to be justified as a response to aggression and threats of aggression. What was wrong, as Janner saw it, was Anglo-French military action despite its admittedly helpful result for Israel.

It was this matter of help that made the issue an agonizing one. No matter how unintentionally, the British government was helping the Israeli cause. Trying to bring down Nasser would itself have been interpreted as helpful. Therefore, pro-Israeli M.P.s in the Labour party necessarily seemed to oppose such British help when they voted with their party. For non-Jewish but pro-Israeli M.P.s, it is true, the problem must have been minor if it existed at all. They did not feel called upon to do any explaining. The most that they suffered was the Conservative charge that they, particularly the Labour leaders, had now deserted the Jews after having supported them before. As one Conservative said, "it is a very cruel thing that the Israelis, in this hour of their tribulation, in this hour when every hand is turned against them, should find that many of the voices to which they have been used to listen have been silent. . . ."[35] The barb was by no means enough to shake the position of the Labour leaders generally. For instance, Hugh Gaitskell, whose previous record was pro-Israeli and whose wife, incidentally, was Jewish, was not shaken at all. He even implied that Israel as well as Britain was wrong when he made his much-quoted statement that what Eden had done, rather than acting as a policeman, "was to go in and help the burglar and shoot the householder."[36] Although Gaitskell and his fellow party leaders did

[34]560 *H. C. Deb.* 55 (6 November 1956).

[35]Captain Waterhouse, 558 *H. C. Deb.* 1660-61 (1 November 1956). Before thus criticizing Labour M.P.s for deserting Israel, Waterhouse (whose Suez group views were previously discussed) explained that he had never defended the Jews, had never "set up as being a Zionist," and that, if anything, his sympathies "lay with the Arabs. . . ." 558 *H. C. Deb.* 1664 (1 November 1956).

[36]558 *H. C. Deb.* 1866 (3 November 1956). Gaitskell's remark was not part of a speech but was rather an interjection between comments by Eden.

subsequently resume their pro-Israeli positions,[37] there is no doubt that the candor of the burglar remark made matters harder for the Jewish M.P.s for whom sympathy for Israel was more important than it was for their party leaders. Jewish M.P.s in the Labour party were identified, despite their own disclaimers, with a party position hostile, at least by implication, to the Israeli action as well as to the British action.

In this circumstance, some reaction from the Anglo-Jewish community had to be expected. Not only would Jews generally sympathize with the Israeli action, but those without close Labour ties would almost certainly welcome the end of what they had regarded as Eden's policy of appeasing the Arabs. For example, despite expressed doubts about the results of Eden's decision, the *Jewish Chronicle* editorialized just after that decision was taken: "Now that the Government has shown the courage to reverse its previous policy its critics oppose it mercilessly." After all, the *Chronicle* added, Eden's government was now doing what its pro-Israeli critics had so frequently demanded, and it seemed "a little harsh that it should be subjected to such a gruelling onslaught by the Labour Opposition."[38] The matter was more pointedly brought to the attention of the Jewish community in the *Chronicle*'s news stories of the following week. One item quoted an East End London rabbi's sharp criticism of the behavior of Jewish M.P.s. In such a crisis, the rabbi said, "Jewish representatives in the Houses of Parliament should not allow themselves to forget their racial origins, irrespective of their political affiliations."[39] Such language was, it is true, extreme as well as offensive in its elevation of Jewish nationalism above both British national and Labour party loyalties. Much less blunt and direct was the *Chronicle*'s long summary story on the parliamentary behavior of Jewish M.P.s. Its lead sentences were:

Amid the vociferous protests of the Labour party against the Government's attitude in the Israel-Egypt clash, Jewish Labour M.P.s were in a difficult position.

The Party Whips won the day, for, to a man, the Jewish members of the Labour Party in Parliament voted against the British and French military intervention in the Middle East.[40]

[37]Examples may be found in speeches by Hugh Dalton and by Aneurin Bevan, 561 *H. C. Deb.* 1293-94 (5 December 1956); 566 *H. C. Deb.* 1337-40 (14 March 1957).

[38]*Jewish Chronicle* (London), 2 November 1956, p. 14.

[39]*Ibid.*, 9 November 1956, p. 5.

[40]*Ibid.*, p. 8.

These remarks were followed by a list of the 17 Jewish M.P.s in the Labour party and by a detailed accounting of their votes during the critical week. The *Chronicle* story carefully discriminated between the parliamentary division of 30 October and the subsequent ones carrying a three-line whip. It was even explained that it was perilous for an M.P. to ignore a three-line whip by voting against his party or by abstaining.

It cannot be said, in light of this reporting, that the *Chronicle* was deliberately stirring its readers to react against Jewish M.P.s. On the contrary, it seems to have been trying, in its main story, to limit the reaction. The paper could not very well be blamed for printing the facts and for printing, as well, a rabbi's attack on Jewish M.P.s and several similarly critical letters (out of many received). [41] Even without any inspiration from the *Chronicle*, however, the Jewish community was certain to be aroused. To make sure that it was, the strenuously and unrestrainedly pro-Suez Beaverbrook press took a hand. Its popular *Sunday Express* columnist, Cross-Bencher, devoted much of a column during the crisis to attacking Jewish M.P.s as well as Gaitskell. The theme of the attack was that it was unexpected and wrong for them not to have supported Israel. Gaitskell was thus subjected to the same criticism as the Jewish M.P.s, since, as Cross-Bencher pointed out, Gaitskell's wife was Jewish and his father-in-law has been "an enthusiastic Zionist all his life." How fantastic, the columnist said, to find Gaitskell "cheering on the cause of Egypt." Also explicitly mentioned as anomalously on Nasser's side were four of the Jewish M.P.s—Silverman, Mikardo, Allaun, and Orbach. Why only these four were mentioned is not clear, but it did happen that each represented a distinctly marginal seat won by a small majority in 1955. In fact, Mikardo and Orbach lost their seats when the next general election did finally come in 1959. But the *Express* was not aiming at any political effect as far off as 1959. There was some cause to expect a general election immediately after the Suez crisis, and, given that contingency, Cross-Bencher aimed specifically at Orbach: ". . . this is the fellow who relies on the Jewish vote to keep him in his shaky Willesden seat. . . . When the next election comes in the New Year, let the Jews of Willesden recall the present performance of Mr. Orbach." [42]

No evidence is at hand to indicate that this threat of Jewish reprisal would have materialized if there had been an early general election.

[41]*Ibid.*, p. 23.
[42]*Sunday Express* (London), 4 November 1956, p. 6.

But a different and more immediate threat did take shape against Barnett Janner. It was directed at his position as president of the Board of Deputies and of the Zionist Federation. Various Zionist groups attacked Janner for failing at least to have abstained from voting in the Labour lobby during the Suez crisis (after 30 October). The culmination of these attacks was a discussion of Janner's position by the Board of Deputies on 18 November. Here Janner defended himself, mainly by trying to distinguish between the Israeli action and the British action. He was upheld by a large majority expressing full confidence in him as Board president. The discussion, however, was "heated," and Janner's critics insisted that to be against British action, which destroyed Nasser's air force, was to be against Israel's interest too.[43] To be sure, Janner's leadership of the Anglo-Jewish community survived, but to have suffered the attack at all was a substantial price to pay for maintaining party regularity.

Party regularity was not the argument that Jewish M.P.s themselves used to justify their position. They preferred to respond, as did Mikardo to a journalist's inquiry as to whether his loyalties were not strained by the Middle East crisis, by saying that they represented the citizens of their respective electoral constituencies. This is the remark that Maurice Edelman quoted at the start of an article he wrote specifically on "The Loyalties Question." Edelman thought that he and other Jewish M.P.s had, as British citizens, "an unquestionable and undivided loyalty: that is to Britain."[44] They might still, Edelman believed, have a concern for Israel and also dislike Nasser, without necessarily condoning the particular Israeli action. His main point, in any case, was that the Jewish M.P. was responsible for judging the British government as a British citizen.

Edelman's view about an M.P.'s responsibility was the only right one. Certainly it was the only one that an M.P. could openly proclaim no matter what opinion he had about Suez. But, within the Jewish community, it was likely to appeal mainly to the sophisticated assimilationist. Thus a Jewish M.P. concerned with Jewish constituents could more clearly defend his anti-Suez stand by stressing, in Janner's manner, the distinction between Israeli and British actions, and by being careful, unlike Edelman, to say nothing against the Israeli attack. David Weitzman, representing (as noted) a heavily Jewish district in North London, provides a good case in point. Speaking just

[43] *Jewish Chronicle* (London), 23 November 1956, p. 1.
[44] *Ibid.*, 9 November 1956, p. 16.

after the crisis week, he attacked the Eden government for having used the Israeli action as an excuse to seize the canal. Relying on Israel's case for the British government's own action was hypocritical, Weitzman said. There was in his mind no justification for Britain using force. But he could not subscribe "to any suggestion that Israel, in any sense of the term, can be described as an aggressor."[45] To make the distinction stick, Weitzman not only had to deny the collusion charges made by some of his Labour colleagues, he had also to insist that even coincidentally or inadvertently Eden was not going to help Israel. He had some aid on this score when Mikardo came to Weitzman's constituency in mid-November. Mikardo said that if Eden had succeeded in bringing down Nasser, then in order to do something dramatic to regain Arab favor, Eden would have had no hesitation in "selling Israel down the river once again."[46] British intervention might thus have done more harm than good—a view echoed later by another Jewish M.P.—on the assumption that Nasser was likely to have fallen without Anglo-French action.[47] In all this, the Jewish M.P.s were well served by Eden's previous reputation for hostility to Israel. They did not hesitate to point out that neither Eden nor his principal supporters had records as friends of the Jews.

It can be observed, therefore, that to survive Jewish reactions, in or out of one's constituency, was not very difficult for Jewish M.P.s who had adhered to the Labour opposition. Surely their troubles were less acute than they would have been if they had deserted their party even to the extent of abstaining in a division subject to a three-line whip. Stanley Evans' experience, as a non-Jewish Labour dissenter, ought to be convincing on this score.[48] A Jewish M.P. representing non-Jewish constituents could not have expected any gentler treatment. One Jewish M.P. said as much, admittedly only in confidence.[49] He did not, it is true, say that it was any such anticipated demand for his resignation by his divisional Labour party that kept him from abstaining. He merely said that abstention would have produced the demand. One can only guess as to the influence of the anticipation on the M.P.'s parliamentary voting behavior.

More direct evidence of the possible consequence of party rebellion

[45]560 *H. C. Deb.* 437 (9 November 1956).
[46]*Jewish Chronicle* (London), 16 November 1956, p. 8.
[47]Barnett Stross, 561 *H. C. Deb.* 1520 (6 December 1956).
[48]See Chapter Six.
[49]In an interview with the author.

comes from the experience of Emanuel Shinwell, who, it will be re-called, was the Jewish M.P. who departed most from his party's position by praising Eden's action in statements made from abroad. For this aberration, Shinwell was subsequently called before his divisional party for an explanation. He did satisfy his local leaders, but the significant point is that Shinwell had to explain at all.[50] He had voted with his party in the only whipped Suez division that occurred while he was in the country. Moreover, he had been the M.P. for virtually the same Durham mining constituency since 1935, an M.P. for another constituency even earlier, a member of the Labour party for 53 years, and in the recent past both a cabinet member and a national leader. If even Shinwell had trouble, however slight, with his local party leaders, it is likely that any other deviating Jewish M.P., especially one more clearly Zionist or pro-Zionist than Shinwell, would have had a great deal more trouble in any ordinary constituency situation. This would have been probable if the M.P. deviated to the extent of abstaining in a whipped division.

4. How Much Cross-Pressure?

The fact that Jewish M.P.s did stay in line with their party is clear. But from this it might be possible to say either that Jewish M.P.s refused to yield to cross-pressure against Labour's position, in part at least because of fear of constituency reprisals, or that there was really no very strong cross-pressure to begin with. The latter possibility cannot be discounted completely since there is no way to measure the degree of cross-pressure so as to be absolutely convincing about its significance. Enough has been said, however, for it to seem likely that at least a few Jewish M.P.s were personally, socially, or politically in situations that made for cross-pressure against their party positions. Conse-quently it is fair to speak of their successfully resisting the cross-pressure except, as has been observed, for fairly minor qualifications and excep-tions. The cross-pressure, it is worth noting again, could well have been in the form of individual convictions and identifications rather than crude external influences. And with respect to the internalized form it is almost certain that most Jews would have had some significant feeling of sympathy for Israel and some desire to welcome British help regardless of its motivation.

[50] *Times* (London), 12 January 1957, p. 6.

Accepting, then, this line of reasoning, in accord with the qualified case made in this chapter, one reaches the conclusion that British party loyalty has been shown, in yet another way, to have been the durable factor in determining political behavior during the Suez crisis. Partisan lines were no more substantially broken by the cross-pressure of a vital minority than by any other cause. Jewish objections within the Labour opposition represented interesting undercurrents, but still undercurrents except for minor and halting appearances here and there during the crisis.

CHAPTER NINE

The Political System

Before a summary analysis of the way in which the British political system worked under the strain of the Suez crisis, it is useful to recall the significance of the issue in recent British history. It was partly because the issue was so deeply significant that it produced so much strain.

For many decades, Britain's role in world affairs was one of the subjects dividing Englishmen along partisan lines. Suez, in this respect, dramatized a continuing but ordinarily less conspicuous division between the upholders of imperial responsibility, chiefly in the Conservative party, and the opponents of traditional power politics, now chiefly in the Labour party. In other words, the part Britain was to play in the world, and particularly how this part was to be played, constituted a focal point in British politics, despite the fact that foreign and imperial policy did not always, or even usually, dominate party ideologies. Thus, although Labour in particular was organized primarily around domestic economic concerns, many of its partisans had a distinctive orientation toward foreign affairs. Certainly much of the Labour leadership did have intellectual commitments with respect to British overseas policy. The Conservative outlook is plainer, however, for the rank and file as well as for party leaders. Imperialism, as has been observed, was even a kind of Conservative ideological cement comparable to socialism in the Labour party. Moreover, it was not just imperialism in the narrow sense that Conservatives cherished. They also regarded their party as the custodian generally for Britain's greatness in world affairs and for the proper discharge of the responsi‧bility that went with greatness.

Through the Suez crisis, the nature of British controversy over the nation's role was not usually over the simple question of whether Britain should be a great power. On the contrary, both sides tended to take such status for granted. The dispute was over the way in which Britain as a great power should behave. Whatever the real facts, even at Suez British critics of intervention seldom argued that the nation was too weak to have acted aggressively. The argument instead was mainly that Britain had acted wrongly and perhaps foolishly. It is understandable that the British in the mid-1950's should still have regarded their nation as a great power. Only very recently Britain had in fact been great in the eyes of the whole world. Now, after an apparent recovery from the austerity and weakness of the immediate postwar period, Britain might well have seemed able to resume some of its old international responsibilities as well as to retain some responsibilities, notably in the Middle East, that it had never fully relinquished. Suez was not the only sign of Britain's world power aspirations in the 1950's. Retention of the imperial ideal, even in its new Commonwealth form, was another. It was not just the Suez group which thought that the national future lay in leadership of the residual Empire. In fact, much of the community, without appreciating the Suez group's conviction that military power was essential to such leadership, believed that Britain could somehow find its place in the world as the leader of the more than 600,000,000 people of the Commonwealth. The decision in 1955 to become a nuclear power reflected the old aspiration.[1]

Although the Suez controversy was thus conducted in Britain under the assumption that the nation remained a great power with imperial responsibility, it must also be stressed that Suez may have been the last great controversy to be so conducted. The old imperial issue, partly perhaps because of the failure at Suez, seemed to have lost its relevance as Britain turned, in the 1960's, to attempt to arrange entry into an integrating Western Europe. The terms of British debate over foreign affairs began to shift from the old imperial and overseas context to a more limited frame of reference.[2] There remain only flickers of the old debate with reference to the final liquidation of British control in

---

[1]The prestige factor in Britain's decision to manufacture the hydrogen bomb is discussed in the author's "Britain and the H-Bomb, 1955-1958," *Review of Politics*, Vol. 21, pp. 511-29 (July 1959).

[2]The consequences of status decline were amusingly but significantly discussed in articles entitled "Learning to Be a 2nd Class Power," *Punch*, Vol. 234, pp. 451-54 (2 April 1958).

Central and East Africa. The clash of imperial and anti-imperial outlooks, affecting British politics off and on since the 1880's, seems unlikely to be vital in the future. The Suez crisis appears to be the last
major mark of a political era. The absence of such subject matter would
mean an eventual change in the basis for partisan alignments. The
Conservative party, in particular, would lose one of its principal
rallying points: the defense of imperial interests and the maintenance of
greatness in world affairs. The importance of such a loss is emphasized
by the intensity of the Conservative partisan commitment in support of
Eden's interventionist policy. In the future, without any greatness to
conserve, it has even been predicted that the Conservative party's
appeal would decline.[3] Or, at least as likely, the party appeal would be
changed and, as in times past, with success. But this is to speculate
about prospective developments. The fact remains that Suez provided
an occasion for the British political system to respond to controversy
over the old and then still lively imperial issue.

As the events of the Suez crisis have been presented, the most striking
general feature of the political system's operation was the maintenance
of the government and its policy by a strictly party majority in the
House of Commons. This feature was striking, however, not because it
was unusual in recent British experience. On the contrary, the effective
functioning of a cohesive parliamentary majority party, along with a
cohesive opposition party, was now the prime characteristic of British
politics—certainly in the era of mainly two-party competition between
Labour and the Conservatives. What was notable, then, about the
Suez controversy was that its political shape did conform to the contemporary partisan norm, even in an extended or exaggerated way,
despite the otherwise unusual aspects of the issue. It is testimony to the
strength of the British political mold of the 1950's that it contained
the Suez conflict within the established channels of government majority versus opposition minority. This was accomplished although
Suez was a foreign policy issue of a type, involving a military commitment, not always dominated by partisan alignments in modern
democratic practice. Furthermore, the Suez commitment was made
without advance mobilization of even majority parliamentary party
support, and despite knowledge that a substantial number of the
government's majority would have disapproved of the commitment if
consulted in advance.

[3]Peregrine Worsthorne, "Class and Conflict in British Foreign Policy," *Foreign
Affairs*, Vol. 37, pp. 419-31 (April 1959).

The last point indicates another important feature of the political system in the Suez crisis: the way in which the crucial decision was made by the executive authority. There is some doubt, as noted in Chapter Five, about the extent to which Prime Minister Eden shared the decision-making with his cabinet. The whole cabinet, it seems likely, was not involved until a fairly late stage (perhaps 25 October or even 30 October), when the Anglo-French commitment might have seemed practically irrevocable. In this perspective, Eden shared his decision-making only with a few key congenial ministers, and, since these ministers were distinctly of his own choosing, he was really the decision-maker. If so, it is well to appreciate that the practice would have been consistent with the tendency, in contemporary British affairs, for the Prime Minister to be a genuine chief executive and not just the first among equals.[4] British executive authority may have become prime ministerial, almost presidential in this respect, rather than collegial in the classical sense of cabinet government. The tendency would surely be in line with what seems to have happened elsewhere in response to the exigencies of policy-making, particularly in foreign affairs, in the mid-twentieth century.

Regardless of the still disputed matter of Eden's relations with his cabinet in late October, there can be no question that the Suez commitment was an executive decision rather than a parliamentary one.[5] Constitutionally, to be sure, this is hardly surprising. It is in accord with both principle and practice in Britain for foreign policy to be made by the executive. Even in the United States, with its presidential-congressional division of powers, the practice if not the principle is for executive determination of foreign policy. But what did seem an aberration from democratic practice, British or American, was for the executive to have committed the nation to war without learning the extent to which the community was prepared to support the commitment, or, knowing this support to be less than that of genuine majority agreement, to have gone ahead anyway. This was hardly in accord with the foreign policy-making model ordinarily thought to prevail in modern Western democracies, although the critics of this working model, like Walter Lippmann, seem to prefer the unfettered executive

[4]John P. Mackintosh, *The British Cabinet* (Toronto: University of Toronto Press, 1962), p. 436.

[5]What is not explored here is the possibility, frequently suggested in private conversations by public persons, that the Prime Minister had become an "odd man" during the Suez crisis.

direction of a responsible leadership.[6] But it should be noted that the Suez intervention, while hardly a monument to successful leadership, does not refute the case for the unfettered executive. Nor does it prove that overwhelming popular support, perhaps determined in advance, is essential for the successful prosecution of a foreign policy involving a military commitment. The fact is that the absence of greater domestic support cannot be established as a crucial factor in the failure of Suez intervention.

Instead, as has been demonstrated, the government was supported in the way that actually counted: by its partisan majority in Parliament. Party solidarity was sufficient to back the government on its decision to intervene and on its later decision to withdraw. Thus parliamentary government in Britain now meant, if it had not before, that a Prime Minister and his cabinet could count on a party majority to support, almost unanimously, their policy both when many parliamentary party members had grave doubts and when that policy subsequently failed. The significance of parliamentary partisanship in this respect is illustrated by the widespread belief that a hypothetical "free vote" in the Commons, before party lines were drawn, would have resulted in a majority against the projected military action. But free votes were, by definition, not allowed on government policy. And Parliament simply did not operate, as it had in the mid-nineteenth century, to overthrow a government. Rather, it functioned so as to debate and criticize the government, but still to support it in the final analysis. The support, derived from the contemporary rigidity of the two-party division, made possible a partisan foreign policy that may be almost uniquely British. Other nations, with less cohesive major parties, might be ill-equipped to maintain such a policy. The United States, although its foreign policy is largely in the hands of an executive whose tenure does not require continuous legislative approval, would face a serious problem in trying to manage a partisan policy supported only by a single American-style uncohesive party. At some point the support of Congress would be needed and this might not be so nearly automatic as British party loyalty makes parliamentary approval.[7] In this respect, an American President may be more in need of prior political support for his actions than a British Prime Minister, and so be more "re-

[6]Walter Lippmann, *The Public Philosophy* (Boston: Little, Brown & Co., 1955).

[7]This seems close to Max Beloff's view of the relative influence of the American legislature. *Foreign Policy and the Democratic Process* (Baltimore: Johns Hopkins Press, 1955).

sponsible" to public opinion. Responsibility to Parliament means little if the majority always feels politically compelled to support decisions even when made solely by the executive.

There is also some doubt about the efficacy of the debating and criticizing function of the British parliamentary process. This is not just a matter of party loyalties precluding the fall of a government as a result of effective debating points. It is also worth asking how suitable the British parliamentary style is for clarifying governmental policy. The much-cherished question period never succeeded in obtaining for M.P.s the crucial information on British military plans before the commitment was made, or any confidential reports after the event— even long after the event. No real parliamentary inquiry ever took place. Therefore, from the standpoint of an effective opposition at least, there might be more to be said for the American legislative committee system. It does provide, especially in Congress, an independent opportunity to press the executive both before and after policy commitments are made.

Despite the apparent absence of opposition accomplishments in Parliament, it is possible that the intense partisan criticism would have been consequential if the government had continued its brief military campaign for several months instead of having to stop for what seemed essentially international reasons. In that event, would the partisan opposition, bolstered by a large portion of independent "informed opinion," have prevented the successful conduct of a longer, more expensive war, inevitably meaning economic hardships at home? Certainly, in that context, the opposition of representatives of nearly half the community would seem to be a more substantial factor than it was during the short week of actual hostilities. The strictly partisan policy, in other words, might not have been viable over a much longer period. Perhaps partly in recognition of this, Eden had planned on a short war, if not quite as short as the aborted intervention. He could not have counted on public opinion moving in his direction during continued hostilities. The fact that it did do so, according to the polls, just after hostilities ended was no sign that the same thing would have happened in more adverse circumstances. The partisan attack might have been more effective as long as it was aimed at ending a war still going on.

Turning back to the main theme of parliamentary partisanship during the crisis, it is important to relate the behavior of the constituency associations to that partisanship. Demonstrably, despite the limited assortment of cases examined, the leaders and most active members of these associations displayed intense partisan commitments on the Suez issue. That they did so, and in greater degree than ordinary party voters, is in accord with what we know about participants in party affairs. Those more active or involved are generally likely to be in more marked conformity with party doctrine than those less active or involved.[8] And those who are active or involved in strictly party associations may be more rigidly orthodox than their elected national representatives, who, while in a way even more active and involved, are nevertheless exposed to sophisticated crosscurrents of opinion. Whatever the reason, on Suez the local Conservative and Labour activists appear to have been strongly in accord with their respective party doctrines. Moreover, it was not just because the pro-Suez and anti-Suez lines were national party doctrines that activists supported those positions. Rather, as shown particularly by Conservative cases, the party activists themselves had views on Suez that were decidedly in accord with the policies of their national leaders.

From the consequent intensification of constituency association opinion, there was, in effect, a reinforcement of the parliamentary alignment over Suez. This is not to say that partisan lines in the Commons would have held any less firmly without association pressure, or threat of association pressure, on M.P.s. There is really no way to know whether more M.P.s would have revolted, or whether those who did revolt would have revolted more persistently and seriously, in the absence of possible local retaliation by those who controlled the candidate selection process. The best guess is that there were probably enough other pressures, mainly parliamentary, to have kept M.P.s in line over Suez. Nevertheless, the crisis did reveal at least a considerable association potential for helping to secure partisan conformity in Parliament. It was, it must be stressed, a potential to secure one kind of conformity: that which represented both the policy of the national leaders and the ideological preference of party militancy. Only the deviation toward the political enemy, as perceived nationally and locally, was subject to punishment at association hands.[9]

Yet this much association pressure is significant. It cannot readily be dismissed simply because there is little evidence of such pressure except

[8]V. O. Key, Jr., *Public Opinion and American Democracy* (New York: Knopf, 1961), p. 442.
[9]The broad problem of controlling moderates and extremists, in any party or movement, is analyzed by Zbigniew Brzezinski, "Deviation Control," *American Political Science Review*, Vol. 56, pp. 5-22 (March 1962).

in the Suez cases. Suez, it may be granted, was an exceptionally emotive occasion, much more likely to produce association reprisals than any ordinary issue. M.P.s are not customarily thus affected by their associations. But, on the other hand, M.P.s do not, on any important issue, ordinarily deviate from their parliamentary parties in the manner of the ten anti-Suez Conservatives and the one pro-Suez Labour M.P. That is, M.P.s do not ordinarily deviate against their parliamentary party's position and, at the same time, against the ideological commitments (to party generally and to the given policy in particular) of their association activists. The usual absence of such deviation may stem from reasons other than constituency association relations. But suppose that those reasons did not exist or were not sufficient to keep certain M.P.s in line (as they were not for the few Suez rebels). Would not the associations then be consequential?

Enough has been suggested here to indicate the relevance of the constituency association pressure, as displayed over Suez, to an understanding of the larger political system. That such pressure should be part of the system has not, however, been generally accepted. Accordingly, after Suez the associations were severely criticized by the British intellectual establishment, including academics, M.P.s themselves, and leader writers for most of the serious national press. The editorial comment of the *Times* was typical; the Bournemouth affair, it said, left "a nasty taste in the mouths of all who are concerned to see representatives of integrity, and no mere delegates, sitting in the House of Commons."[10] The *Times* quoted Burke, as did almost all critics of the associations. But plainly this Burkean view of how M.P.s should function does not correspond to the realities of contemporary British party politics; nor, as Burke himself learned, did it correspond with the way politics worked even in late eighteenth-century Bristol.[11] True, the modern British Burkeans would not deny the democratic electorate's power eventually to get rid of an M.P. whose convictions differ from its own. What is objected to is that the small portion of the electorate composing a local party's leadership should have this power, and that it should use it in the manner of a lynch mob in immediate retaliation

[10]*Times* (London), 3 October 1958, p. 7.

[11]What actually happened to Burke is worth looking at along with his more familiar classic apologia. There is a most judicious account by Ernest Barker, "Burke and His Bristol Constituency, 1774-1780," in his *Essays on Government* (London: Oxford University Press, 1951), chap. 6. More details are supplied in a somewhat antiquarian manner by G. E. Weare, *Edmund Burke's Connection with Bristol, from 1774 till 1780* (Bristol: Wm. Bennett, 1894).

against a deviating M.P. This latter point about method, while much was made of it concerning Nicolson and Evans, does not seem crucial. The association's power would be as great if it waited a few extra months before formally rejecting its M.P., or even if it merely threatened to do so. There is a strong practical reason for an association, once dissatisfied with its M.P., to secure quickly a new prospective general election candidate to fill the role which a locally disowned M.P. can no longer play at party meetings.

Accordingly, the significant question is whether the associations should have the power at all to reject their M.P.s for their deviations. Once posed this way, the answer—given the British political system— has to be yes. It would be ridiculous to suggest that the groups which select candidates should not be able to reject them. If one wants to take away the power to reject, then the power to select must be shifted as well. It makes little sense to say that an M.P., when he is being rejected by the same group which selected him, should be able to appeal beyond this group to a larger section of the local electorate. Unless the British critics wish to substitute something like an American-style primary method of candidate selection—and they assuredly do not— then the power of constituency associations has to be borne.[12]

More significantly, any shift in power from the associations might alter the basic arrangement for carrying on British parliamentary government. That arrangement, resting as it does on virtually complete party cohesion in the Commons, appears incompatible with a method of candidate selection which would transfer an M.P.'s loyalty from the zealous faithful of his association to those who are merely party voters. Such a transfer would have the effect, as it does in those American states where the primary is really effectual, of freeing the legislator from a complete dependence on party supporters for his political survival. This would not only allow an M.P. to use his own judgment; it would also subject him increasingly to the cross-pressures of various local interest groups. Both results would tend to work against parliamentary cohesion.

[12]This assumes that critics of constituency association power in candidate selection do not wish to substitute a complete central office control. That is a possibility, more realistic in Britain than an American-style primary, and it would evidently provide a greater appearance of toleration in a crisis like that over Suez. But it would open the way to a long-run imposition of orthodoxy and regularity almost certain to be objectionable to critics favoring individuality and independence in their M.P.s. Furthermore, central control of candidature, in much greater degree than now exists, would deprive constituency activists of one of the functions ʲustifying activism.

The British model of M.P.–constituency association relations is an integral part of the nation's working form of parliamentary government. Only the dislike of many Englishmen for the way that model functioned during the Suez crisis obscured this principle. But even at the time, it was not obscure to an old hand at the maintenance of parliamentary party cohesion. Thus Earl Attlee, in a magazine debate with one of the anti-Suez Conservatives, wrote that there are "few, if any, Members who get into Parliament on account of their own qualities. They are elected because the politically active citizens select them as expressing broadly their views, and because these same citizens have worked to persuade a majority of the electors to support them."[13] So, Attlee continued, if an M.P. fails to support the government or fails to act with the opposition in its efforts to turn the government out, he acts contrary to the expectations of those who have put their trust in him. It follows for Attlee that when in disagreement with his party on a major issue, an M.P. should submit the issue to his local association and resign if the association so wishes. However, such a situation, as Attlee indicates, arises but rarely. The rules of the game are too well understood by almost all of the participants. M.P.s know what their parties expect by way of loyalty to the national cause, and they know that such loyalty is of the essence of British politics. In Attlee's words, the party leader requires disciplined troops "unless one is prepared to lose the battle."[14] In this perspective, constituency associations are the ultimate sanction for rules usually observed for other reasons.

One can agree with Attlee about the role of constituency associations in preserving parliamentary party cohesion without sharing the dismay, first reflected by Ostrogorski and now by British liberals, concerning the power of the associations. Really how one regards this power depends on how one values the strong parliamentary party cohesion to which it contributes.

During the Suez crisis, this party cohesion, so manifest in Parliament and in the constituency associations, did not grossly distort the views of ordinary voters. The bulk of the electorate, ordinarily voting either Labour or Conservative, did tend to have views on Suez that coincided with those of their elected party representatives. But the tendency was

---

[13]"Party Discipline Is Paramount," *The National and English Review*, Vol. 148, p. 15 (January 1957). Attlee's piece is published along with Sir Edward Boyle's case for only a slightly looser interpretation of party discipline—one just loose enough to justify his own Suez deviation.

[14]*Ibid.*, p. 16.

not nearly so uniform, especially on the Labour side, as it was in Parliament or among party activists. Moreover, some of the tendency of ordinary Conservative voters to be pro-Suez and of ordinary Labour voters to be anti-Suez might have been the result of wanting to follow their respective parties on Suez or on any other issue once each party had assumed its position. Or, more probably, party leaders might have been effective, once the crisis began, in persuading their respective electorates to adopt particular Suez views. This seems to have been true in the Conservative case. For thus persuading their own voters, party leaders were reinforced by the nearly straight partisan alignment of the press—Conservative papers being pro-Suez and Labour (and liberal) papers being anti-Suez. The press, more generally as well, contributed to the partisan division outside of Parliament. Consequently, it is understandable that the division of public opinion, while not so strictly partisan as the parliamentary division, was mainly significant for its fairly high degree of partisanship over Suez. The exceptions, at any rate, were not sufficient to produce any substantial feedback effect on parliamentary behavior. Even an unusual nonparty cross-pressure, examined at length in the previous chapter for its influence in the parliamentary Labour party, turned out to have no major effect on the behavior of relevant M.P.s.

At the end, then, of this case study, it can be fairly concluded that Britain's Suez experience displayed a rigidly partisan political mold that appears to be a response of the parliamentary system to problems facing a major democratic nation in the first half of the twentieth century. This response includes the development of two major parties, each maintaining cohesive parliamentary organizations and each backed by considerable external memberships recruited on national issues. The result has surely been stable executive government in an era in which parliamentary government elsewhere has had hard times. Unlike France of the Third and Fourth Republics, for example, Britain has been assured of continuity for its policies. Its executive is almost as likely to remain in office as is the American President with his fixed term of office. And the British Prime Minister is more likely than the American President to be assured of support while he remains in office. So much, or nearly so much, stability seems to be a necessity for a nation with major problems, especially external ones. In this respect, Britain seems to have been well served by its political system.

Whether this kind of stability will always be useful to Britain is another matter. So is the question whether it will always seem useful enough, in days of lesser national power and fewer major foreign responsibilities, for the British to pay the price of partisan rigidity that goes with the achievement of executive stability. In the future, there may be more room for a third party, like the reviving Liberals, and for less cohesive parliamentary parties. The strict two-party division exhibited in the Suez experience may be a period piece and not the shape of British parliamentary government for all time. Its advantages may come to be seriously questioned, as they were by Eden's opponents during the Suez crisis.

Index